CORPORATE INSOLVENCY IN PRACTICE: AN ANALYTICAL APPROACH

Clare Campbell and Brian Underdown

Paul Chapman
Publishing Ltd

Clare Campbell has lectured at the University of Sheffield for 15 years and is responsible for the company law course. She has also taught on the European Communities law course. She is a consultant editor to the journal *The Company Lawyer*, and is the author of numerous articles and notes on insolvency law matters.

Brain Underdown is Professor of Accounting at Sheffield University. He graduated from Leeds University and worked as a management accountant in engineering, food processing and steel. He completed an MA by research at Sheffield University where he was appointed to the staff in 1971. He is co-author of several books on accounting, including *Accounting in a Changing Environment*, *Accounting Theory and Practice*, *Accounting Theory and Policy Making*, *Financial Accounting*, *Advanced Financial Accounting* and *Cost Accounting*.

Copyright © 1991 Clare Campbell and Brian Underdown

All rights reserved

First published in 1991 by
Paul Chapman Publishing Ltd
144 Liverpool Road
London
N1 1LA

No part of this publication may be reproduced, stored in a retrieval system, or transmitted, in any form or by any means, electronic, mechanical, photocopying, recording or otherwise, without the prior permission of Paul Chapman Publishing Ltd.

British Library Cataloguing in Publication Data
Campbell, Clare
  Corporate insolvency in practice: an analytical approach.
  1. Companies. Insolvency
  I. Title II. Underdown, Brian 1935–
  332.75
  ISBN 1-85396-085-3

Typeset by Best-Set Typesetter Limited, Hong Kong
Printed by St. Edmundsbury Press, Bury St. Edmunds
Bound by W. H. Ware, Clevedon, Avon.
A B C D E 5 4 3 2 1

Contents

Series Editor's Foreword	vi
Preface	vii
Acknowledgements	viii
1 THE INSOLVENCY PROCESS	1
Environmental and managerial factors	1
Performance indicators	3
Response to deterioration in performance indicators	4
Detection by outsiders	9
Action taken	9
Turnaround	10
Insolvency	10
Insolvency practitioners	11
Administration	12
Administrative receivership	13
Liquidation	14
References and further reading	14
Notes	15
2 CAUSES OF CORPORATE FAILURE	17
Main causes of failure	17
Profiles of company failure	23
Case study: budgetary planning at Jay plc	25
References and further reading	32
3 INDICATORS OF BUSINESS FAILURE	33
Solvency analysis	33
Traditional ratio analysis	34
Predictive models	39
Measuring funds flow	41
Improving the predictability of accounts	45
Qualitative analysis	46
References and further reading	48

iv   Contents

4	ASPECTS OF LIQUIDITY MANAGEMENT	49
	Principles of working capital management	49
	Cash management	51
	Cash budgeting	51
	Increasing the efficiency of cash management	52
	Managing trade debtors	53
	Stock	57
	Summary	59
	References	60

5	COMPANY TURNAROUND	61
	Evaluation stage	62
	Change of top management	64
	Emergency action stage	64
	Developing corporate recovery strategies	65
	Implementing and monitoring the plan	68
	Turnaround specialists' skills and experience	69
	Case study: Northern Manufacturing Ltd.	69
	References	72

6	PROCEDURES FOR DEALING WITH INSOLVENCY	73
	Informal procedures	73
	Formal procedures without the need to involve an insolvency practitioner	74
	Formal procedures necessitating the involvement of an insolvency practitioner	75
	References and further reading	81
	Notes	81

7	ADMINISTRATION: PURPOSES AND PROCEDURES	83
	Introduction	83
	Circumstances in which administration will be an appropriate remedy	84
	Conditions for making an administration order	85
	Procedure on application for an administration order	86
	The consequences of an administration petition	88
	Duties of administrators	90
	Termination of the administration	92
	Case study: Northern Loans Ltd	93
	References and further reading	101
	Notes	102

8	ADMINISTRATIVE RECEIVERS: PURPOSES AND PROCEDURES	105
	Fixed and floating charges	105
	Procedure for appointment	112

	The status of the administrative receiver	116
	Resignation and removal of administrative receivers	117
	Case study: Any Windows Ltd.	118
	References and further reading	128
	Notes	128

9 TRADING AND SALE BY ADMINISTRATORS AND ADMINISTRATIVE RECEIVERS — 131

Introduction	131
Preliminary stages	132
Powers in relation to trading	135
Duties in relation to trading	139
Powers in relation to sale	140
Duties in relation to sale	143
Enforcement of duties in relation to trading and sale	145
Powers and duties as office-holders	146
Conclusion	148
Case study: Any Yarn Ltd.	148
References and further reading	155
Notes	156

10 LIQUIDATIONS — 159

Introduction	159
Procedures	160
Status, powers and duties of the liquidator	162
Compulsory liquidations	165
Termination of liquidation	174
Case study: Any Name Ltd.	175
References and further reading	188
Notes	188

Table of cases	191
Table of statutes	195
Table of statutory instruments	197
Index	198

Series Editor's Foreword

When the economy is booming the number of corporate liquidations is less than the number of new registrations. When the economy is in recession there is plenty of work for receivers and liquidators. But whatever the state of the economy there are always some companies which, through poor financial management, have severe cash-flow problems and are technically insolvent. Insolvency is a fact of business life.

In the first part of their book Campbell and Underdown discuss the causes of insolvency, the lead indicators of business failure and the way management can improve their cash flows to avoid insolvency. The second part of the book assumes that management has not been able to turn the company around, and describes the informal and formal procedures for dealing with insolvency, and the role and duties of administrators, administrative receivers and liquidators.

Thus, *Corporate Insolvency in Practice* is far from a dry legal text dealing only with the last rites of companies. It recognizes that not all insolvent companies become the subject of winding-up orders and gives useful advice to managers on how they can help their companies become solvent once again. It also utilizes the disciplines of economics, financial management and law to produce an interdisciplinary approach to insolvency which is missing from all other books on the subject.

Campbell and Underdown have also skilfully integrated theory with practice, giving due attention to the most recent research on company failure prediction, as well the detailed provisions of the Insolvency Act 1986 and its implications for directors and insolvency practitioners. Furthermore, they make extensive use of case study material to bring the subject to life and to provide material for critical discussion. In this way, the authors have written a book which can be used in the classroom by degree and professional students and as an up-to-date reference text by managers, directors and insolvency practitioners.

Without doubt, *Corporate Insolvency in Practice* is a book of high quality, originality and broad appeal. I am delighted, therefore, that it now joins the other books of excellence in the Paul Chapman Series in Accounting and Finance, and I am sure it will soon become one of the classic texts in the field of insolvency.

Michael Sherer

Preface

This book developed from a research project which investigated the impact within the South Yorkshire area of the rehabilitative provisions relating to corporate insolvency introduced by the Insolvency Act 1986 and the response of the local accountancy and legal professions to these provisions. This research also sought to assess the effect of the Insolvency Act and the Company Directors Disqualification Act 1986 on the conduct of directors of companies in financial difficulties.

One finding of the research was that writers on corporate insolvency have tended to adopt either a legal, economic, managerial or financial perspective when dealing with issues related to insolvency. Although the relationship between these aspects is of the utmost importance in determining individual behaviour, it is rarely explored. The result is that developments in practice are proceeding faster than the literature and the implications of these developments do not always receive the attention they deserve.

The objective of this book is to integrate the traditional approaches to insolvency and to deal with the subject in an analytical manner. Case studies are introduced at appropriate places in the text in order to facilitate our approach.

We believe that this book will be suitable for the following uses:

(1) for university and polytechnic courses in accounting, law and business studies, especially where such courses adopt an interdisciplinary or case-study-based approach to insolvency law;
(2) as preparation for the examinations of the various professional bodies which include an in-depth knowledge of corporate insolvency;
(3) to cater for the needs of the businessman, manager or general reader who requires an up-to-date survey of corporate insolvency.

Acknowledgements

We wish to place on record our gratitude to many individuals for the advice and help which they have given us in the course of writing this book. In particular, we thank Edward Klempka and David Stokes of Cork Gully, Andrew Mayberry and Colin Duckworth of Hart, Moss and Copley & Co., Richard Betts of Grant Thorton, Ron Harding of Pannell Kerr Forster, Josephine Maltby of Sheffield University and Marianne Lagrange of Paul Chapman Publishing.

Our thanks are due to Professor Paul Wiles of Sheffield University, whose advice and guidance was of great assistance at the beginning of the research. We also owe a debt of gratitude to Dr Jacqueline Dunn, whose encouragement was an inspiration for the research; it is with sadness we record she was not able to see it bear fruit.

We are also grateful to Jean Hopewell, Shirley Peacock and Audrey Rixham for cheerfully typing (and retyping) the drafts.

Responsibility for errors or omissions is ours alone.

The law is stated as at 1 May 1990.

Clare Campbell
Brian Underdown

1
The Insolvency Process

An insolvent company is unable to meet debts when they fall due. It runs out of cash and ceases trading. There are two reasons why companies become insolvent.

First, a company typically gets into financial difficulties when a poor trading performance leads to inadequate profits over a period of years and this is followed by a cash crisis. Generally, over the longer term, there is a close relationship between the level of profits earned and the amount of cash generated. Long-run solvency depends on long-run profitability. The importance of the long-run in the determination of insolvency is reflected in a recent definition of solvency: 'solvency refers to the availability of cash over the longer term to meet financial commitments as they fall due' (IASC, 1988). Companies become insolvent because their managements fail to develop adequate longer-term strategic plans to deal with problems of profitability and cash flow.

Second, a surprising number of companies that have been generating satisfactory profits fail because they run out of cash. In these cases, inadequate attention has been given to liquidity (or working capital) management. If, for example, a business grows rapidly the resulting increase in stock and debtor levels can cause an acute cash-flow crisis. Failure to limit a company's growth to a rate at which increased working capital needs can be financed is known as 'overtrading'.

The purpose of this chapter is to introduce the various components of the insolvency process and the factors that determine the behaviour of management in response to these components. These are illustrated in Figure 1.1. The Roman numerals in the figure cross-refer to the remaining sections of this chapter.

ENVIRONMENTAL AND MANAGERIAL FACTORS (I)

The success of any business enterprise is determined by the interaction of two major sets of factors. First, a variety of factors emanate from outside the business itself. These environmental variables are beyond the control of business management and include such environmental conditions as shifting

2 Corporate Insolvency in Practice

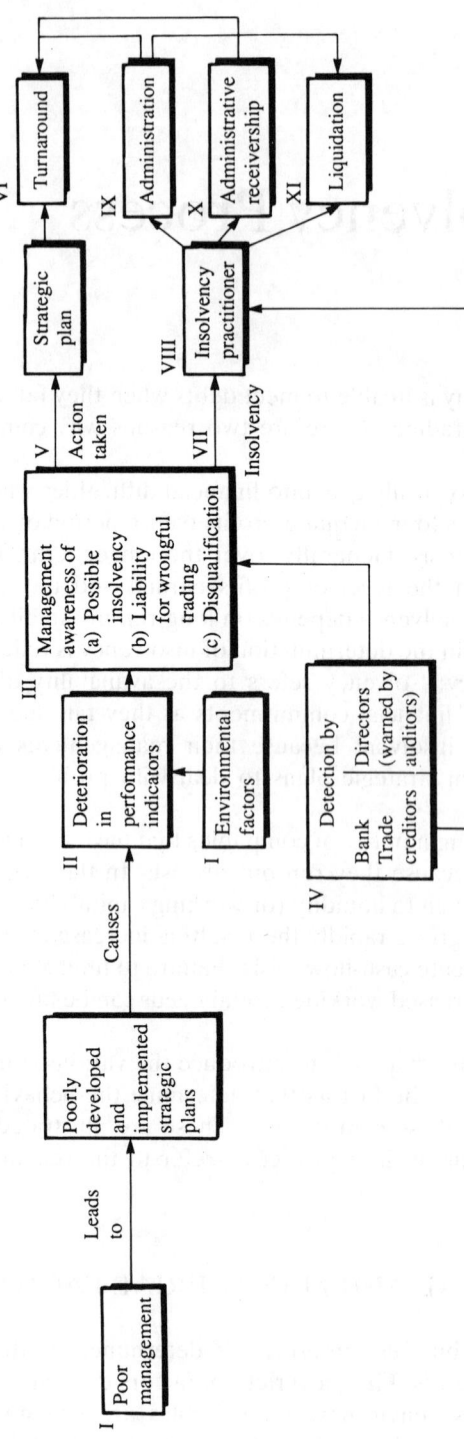

Figure 1.1 *The insolvency/failure process*

preferences, attitudes and behaviour of consumers, adverse movements in commodity prices, changes in government policy and cyclical market forces.

The other major factors that determine business success emanate from inside the firm and encapsulate the ability of management to develop and implement planning strategies that fit the business to the environment. Strategic planning is, by definition, an exercise in forward thinking aimed at attaining specific company goals at some point in the future. In an environment characterized by change, uncertainty and even turbulence, the ability to adapt to changing circumstances is essential to business survival and success. Therefore, our previous identification of environmental variables as uncontrollable does not imply that they should be omitted from the planning process. On the contrary, the probability of changes in the environmental factors and the effects of such changes on future business performance should be taken into account if an enterprise is to survive and prosper.

PERFORMANCE INDICATORS (II)

A company is accountable to many groups who need to receive performance results in order to evaluate the actions taken by management. For example, shareholders and creditors expect the company to provide certain financial performance results in terms of profitability, growth and liquidity. A variety of other stakeholders in the business, such as employees, suppliers and the community, expect certain performance results in terms of employment stability and advancement, creditworthiness and environmental protection issues. The degree to which a company meets its responsibilities is measured by performance indicators. Therefore, the firm meets its responsibilities by formulating and executing strategic plans, the outcome of which can be evaluated by the performance indicators. These are derived from published financial accounts and measure certain financial relationships. They often take the form of ratios or percentages i.e. numbers which express the relationship of one financial magnitude to another, such as that of profit to invested funds. A ratio or percentage is compared with a standard. The standard used may be the corresponding figures from competitors' company accounts or the corresponding industry average in respect of the current period. Alternatively, the standard may be the corresponding figure for the same company in respect of past periods.

Where the enterprise is heading towards financial failure all the stakeholders need to be aware of the situation so that they can protect their interests as far as possible. Hopefully, timely action will result in either the avoidance of collapse or the avoidance of loss by interested parties. Chapter 3 discusses the extent to which the analysis and interpretation of the financial statements of companies assist in predicting insolvency. In isolation, such statements do not provide an adequate basis for this purpose. The analysis of these historical statements may indicate financially comfortable conditions or satisfactory trends in key ratios. However, our concern in prediction is with the uncertain future. For this reason the success of a company depends more on the soundness of its plans than on that of its past financial position.

Research studies have concentrated on business failure (i.e. firms that have ceased to trade) rather than insolvency. This may be because failure is a historically recorded fact whereas insolvency is a condition. The timing of the onset of insolvency may be determined from the inability of a company to pay its debts as they fall due. This in turn may be evidenced by undue delays in paying creditors; writs issued against the company against which there is no defence and payment is not made; dishonoured cheques and repossession of creditors' goods on the company's premises. However, insolvency may be remediable, whereas failure is final. In Chapter 6 we examine the various mechanisms for dealing with insolvency, some of which provide for a turn-around in the fortunes of the business, some of which end in liquidation and distribution of what assets remain. Therefore a study of indicators of approaching failure can be expected to be relevant also to insolvency.

RESPONSE TO DETERIORATION IN PERFORMANCE INDICATORS (III)

Unless management responds to a deterioration in performance indicators by taking remedial action, the company will sink into insolvency and thereafter failure. The catalyst leading to such action may be either an internal one or a response to pressure from outside the company.

Essential to the understanding of the failure process is a realization of the impact of legal liabilities on the response of management to the decline in business performance. These legal liabilities stem from changes introduced by the Insolvency Act 1986 and the Company Directors Disqualification Act 1986.

Wrongful trading

Companies trade with the privilege of limited liability which insulates their shareholders and, to some extent, their directors from personal liability for corporate debts.

In the light of growing disquiet with the abuse of limited liability by reckless and irresponsible directors who continued trading when corporate collapse was almost inevitable, causing greater loss than necessary to creditors, the Cork Committee[1] (which reviewed the law of corporate insolvency) recommended that a new civil liability be introduced to enable creditors to obtain compensation from such directors. This new liability springs from section 214 of the Insolvency Act 1986, which imposes personal liability on directors for wrongful trading. Upon application made by the liquidator in a compulsory or a creditors' voluntary winding-up proceeding, the court may order that any person who is or who has been a director of the company is liable to make such contribution to the company's assets as the court thinks proper.

An analysis of section 214 will demonstrate its wide potential and its significance for anyone concerned with the diagnosis of corporate failure. First, the section requires that the company should have gone into insolvent liquidation.[2] Thus, liability under this section cannot be enforced in any other type of insolvency proceeding. Second, the liquidator must show that:[3]

> at some time before the commencement of the winding up of the company, that person knew or ought to have concluded that there was no reasonable prospect that the company would avoid going into insolvent liquidation.

Finally, a director can escape personal liability if he can discharge the heavy burden of showing that he took 'every step' with a view to minimizing the potential loss to the company's creditors.[4]

The section, which is a potent weapon in changing directors' behaviour in the event of the likely failure of the company's business, contains two critical points. The first difficulty is ascertaining the 'moment of truth', i.e. the time when the directors realized or ought to have realized that there was no prospect of avoiding insolvent liquidation. The CBI, in its advice to directors on the introduction of liability for wrongful trading, commented adversely on the vagueness of the test.[5] For example, would a director who was alerted by the performance indicators and forecasts based thereon that insolvency might occur in the foreseeable future, be potentially liable for wrongful trading for his failure to act perhaps even two or three years before the company went into liquidation?

Judicial guidance on the question of recognizing when a company will go into insolvent liquidation is to be found in the case of *Re Produce Marketing Consortium Ltd*.[6] The company, in that case, acted as an import agent in the fruit trade, its only source of profits being through commission charged on the gross sale price of fruit imported through its agency. Its gradual decline towards failure was discernible from the accounts. In 1980 it traded profitably and assets exceeded liabilities but, by the year ending 30 September 1985, the position had reversed and the company had suffered a loss of £55,817 and its excess of liabilities over assets stood at over £114,000; its overdraft exceeded £91,000, which was well above its borrowing limit. In early 1987 its bank began dishonouring cheques and the company's auditors warned the directors of their potential legal liability for fraudulent trading. The company eventually went into creditors' voluntary liquidation in October 1987 and the liquidator sought and obtained an order for compensation against the two directors of £75,000 each.

The court held that the directors knew from what documentary evidence was actually available to them that the turnover figure for 1985/6 was such that a substantial loss was likely to be incurred. Furthermore, as section 214(4) indicates, a director will incur liability if there are facts which he ought to have known or ascertained. Thus, it was held that information in the accounts, which should have been available and which would have enabled the directors to assess the extent of the excess of liabilities over assets was to be taken into consideration. Consequently the directors should have ascertained that as from the end of July 1986, more than fourteen months before the company was wound up, there was no reasonable prospect of avoiding insolvent liquidation.

The degree of knowledge and the quality of deductions which are to be made by the directors are to be judged by both an objective and a subjective standard. Thus, the facts which the director ought to know or ascertain, the conclusions he should reach and the steps he should take are those which would be taken by a reasonably diligent person having both:[7]

(i) the general knowledge, skill and experience that may reasonably be expected of a person carrying out the same functions as are carried out by that director in relation to the company, and
(ii) the general knowledge, skill and experience that director has.

The second critical point in interpreting the section is that a director can escape liability if he can show that he took 'every step' to minimize the potential loss to the company's creditors. However, the section gives no guidance as to what steps might be taken. Presumably, calling in a 'company doctor', injecting more capital, pursuing plans to achieve a turnaround and consulting and acting on the advice of a licensed insolvency practitioner would all constitute 'steps' designed to minimize the harm to creditors. If the company's parlous condition would not benefit from any remedial action, the only step available for minimizing loss to creditors would be to put the company into immediate liquidation.

Once a finding of wrongful trading has been made, the court can make a declaration that the person concerned should make such contribution as the court thinks fit to the company's assets. Furthermore, if the person found liable for wrongful trading has any debt or obligation due from the company to him, the court can order that the compensation payment be a charge on such debt or obligation.[8] Finally, a director who has participated in wrongful trading may be disqualified under the terms of section 10 of the Company Directors Disqualification Act 1986.

Section 214 on wrongful trading may well act as a catalyst bringing about in the long term an alteration in managerial behaviour. The result of the introduction of this liability may well be that advice is sought at an earlier stage in the financial crisis and this may have the effect of maximizing the chances of a successful turnaround or minimizing further loss to creditors.

Disqualification orders

Allied to the liability for wrongful trading, the directors of a company which has become insolvent also run the risk of a disqualification order being made. Such an order, under which a director or shadow director is prevented from acting as a director (whether directly or indirectly) or from in any way being concerned in the promotion, formation or management of a company, is made under the Company Directors Disqualification Act 1986.

There are three main categories of cases in which the court may make a disqualification order:

(1) where there has been general misconduct in the affairs of the company or misconduct or fraud in relation to the promotion or management of the company;
(2) disqualification for unfitness;
(3) disqualification after a liability has been imposed for wrongful trading.

Briefly, the situations covered by (1) will include breaches of company law and of the general criminal law relating to the formation and running of companies, including the commission of indictable offences in the running of the business;[9] persistent failure to observe the regulatory requirements of the companies legislation relating to the filing of accounts and returns[10] and convictions in relation to such failures.[11] The notion of an 'offence connected with the management of a company' is capable of very wide interpretation.[12]

The second, and increasingly important ground for disqualification is a finding of unfitness to be concerned in the management of a company.[13] The evidence of such unfitness will primarily be provided in the report which the insolvency practitioner, who is dealing with the company's affairs as 'office-holder' (e.g. as liquidator, administrator or administrative receiver) is obliged to prepare on the conduct of all directors of the company with which he is dealing.[14] The format and timing of such reports is regulated by the Insolvent Companies (Reports on the Conduct of Directors) No. 2 Rules.[15] If the Secretary of State, or in the case of a company in compulsory liquidation the Official Receiver, considers that it is expedient in the public interest that a director or shadow director be disqualified, an application may be made to the court for such an order to be made. Once the court is satisfied that the director's conduct is such as to render him unfit to be concerned in corporate management, there is no discretion as to whether to disqualify; disqualification is mandatory for the minimum period of two years. The maximum period of disqualification under section 6 of the Company Directors Disqualification Act 1986 is fifteen years.

In determining whether a director's or shadow director's conduct has rendered him unfit to be concerned in the management of a company, the court has to consider the matters referred to in Schedule 1 of the Company Directors Disqualification Act.[16] The significance of this Schedule is that it operates as a kind of 'statement of practice' against which the director's conduct may be measured. The matters which are to be considered include:

(1) any misfeasance or breach of fiduciary or other duty by the director in relation to the company;
(2) misapplication of company funds;
(3) the director's responsibility for the failure of the company to fulfil its accounting and reporting obligations under the Companies Acts;
(4) the extent of the director's responsibility for the company's insolvency;
(5) the director's responsibility for the company's failure to supply any goods or provide services which have been paid for in advance;

(6) the extent of the director's responsibility for the company entering into a transaction which is a preference or which defrauds creditors;
(7) the extent of the director's responsibility for the failure to call a creditors' meeting in the event of a creditors' winding up;
(8) the extent of the director's failure to deal with administrative matters as requested by the insolvency practitioner dealing with the company's affairs and his failure to co-operate with such practitioner.

As can be seen, the list of actions or omissions which can be taken into account is extensive. An examination of some of the cases which have been brought before the courts reveals the types of conduct regarded as most reprehensible in assessing the director's conduct. The courts have been particularly critical of the use of amounts retained on account of PAYE, national insurance contributions and VAT to finance current trading, which, upon a company's insolvency leaves the Crown as a substantial creditor for these sums. For example, in *Re Stanford Services Ltd*[17] the court strongly criticized directors who had continued to trade while owing very substantial sums to the Crown in respect of PAYE, VAT and national insurance; it was said that the Crown was an 'involuntary creditor' in this regard, unable to protect its position in the same way as ordinary trade creditors, and that, as the taxes were 'collector taxes', they were held on 'quasi-trust' for the Crown.[18]

Also considered reprehensible is the under-capitalization of the business either on start-up or during its trading history.[19] Although there is no statutory minimum capital requirement for private companies, the courts have taken into account the irresponsible conduct of directors who have permitted companies to commence business with woefully inadequate start-up capital and which effectively operate on creditors' funds.

Finally, failure to file annual accounts and returns and to maintain adequate records is a ground for disqualification especially where the director concerned has some special responsibility or knowledge in the area of accounting.[20]

A director cannot escape possible disqualification by pleading that he left all the decision-making to other members of the board.[21]

From the figures published by the Insolvency Service of the Department of Trade (see Table 1.1), it is clear that there is a 'get tough' policy in relation to reckless and continually defaulting directors. Directors whose conduct falls below the accepted standard of commercial competence may well find that a disqualification order is made to protect the public from their activities. Once

Table 1.1 Disqualification of directors in Great Britain

	Total	Up to 5 years	More than 5 years
1987	159	109	50
1988	332	268	64
1989 (to 30 June)	155	123	32

again, the best strategic plan for a director of a company in financial difficulties would be to obtain the advice of an insolvency practitioner with a view to working out a rescue plan at the earliest possible moment.

DETECTION BY OUTSIDERS (IV)

The warning signs that can be derived from company accounts have implications for those outside the company, especially its bankers and accountants. Bankers are well placed to act as watchdogs. Since their money is at risk, they can establish direct contact with management at the highest level. They are in a position to spot the early warning signs such as the company exceeding its overdraft limits, evidence of cash-flow problems, problems with trade debtors, etc., long before these problems show up in the annual accounts. However, although they can monitor for signs of corporate failure, the bank's response to such signs may well have to be circumspect. There is a danger that if it makes recommendations or, even more so, gives instructions, to the directors, the bank may itself incur liability for wrongful trading should the company subsequently go into insolvent liquidation.[22] Similarly, in their capacity as auditors, accountants are well placed to warn the directors when they are examining the finances of a potentially failing company.

The introduction of the Insolvency Act 1986 and the Company Directors Disqualification Act 1986 with its penalties for directors has helped to make management more aware of the need to seek help before the company's problems become terminal. It has also given leverage to bankers and other creditors enabling them to compel directors of ailing companies to take their responsibilities more seriously.

ACTION TAKEN (V)

The action taken by directors in response to the recognized financial crisis may follow one of two routes.

First, if the company is not already insolvent, the management may well be advised to respond either by themselves devising a rescue plan, if they are confident that they have the necessary expertise, or – perhaps a more likely strategy – to obtain the help of a 'company doctor' or investigating accountant who will put forward a turnaround plan. This will involve evaluating the reasons for, and the severity of, the company's financial crisis; developing a corporate recovery strategy and implementing and monitoring the plan. These elements of a corporate turnaround are examined in detail in Chapter 5.

Second, if the company is insolvent, the directors' response should involve taking the advice of a professional insolvency practitioner with a view to putting into effect one or more of the informal or formal mechanisms for dealing with an insolvency. Ultimately the insolvency practitioner may be able to achieve a turnaround or the situation may be such that the only feasible outcome is the liquidation of the company so as to avoid further loss to creditors.

The following sections will assist in understanding the remaining steps in the insolvency process as referred to in Figure 1.1.

TURNAROUND (VI)

Corrective action can result in a turnaround, which may be defined as an improvement in company performance from a lower than normal to a satisfactory rate of return on capital employed, which then ensures the long-term viability of the company.

Slatter (1984) undertook a study of publicly quoted companies in the United Kingdom over a fifteen-year period. For the purpose of the study a company was defined as in need of a turnaround if inflation-adjusted profits declined in more than three successive years. Using this definition, 21 per cent of 2,100 companies surveyed were, at some stage, in need of a turnaround. Of the 437 so identified only 102 managed a successful recovery. The remaining companies were either wound up or, more commonly, acquired by other companies.

A similar survey by Bibeault (1981) in the USA found that 27 per cent of US quoted companies were in need of a turnaround over a ten-year period. In this study a turnaround was defined as the existence of a loss situation or severe decline in profits of 80 per cent or more in a single year. According to this study, only a third of these companies were successful turnarounds.

Two major lessons follow from these surveys: first, there is a need for a company's financial health to be more carefully monitored; second, management should be aware of the various strategies available to assist in corporate reconstruction and recovery. With regard to the first lesson, Kibel (1982) offers valuable advice on the course to be followed if the health of a company is to be maintained:

(1) set and maintain clear objectives;
(2) maintain and update corporate strategy;
(3) have an annual corporate health check-up;
(4) emphasize true balance sheet reporting;
(5) understand the law.

The second lesson will be discussed in Chapter 5.

INSOLVENCY (VII)

In assessing whether a company is insolvent, any of the various alternative tests defined in section 123(1) of the Insolvency Act may be taken into account. These are:

(i) if a creditor (by assignment or otherwise) to whom the company is indebted in a sum exceeding £750 then due, has served on the company, by leaving at the company's registered office a written demand requiring the company to pay the sum so due, and the company has for three weeks thereafter neglected to pay the sum or to give security for its payment to the reasonable satisfaction of the creditor, or
(ii) if execution or other process issued on a judgment, decree or court order in favour of a creditor of the company is returned unsatisfied in whole or in part, or
(iii) if it is proved to the satisfaction of the court that the company is unable to pay its debts as they fall due.

Under section 123(2) a company is deemed to be unable to pay its debts if it is proved to the satisfaction of the court that the value of the company's assets is less than the amount of its liabilities, taking into account its contingent and prospective liabilities.

The legal definition of insolvency thus encompasses both ends of a spectrum ranging from 'cash' insolvency proved by an inability to pay debts after a statutory demand or without making complex arrangements to pay,[23] even if the company's assets would be sufficient to meet all its liabilities on a liquidation. It also embraces 'balance sheet' insolvency where the assets are insufficient to cover all liabilities. This latter test is particularly stringent because, for example, prospective liabilities under continuing unprofitable contracts could be brought into consideration, as may be the calling in of an unsecured overdraft facility. Similarly, a possible contingent liability[24] under an uninsured civil claim or the possibility of the calling in of an intra-group guarantee could be brought into the calculation of the solvency of the business. The result of the width of this definition is that many apparently solvent companies could potentially be in a position of insolvency or likely insolvency.

INSOLVENCY PRACTITIONERS (VIII)

An insolvency practitioner is a person who is responsible for a company's affairs in a insolvency context, whether as a supervisor of a voluntary arrangement, an administrator, an administrative receiver or a liquidator. These roles are examined in Chapter 6.

Figure 1.1 shows how an insolvency practitioner can be seen to occupy two roles: 'company doctor' and 'company undertaker'. Turnaround will invariably involve a practical, executive role in rebuilding the structure and fabric of a company with a view to achieving its long-term recovery for the benefit of all stakeholders. The achievement of a turnaround calls for the application of managerial, financial and entrepreneurial skills because it is more commercially orientated than the more traditional approach taken by insolvency practitioners prior to the 1986 Act.

If the insolvency practitioner's role is to dismantle the business for subsequent sale or realization of its constituent elements, he will be called on to utilize skills in negotiation and financial and organizational management.

Prior to the Insolvency Act 1986 there was considerable criticism in accounting and legal circles of the activities of 'cowboy' liquidators – that is, unqualified persons, who may be friends or even relatives of the directors of an insolvent company, who could be relied on not to investigate the affairs of management.[25] They might also assist in the sale of any remaining assets at a discount price to the directors of the insolvent company, without due investigation, and in circumstances which gave rise to suspicion of sharp practice, leaving these directors, shorn of responsibilities to disappointed creditors, to start trading afresh through the medium of a newly incorporated company bearing a name similar to that which had just been liquidated. This was the so-called 'Phoenix syndrome'.

One of the major reforms introduced into insolvency law as a result of the Cork Committee proposals is the imposition of proper controls over the licensing of insolvency practitioners and the monitoring of the qualifications and performance of such individuals.[26]

An insolvency practitioner must be authorized to act, either by virtue of his membership of a recognized professional body, having been permitted to do so by fulfilling the requirements of such a body as regards education, training and experience, or by obtaining authorization from the Secretary of State for Trade.[27] Additionally, an insolvency practitioner must ensure that there is in force security for the proper performance of his functions, in the form of a professional indemnity bond. The Insolvency Practitioners' Regulations 1986 prescribe that the amount of the general bond must be £250,000 and, in relation to any specific appointment, the insolvency practitioner is to obtain, as soon as possible after appointment, insurance cover in respect of the appointment based on the value of the assets comprised therein.[28] Section 389 of the Insolvency Act provides that it is a criminal offence to act as an insolvency practitioner if a person is not qualified to do so.

ADMINISTRATION (IX)

The Insolvency Act 1986 introduced a procedure to facilitate the rescue and rehabilitation of companies in financial difficulties, through the appointment of an administrator. In the circumstances specified in the Act, the company, its directors or any of its creditors may apply to the court for an order that the affairs of the company be put under the control of an administrator (who must be a licensed insolvency practitioner) who will examine its business and the circumstances leading to its current position and make proposals designed either to (1) achieve a turnaround with the survival of the company and its business, or (2) come to an arrangement with the company's creditors and shareholders with a view to reorganizing its affairs or (3) make plans to achieve a better realization of the company's assets than would be achieved on a winding up.[29]

The idea behind the administration procedure is that it permits a breathing space during which plans for a rescue can be finalized or the sale of the business as a going concern can be negotiated. In order that the administrator is freed from the pressing claims of creditors, which might hinder these plans from coming to fruition, the Insolvency Act introduces a new idea – a moratorium immediately upon the presentation of the petition, providing immediate relief against creditors' claims until the hearing of the petition.[30] In the event of an administration order being granted, the moratorium on enforcement by creditors continues until the discharge of the order.[31]

The procedures associated with administration and the powers given to the administrator to assist him to achieve a turnaround are considered in Chapters 6, 7 and 9.

ADMINISTRATIVE RECEIVERSHIP (X)

Where a major creditor, such as a bank or financial institution, has lent money to a company, it will usually take some security interest over the company's assets as a protection against default in repayments. If this security is in the form of a floating charge over substantially all of the company's assets (the nature of such a charge will be examined in Chapter 8), the creditor may, in certain circumstances, appoint an administrative receiver. Such an insolvency practitioner has extensive rights over the company's assets and undertaking, including the power to manage the business as well as to sell assets covered by the charge. This full managerial power gives the administrative receiver the authority he needs to implement a rescue plan designed to save the profitable parts of the business provided that such a plan is in the interests of the appointing creditor.

An administrative receiver appointed under the auspices of a floating charge should be distinguished from the receiver appointed under a fixed charge over specific items of corporate property. A receiver appointed by the holder of a fixed charge has no power to continue the business of the company and thus cannot effect a turnaround or implement a rescue plan.

Turnaround by an administrative receiver will usually be in the secured creditor's interests (and also often in the interests of unsecured creditors and other stakeholders in the company) if it improves the chances of the recovery of the loan by the creditor or if the creditor thereby maintains a continued trading relationship with the debtor company. There may also be other business or social reasons why a secured creditor might prefer to implement a rescue through the appointment of an administrative receiver, rather than stand back and see the company sink into insolvent liquidation. Administrative receivership is examined in Chapter 8.

LIQUIDATION (XI)

Liquidation is the process whereby the assets of the company are realized and distributed among its creditors according to their legal priority and entitlement.

The usual mode adopted is for the directors to recommend that the shareholders pass an extraordinary resolution to put the company into voluntary liquidation.[32] In the case of an insolvent company, the shareholders' resolution will be followed by a creditors' meeting which will receive and consider the directors' statement of affairs indicating the extent of the company's insolvency.[33] The meeting will also nominate the liquidator, and the creditors, if they wish, may elect a liquidation committee to assist and supervise the liquidator. The company is then wound up by the liquidator without the necessity for the intervention of the court. The statistics reproduced in Table 1.2 demonstrate that the creditors' voluntary liquidation is the most often used of the insolvency procedures.

Table 1.2 Corporate insolvencies in England and Wales

	Total	Compulsory liquidations	Creditors' voluntary	Administrations	CVAs
1986	14,405	5,205	9,201	—	—
1987	11,591	4,116	7,323	131	21
1988	9,672	3,667	5,760	198	47
1989 (to 30 June)	5,515	1,999	3,424	72	20

Alternatively, the company may be wound up by the court in a compulsory liquidation. The procedure is commenced by a petition to wind the company up, presented for one or more of the reasons stated in section 122 of the Insolvency Act 1986. In the case of an insolvent company, the usual reason is that the company is unable to pay its debts as they fall due, as defined in section 123.[34] If the directors cannot be persuaded to recommend, or the shareholders to pass, the necessary resolution to put the company into voluntary liquidation, then the creditors may be compelled to petition for a compulsory winding-up order. This is an expensive procedure, involving the investigation of the company's affairs by an official of the Department of Trade known as the Official Receiver.[35] It is best reserved for complex insolvencies requiring investigation or for cases where, for technical reasons, voluntary liquidation is not possible. The various procedures for both voluntary and compulsory liquidation are examined in Chapters 6 and 10.

REFERENCES AND FURTHER READING

Bibeault, D. (1981) *Corporate Turnaround*, McGraw-Hill, New York.
CBI (1985) *Insolvency Law Changes and Directors*, Consultative Document, CBI, London.

International Accounting Standards Committee (IASC) (1988) *Framework for the Preparation and Presentation of Financial Statements*, IASC, London.

Kibel, H. R. (1982) *How to Turnaround a Financially Troubled Company*, McGraw-Hill, New York.

Sealy, L. (1989) *Disqualification and Personal Liability of Directors*, 3rd edn, CCH Editions, Bicester.

Slatter, S. (1984) *Corporate Recovery*, Penguin, Harmondsworth.

NOTES

1. *Insolvency Law and Practice*, Report of the Insolvency Law Review Committee, Cmnd. 8558 (1982). See especially paras. 1776–1777.
2. S. 214(2)(a).
3. S. 214(2)(b).
4. S. 214(3).
5. CBI (1985) pp. 6–7.
6. (1989) 5 BCC 569.
7. S. 214(4).
8. S. 215(2).
9. CDDA 1986, s. 2(1).
10. CDDA 1986, s. 3(1). Note that persistent default is conclusively proved by showing that in five years ending with the date of the application, the director has been adjudged guilty (whether or not on the same occasion) of three or more defaults in relation to reporting requirements. See also *Re Arctic Engineering Ltd* [1986] 1 WLR 686.
11. CDDA 1986, s. 5.
12. *R v. Georgiu* (1988) 4 BCC 322.
13. CDDA 1986, ss. 6–9.
14. CDDA 1986, s. 7(3).
15. S.I. 1986 No. 2134.
16. CDDA 1986, s. 9.
17. (1987) 3 BCC 326.
18. This approach was followed in *Re Churchill Hotel (Plymouth) Ltd* [1988] BCLC 341.
19. *Re Dawson Print Group* [1987] BCLC 601. See also *Re Churchill Hotel (Plymouth) Ltd* [1988] BCLC 341 and *Re D. J. Matthews (Joinery Design) Ltd* (1988) 4 BCC 513.
20. *Re Stanford Services Ltd* [1987] BCLC 607; *Re Lo-Line Electric Motors Ltd* [1988] BCLC 698; *Re Majestic Recording Studios Ltd* (1988) 4 BCC 519; *Re Cladrose Ltd* (1990) 6 BCC 11; *Re J. & B. Lynch (Builders) Ltd* [1988] BCLC 376.
21. *Re Majestic Recording Studios Ltd* [1988] 4 BCC 519.
22. See *Re A Company (No. 005009 of 1987)* [1989] BCLC 13, in which the court refused to strike out an action for wrongful trading against a bank. The allegation was subsequently dropped.
23. *Byblos Bank v. Al-Khudhairy* (1986) 2 BCC 99.
24. A contingent liability is one that potentially exists under a current legal commitment and may or may not arise depending upon the happening of an event or the occurrence of a circumstance.
25. See Cmnd. 8558, para. 756.
26. Insolvency Act Part XIII – Insolvency Practitioners and their Qualification.
27. Ss. 388 and 391. The recognized professional bodies are scheduled in the Insolvency Practitioners (Recognised Professional Bodies) Order 1986 (S.I. 1986 No. 1764): the Chartered Association of Certified Accountants; the Insolvency

16 Corporate Insolvency in Practice

   Practitioners Association; the Institute of Chartered Accountants in England and Wales; the Institute of Chartered Accountants in Ireland; the Institute of Chartered Accountants of Scotland; the Law Society; the Law Society of Scotland.
28 Insolvency Practitioners Regulations 1986 (S.I. 1986 No. 1995), reg. 10.
29 S. 8.
30 S. 10(1).
31 S. 11(3).
32 S. 84(1)(c).
33 S. 98.
34 See p. 11.
35 S. 132.

2
Causes of Corporate Failure

In this chapter we consider the main causes of corporate failure, and the profiles which are associated with this event. According to economic criteria, 'failure' means that the realized rate of return on invested capital, with allowances for risk considerations, is significantly lower than prevailing rates on similar investments. Economic failure may lead to legal failure. In the latter case 'failure' refers to a company whose performance is so poor that sooner or later it is forced to take immediate action or go into liquidation.

MAIN CAUSES OF FAILURE

A knowledge of the causes of company failure can enable the identification of a potential problem before circumstances become too serious. It is important, therefore, to trace some of the steps which lead to failure and even more important to search for ways to avoid those steps. It is often not easy to determine one precise cause of failure in any individual case. Frequently it is the result of several factors leading up to one event which immediately brings failure.

In almost all the studies of corporate failure a list of causes contributing to failure has been developed (Ross and Kami, 1973; Argenti, 1976; Schendel, Patton and Riggs, 1976; Slatter, 1984; Grinyer, Mayes and McKiernan, 1988).

Figure 2.1 illustrates how these causes may be grouped to track the process of decline.

Changes in the environment fail to provoke a suitable response from corporate management because defects exist in the management team. These defects result in the lack of an adequate control system within the company which can fit the business to the environment. The result is an imbalance in operations. Finally, the diagram shows that environmental changes (in the form of high interest rates, inflation, tight markets, industrial unrest and economic uncertainty) take their toll on the most well-managed operation.

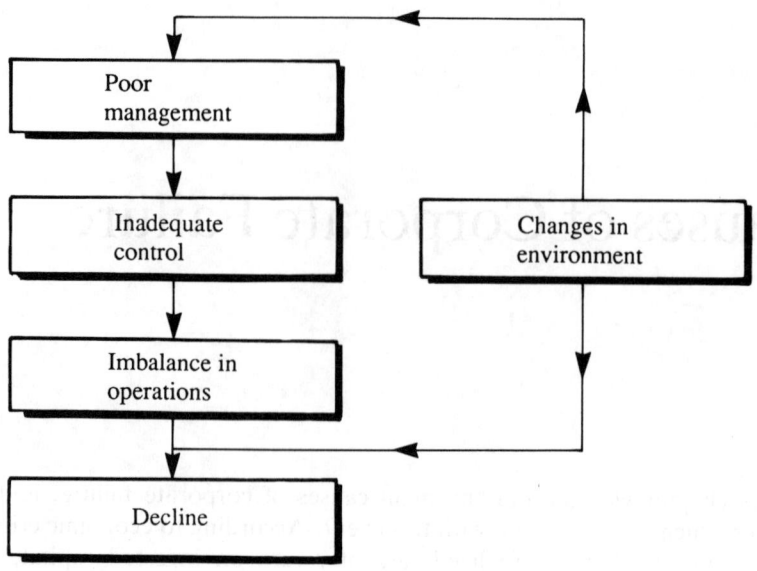

Figure 2.1   The process of decline

Poor management

Case studies consistently show that the majority of corporate failures stem from poor management. A good management team reacts to unfavourable circumstances and is able to take action leading to recovery; poorly managed businesses collapse. Blame for management failure is usually directed towards the top. In essence five top management defects can be identified: a domineering executive, inadequate management depth, an unbalanced administrative team, an uninvolved team and a weak finance function (Norgard, 1987).

Many authors have stressed the importance of management creating a clear set of shared values in the company (Peters and Waterman, 1982). A strong culture makes for a highly successful company. All employees know the goals of the organization and they set the pattern for opinions and actions. It is generally recognized that loss of morale and lack of enthusiasm are very obvious factors contributing to corporate decline.

Changes in the environment

Change in overall market demand is an important factor affecting corporate performance. A contraction of economic activity can cause many companies to fail. A company which has an inadequate management may show satisfactory financial results when times are good and sales are strong. But a tight economy uncovers corporate weaknesses, forcing many of the marginal companies out of existence. Also, government policy can have an influence on a company and its industry. The British government's high interest rate policy resulted in a significant surge in company failures in the second half of 1990. The number of companies going into receivership during this period nearly matched the total of the previous year. An increase in the minimum lending rate causes an increase in expenditure for all companies with bank overdrafts. This is particularly serious for companies whose capital gearing is high and which have unrealistic debt repayment schedules.

Individual industries may be affected by competitive pressure in the form of (1) product competition and (2) price competition. The product life-cycle concept provides a useful framework for analysing competitive pressure. The idea of the life-cycle is that, after an initial start-up period, successful products go through phases of growth, maturity and, eventually, decline as new and improved products are brought on to the market. The length of the cycle varies from one industry and product to another. The basic idea is that all products become obsolete as new technology is developed or existing technology improved, or substitute products are introduced and consumer preferences change. A firm that fails to respond to these changes is likely to find itself heading towards extinction.

According to Slatter (1984) severe price competition from overseas competitors is probably the most common cause of decline in manufacturing industry in Britain and other Western countries. Cars, motor cycles, ball bearings, carpets, cutlery, machine tools, textiles, paper, television and household appliances are examples of whole sectors of the economy where individual companies have declined due to price competition.

Inadequate control

Poor management leads to inadequate control in the form of:

(1) poor planning and decision-making;
(2) inadequate financial control;
(3) lack of marketing/sales effort.

Poor planning and decision-making

There is almost complete agreement among specialists in the field that companies fail because they have either not noticed a change in the business environment or not responded to it. Planning provides a framework by which economic and business conditions are evaluated, and most causes of failure can be grouped under the heading of poor planning. If managers do not plan ahead, problems are dealt with on a day-to-day basis and the wrong decisions or no decisions are made. Companies are not able to respond to changes in their business environment.

Planning consists of four steps.

(1) Assessing the environment in which the company operates by reference to the external factors which are likely to affect its operations: for this purpose, forecasts must to be made which attempt to predict what will happen in the future with and without policy changes.
(2) Assessing existing resources, for management is concerned with making the most efficient use of scarce resources.
(3) Determining the strategy for achieving stated objectives by means of an overall plan which specifies strategic goals: strategic planning attempts to find ways of adjusting to and exploiting environmental changes.
(4) Designing a programme of action to achieve selected strategic goals by means of both long-range and short-range programmes, the latter covering a period of a year or less and containing sets of instructions of the type found in annual budgets.

Inadequate financial control

In the absence of a basic control system a company does not know where it has been, and does not have the information needed to tell it where it should be going or how to get there. The following major defects exist.

(1) Lack of budgetary controls: a company needs not only a clear system of budgets which sets out what it is expected to achieve, it also needs a means of assessing performance against targets and procedures for taking corrective action where necessary. The case study at the end of this chapter illustrates how budgets are prepared.
(2) Lack of cash-flow forecasts ensures that management does not know what the future borrowing requirements are likely to be. To ensure survival in difficult trading conditions, management should attempt to maximize the company's main source of secure funding – its internal cash generation. Deterioration of a company's cash flow is a key indicator of problems ahead. In the final analysis, negative cash flows – not annual profitability – lead to insolvency.
(3) Lack of cost information: it is necessary for a firm to ascertain the profitability of each different part of its activities. In particular, managers need to know the contribution from their products and whether selling prices provide the company with a profit. A firm will quickly be in trouble if it operates with an unrealistic pricing policy, and it will not survive for long if it continually sells below cost.
(4) Poor credit control: in an attempt to increase sales or build up good relations a business may be lax in controlling its debtors' accounts and extend credit to customers who are habitually slow in paying their bills. At best, this can force the company to become a slow payer itself and so damage its reputation with suppliers. At worst, it can lead a company to a cash crisis if excessive funds become tied up in debtors' accounts and/or a large account goes bad and proves uncollectable.
(5) Excessive drawings: a common mistake made by people who have

recently started their own business is to draw far too much from the business by way of wages, entertainment expenses, expensive cars and other extravagances. Often, because they are working twice the hours and carrying twice the responsibility, they feel entitled to greater rewards than in their previous occupations. They fail to realize that ploughing back profits into their business may, in the short run, be the only way of funding its growth and countering the effects of inflation.

Many of the defects described in this section will be discussed in greater detail in Chapter 4.

Lack of marketing/sales effort

According to Gaffney (1983) some 20 per cent of small business failure is attributable to marketing errors. All too often knowledge of markets and competition is poor, marketing channels are not established, marketing methods are weak, and selling is not aggressive; the initial market research may have been half-hearted. Many small manufacturers are product-orientated and they are inclined to concentrate on the design and production of goods at the expense of marketing.

Imbalance in operations

Inadequate control can cause an imbalance in operations which takes the form of one or more of the following:

(1) inadequate financial resources;
(2) high gearing;
(3) high cost structure;
(4) over-expansion;
(5) big projects, acquisitions.

Inadequate financial resources

It is essential for a company to have adequate capital resources if it is to operate successfully. Failure can result from:

(1) insufficient capital or loan facilities. This ensures that many small businesses are doomed at an early stage of their existence. According to the Cork Committee:

> Trading when a business is heavily under-capitalised will often come within the concept of 'wrongful trading'. Those responsible for carrying on trading with insufficient share capital and reserves may well find themselves guilty of wrongful trading and accordingly subject to a personal civil liability in this respect. We believe that our proposals will encourage directors to satisfy themselves that their companies are adequately capitalised when regard is had to the scale of their operations and the level of the commitments into which they are proposing to enter; and that the new concept of wrongful trading will

go a long way to meet the criticisms of those who complain of the absence of a statutory minimum paid-up share capital for all trading companies (a matter for which the remedy lies outside our terms of reference).

(Cork Committee Report, CMND 8558, para 1785)

(2) over-dependence on loans or overdrafts as a source of capital. This ensures that a large measure of control of the business is inevitably lost. All management's major actions are subject to review by the bank and when the going grows difficult they are entirely in the hands of the bank as to continuation of the business.

High gearing

When the proportion of fixed-interest commitments or fixed-interest capital is high, the company is said to be highly geared. Therefore, high gearing directs a significant proportion of gross profits towards financing loan capital, with the result that the company becomes vulnerable to fluctuations in trading conditions.

Loan capital is a more secure form of investment than equity capital, and interest payments can be charged as expenses against profits, thereby reducing tax liability. For these reasons loans are highly attractive, especially when a company is starting up and has difficulties in obtaining sufficient capital.

The effect of gearing on profits will be considered in Chapter 3.

High cost structure

If a company with a high cost structure sets selling prices which are similar to those of its competitors the resulting lower margins will generate less profit and result in an additional borrowing requirement. With less funds available than competitors the company will not be able to invest so much in new product development and marketing, and consequently will be less capable of building and defending its market position.

A high cost structure could result from high interest costs, low labour productivity or over-investment in fixed assets. The last factor ties up cash or other funds so that they are no longer available to management to meet other obligations. As a company expands there is a need for greater investment in fixed assets. If the company can continue to operate at this capacity, profits will continue. However, if production declines significantly the company is in a difficult position. Fixed costs are not used fully and as a result the depreciation charge against net income is unduly high for the level of production. These costs are committed and little can be done in the short run to affect their total. If the reduction in production is permanent, action must be taken to eliminate some of the unprofitable divisions and dispose of their assets. A high cost structure can also result from over-investment in stocks. Carrying a large amount of stocks results in excessive storage costs, such as warehouse rent and insurance coverage, and the risk of spoilage and obsolescence.

Over-expansion

Over-expansion can cause two problems.

(1) Overtrading, when a business expands faster than its ability to finance itself. The cost of increased borrowing becomes a drain on cash flow and shrinking margins impair profitability. Profits tend to be short term, with turnover having priority over cost per sale.
(2) Managerial problems, where the business outruns its ability to manage itself. Usually a major difficulty is the proprietor's inability to delegate. Expansion must be planned, just as any other business activity.

Big projects, acquisitions

If a company attempts anything large relative to its own size, the risks of failure necessarily become much more important. As a rule of thumb, a firm should not enter into a contract which, if it went wrong, would by itself cause the company to fail. The reasons for big projects failing are usually related to poor design, poor planning and poor control.

Similarly, poor acquisitions can bring a firm down. Slatter (1984) identifies three ways in which an acquisition can cause the acquirer to fail: first, because the acquired company is weak; second, because too high a price is paid; and, last, because the acquirer fails, through poor management, to turn the new business to its advantage.

Combination of causes

Most writers on corporate failure agree that it is rarely the case that any one of the causes described above is sufficient to lead to relative decline. Usually it is a combination of causes that undermines the performance of a company and threatens its survival. Grinyer, Mayes and McKiernan's (1988) research showed that many of the companies in their sample that suffered relative decline exhibited (a) adverse economic factors, (b) a high cost structure, (c) poor management, (d) inadequate financial control and (e) big projects that failed.

PROFILES OF COMPANY FAILURE

Over a decade ago insolvency expert John Argenti (1976) constructed a model of the three prevailing types of corporate failure:

(1) small companies, newly founded, which never got going;
(2) high rollers, i.e. firms which not only get off the ground but quickly reach spectacular heights before crashing down;
(3) larger, more established companies which usually have a broader-based management and are publicly owned.

Small companies

Failed companies of this size never rise above a poor level of performance. Up to 60 per cent of business failures in any one year occur in businesses that are less than three years old (Ganguly and Bannock, 1985).

Many of their proprietors lack essential entrepreneurial skills. It is not uncommon, for example, for an experienced plumber to open a plumbing retailing firm: what the plumber may not realize is that managing the retailing firm requires far different and broader skills from those he has acquired as a plumber. For this reason we frequently see a company out of balance. The owner may bring to it a sales orientation but have no financial knowledge; or the owner may have creative talents but be weak in implementation. While major weaknesses can often be corrected, or supplemented through staff additions, the owner must recognize his or her limitations and arrange for these missing skills to be brought into the organization.

The success of a new venture often depends on the influences which motivate the entrepreneur. One study of 200 new start-ups (Turok and Richardson, 1989) found that unemployed people who set up in business are motivated more by a desire to achieve employment than to achieve independence or financial reward. In turn, they are more likely to fail than employed people who establish their own firms and whose motivation is most likely to be a desire to achieve independence. Three quarters of the founders of businesses that ceased trading were previously unemployed, compared with less than one third of those who were still trading. Therefore, businesses started by unemployed people are less likely to survive.

The small company is less likely to survive a significant downturn in its trade than the other two types of company. By reason of its size it has limited resources with which to rebuild. It will also be hampered in its turnaround efforts by its own shallow management capabilities. When trouble strikes, the small business owner may have little idea of where to turn, just as he or she has little idea of what to do. The net result is that the company may fade away with no attempt to achieve a turnaround.

However, the smaller company also has considerable, often overlooked strengths that can be decisive in a downturn. First, the company has great flexibility in its options, and is free of the constraints and complexities of large companies. It can change form and shape with remarkable simplicity. For example, a surprising number of small companies that were dependent on the steel industry survived the recession in the early 1980s. Many were able to develop new processes (e.g. rolling paper) and new markets abroad. Second, the owners of small businesses may bring to a turnaround a greater determination to succeed than the managers of large companies, if only because they may have more at stake in a professional sense.

High rollers

Only a small percentage of all companies are high rollers. Unlike the case with most small companies, the characters who head high rollers are colourful, flamboyant people whose enterprises capture the imagination of the investing public, fuelling the company to fantastic heights where even more money can be attracted. But these companies are founded with the same kind of management defects as the small companies that fail. Unfortunately, as such a company rapidly expands the proprietor does not introduce formal management procedures, with the result that the defects that existed at the beginning are not corrected. After a certain point, turnover grows but profits remain the same. The company is clearly overtrading. Bankers refuse further advances and the company collapses.

Large companies

In contrast to the previous two types, the larger companies which collapse are usually professionally managed and publicly owned. These are mature companies that have become sluggish or lost touch with their markets. Many have enjoyed years of profitable operation before going into decline. They generally go through three stages on the way to failure: initial downturn, plateau and final collapse. A company with a reasonably strong balance sheet can plateau for years without coming to grips with its problems.

These companies have a greater chance of turnaround because they are so solidly based. The greater the size of the troubled company the more profound the effect of failure and the greater the support for survival. The large company also has a greater reservoir of assets with which to rebuild and the mature organization has greater management strength and the ability to attract an effective turnaround team. Also, the government may be unwilling to allow collapse. Unemployment is a major concern and the collapse of a large company often leads to the failure of others. However, job losses may have to be faced if a company is to be run efficiently, because failure may be caused by over-staffing, leading to poor productivity.

Strategies for survival

In spite of the differences between the three types of companies considered above, corporate survival depends on remarkably similar strategies (Goldstein, 1988). An ailing company must:

(1) recognize its problems and face them squarely;
(2) stem losses, marshal resources and stabilize itself for the turnaround;
(3) understand the causes of decline, evaluate its present position and design a long-term turnaround programme;
(4) restructure its debt, regain profitability and position itself so that it can go forward as a stable, healthy enterprise.

Case Study
Budgetary Planning at Jay plc

At Jay plc financial planning begins with the setting of the company's financial objectives and the adoption of broad guidelines of financial strategy to reach these objectives. The board of directors, following a comparison with the company's competitors and a consideration of prevailing general economic conditions, concludes that Jay plc should be earning at least a 14 per cent return after taxation on total assets employed. In the previous two years Jay plc has earned returns of 13 and 12 per cent. Accordingly, the directors have made it clear to top-level managers of the company that reaching a 14 per cent return on capital employed is the number one financial objective for the next year.

The effective use of budgetary control procedures represents the most effective means of reaching the company's financial target. The method of co-ordinating planning budgets for the company as a whole and the final outcome of the process is given below.

Step 1: Sales budget

Budgetary planning begins with the sales budget. The other budgets are based directly or indirectly upon this budget. The sales budget is prepared from sales forecasts, which incorporate estimates of the levels of sales at different prices. Once the sales forecast is completed, the sales budget may be derived from the target sales established both as regards price and sales volume. The sales forecast is developed by accumulating sales projections from the sales departments, market studies, extrapolation of current sales and statistical analysis involving such factors as gross national product, personal incomes, employment and price levels.

Profit planning for next year usually requires more than one cycle of effort by the various managers involved in the budgetary process. Initially, when all the details and separate parts of next year's profit budget are finally put together and summarized, the budgeted profit and loss account may reveal that the operating profit for the next year would not be enough for the company to earn a sufficient rate of return on its assets. Therefore, the management would 'go back to the drawing board' to try to find ways of improving the profit plan. From this process the management of Jay plc sets the sales price at £10 per unit and prepared the sales budget as follows:

	1st quarter	2nd quarter	3rd quarter	4th quarter	Total
Units					
Yorkshire	10,000	12,000	14,000	16,000	52,000
Lancashire	4,000	5,000	6,000	7,000	22,000
	14,000	17,000	20,000	23,000	74,000
Value (£)					
Yorkshire	100,000	120,000	140,000	160,000	520,000
Lancashire	40,000	50,000	60,000	70,000	220,000
	140,000	170,000	200,000	230,000	740,000

Step 2: Cost of goods sold budget

From the estimate of sales volume the budget director can prepare an estimate of cost of goods sold. On the basis of past experience and recent trends, he estimates that the cost of the product will be £5 per unit. The cost of goods sold budget is prepared by applying this unit cost to the numbers of units to be sold:

	1st quarter	2nd quarter	3rd quarter	4th quarter	Total
Units (step 1)	14,000	17,000	20,000	23,000	74,000
Cost of sales (£)	70,000	85,000	100,000	115,000	370,000

Step 3: Purchases budget

The sales budget provides the basis for planning purchases and stocks of the necessary merchandise. Jay plc has 4,000 units on hand in stock at the beginning of 19X1. The purchasing department decides that it should have the following quantities on hand at the end of each quarter to maintain an ample safety margin in relation to the sales volume: first quarter 6,000 units; second quarter 7,000 units; third quarter 8,000 units; fourth quarter 9,000 units. The purchasing department also supplies information about the estimated costs of the purchases, £5 per unit throughout the year. This information is summarized in the purchases budget as follows:

	1st quarter £	2nd quarter £	3rd quarter £	4th quarter £
Desired closing stock	6,000	7,000	8,000	9,000
Add: sales	14,000	17,000	20,000	23,000
Total required	20,000	24,000	28,000	32,000
Less: opening stock	4,000	6,000	7,000	8,000
Purchases required	16,000	18,000	21,000	24,000
Price per unit	5	5	5	5
Total purchases	80,000	90,000	105,000	120,000

Step 4: Selling expenses budget

The sales department management provides estimates of the expenses that will be incurred in achieving the sales shown in the sales budget. These are based on past experience, current trends and plans for future operations. From the data submitted by the sales department the budget director prepares a selling expenses budget showing estimated expenses for each quarter and for the year:

	1st quarter	2nd quarter	3rd quarter	4th quarter	Total
	£	£	£	£	£
Salaries	17,000	21,000	25,000	28,000	91,000
Expenses	6,000	7,000	8,000	9,000	30,000
Advertising	4,000	4,500	5,000	6,000	19,500
Other	2,000	2,500	3,000	3,000	10,500
	29,000	35,000	41,000	46,000	151,000

Step 5: Administrative expenses budget

Executives at the general administrative level provide estimates of the administrative expenses expected during the year. Many of these are fixed in nature and do not vary with the predicted sales volume. From the data submitted the budget director prepares an administrative expenses budget:

	1st quarter	2nd quarter	3rd quarter	4th quarter	Total
	£	£	£	£	£
Salaries	10,000	13,000	14,000	18,000	55,000
Stationery	2,000	2,000	2,500	2,500	9,000
Other	3,000	3,000	3,500	4,500	14,000
	15,000	18,000	20,000	25,000	78,000

Step 6: Payment on purchases budget

From the purchases budget, the budget director can prepare a budget showing payments to be made on purchases during each quarter. Jay plc pays 50 per cent of its accounts during the quarter in which the purchases are made and pays the remaining 50 per cent during the following quarters. Creditors of £50,000 from 19X0 are unpaid at the beginning of the year. The payment on purchases budget is shown below:

Purchases made during	1st quarter	2nd quarter	3rd quarter	4th quarter	Total
	£	£	£	£	£
4th quarter 19X0	50,000				50,000
1st quarter 19X1	40,000	40,000			80,000
2nd quarter 19X1		45,000	45,000		90,000
3rd quarter 19X1			52,500	52,500	105,000
4th quarter 19X1				60,000	60,000
	90,000	85,000	97,500	112,500	385,000

Step 7: Receipts from debtors budget

The accounting department submits data about predicted receipts from debtors. Jay plc makes all its sales on credit. Past experience indicates that 40 per cent of sales on credit are collected during the quarter in which they are made and the remaining 60 per cent are collected in the following quarter. During the first quarter the company expects to collect £60,000 cash on 19X0 sales.

Sales made during	1st quarter	2nd quarter	3rd quarter	4th quarter	Total
	£	£	£	£	£
4th quarter 19X0	60,000				60,000
1st quarter 19X1	56,000	84,000			140,000
2nd quarter 19X1		68,000	102,000		170,000
3rd quarter 19X1			80,000	120,000	200,000
4th quarter 19X1				92,000	92,000
	116,000	152,000	182,000	212,000	662,000

Step 8: Cash budget

The cash budget consists of the estimates of cash receipts and cash payments considered in steps 3, 4, 5, 6 and 7. The opening balance for the year is £10,000. Dividends of £40,000 are to be paid in the fourth quarter. Corporation tax of £50,000 is to be paid in the fourth quarter.

	1st quarter	2nd quarter	3rd quarter	4th quarter	Total
	£	£	£	£	£
Opening cash balance	10,000	(8,000)	6,000	29,500	10,000
Cash receipts (step 7)	116,000	152,000	182,000	212,000	662,000
Total cash available	126,000	144,000	188,000	241,500	672,000
Cash payments					
Purchases (step 6)	90,000	85,000	97,500	112,500	385,000
Selling expenses (step 4)	29,000	35,000	41,000	46,000	151,000
Administrative expenses (step 5)	15,000	18,000	20,000	25,000	78,000
Dividends				40,000	40,000
Corporation tax				50,000	50,000
Total payments	134,000	138,000	158,500	273,500	704,000
Closing balance	(8,000)	6,000	29,500	(32,000)	(32,000)

The cash budget provides a clear view of the timing of both cash inflows and cash outflows over a given period. We saw in Chapter 1 that a company must always have enough cash available to meet liabilities when they fall due. In our example, Jay plc faces a cash deficiency in the first and fourth quarters. The company must plan, therefore, how to obtain a borrowing facility to cover the forecast deficit.

Step 9: Budgeted profit and loss account

The purpose of the budgeted profit and loss account is to summarize and integrate all the operating budgets so as to measure the company's income.

		£
Sales (step 1)		740,000
Cost of goods sold (step 2)		370,000
Gross margin		370,000
Selling expenses (step 4)	151,000	
Administrative expenses (step 5)	78,000	229,000
Net profit before tax		141,000
Tax (35%)		49,350
Net profit after tax		91,650

Step 10: Budgeted balance sheet

The final step is the projection of the budgeted results on the firm's financial position at the end of the year. The accountant takes the balance sheet for the end of the current year and combines these data with the transactions reflected in the various budgets to obtain an estimate of the balance sheet at the end of next year.

	£	£	£
Fixed assets			
Land and buildings			600,000
Current assets			
Stocks		45,000	
Debtors		138,000	
Cash		(32,000)	
		151,000	
Creditors: amounts falling due within one year			
Creditors	60,000		
Tax	49,350	109,350	41,650
			641,650
Capital reserves			
Called-up share capital			575,000
Retained profits			66,650
			641,650

Conclusion

Jay plc's directors formulated a 14 per cent return on capital employed as the number one financial objective for next year. The budgeted figures show that this target is expected to be achieved:

$$\text{Budgeted return on capital employed} = \frac{£91,650}{£641,650} = 14.3\%$$

However, the cash budget shows that the company is expected to face a cash deficiency in the first and fourth quarters. In addition to planning a borrowing facility, there may be opportunities to improve liquidity management. This is the subject of Chapter 4, where we consider various methods for accelerating cash inflow and delaying the outflow to minimize cash requirements.

REFERENCES AND FURTHER READING

Argenti, J. (1976) *Corporate Collapse*, McGraw-Hill, New York.
Cork Committee Report, CMND 8558, para. 1785.
Gaffney, M. (1983) Small firms really can be helped, *Management Accounting*, February.
Ganguly, P. and Bannock, G. (1985) *U.K. Small Business Statistics and International Comparisons*, Paul Chapman Publishing, London.
Goldstein, A. S. (1988) *Corporate Comeback – Managing Turnarounds and Troubled Companies*, Wiley, New York.
Grinyer, P. H., Mayes, D. G. and McKiernan, P. (1988) *Sharpbenders – The Secrets of Unleasing Corporate Potential*, Basil Blackwell, Oxford.
Norgard, R. (1987) Forecasting corporate failure, *The Chartered Accountant in Australia*, August.
Peters, T. S. and Waterman, R. H. (1982) *In Search of Excellence: Lessons from America's Best-Run Companies*, Harper & Row, New York.
Ross, J. E. and Kami, M. S. (1973) *Corporate Management in Crisis*, Prentice-Hall, Englewood Cliffs, New Jersey.
Schendel, D., Patton, G. R. and Riggs, J. (1976) Corporate turnaround strategies: a study of profit decline and recovery, *Journal of General Management*.
Slatter, S. (1984) *Corporate Recovery*, Penguin, Harmondsworth.
Turok, I. and Richardson, P. (1989) *Strathclyde Papers on Planning, Supporting the Start-Up and Growth of Small Firms*, University of Strathclyde.

3
Indicators of Business Failure

We saw in Chapter 1 that the future likely success of a business can be predicted by either:

(1) analysing the quality of its management and the resulting strategic plan and/or its implementation (causes of failure), or
(2) observing the performance indicators (symptoms of failure).

Although corporate collapse is usually dramatized in the media as a sudden occurrence, this is almost never the case. Corporate failure is the result of a long-term deterioration in financial performance. Early warning signs do exist in the business world which can be spotted early enough to trigger action which would prevent ultimate failure. Furthermore, the health of a company can be determined in a way similar to that of an individual. Thus, an enterprise which subjects itself to a regular review programme is most likely to identify warning signs of 'sickness' early enough to take corrective action.

This chapter examines the warning signs that can be derived from published company accounts. If management recognize that problems exist at an early date they can save many of the resources which are wasted during a prolonged period of decline. The authors' research shows that many companies which collapse do not have the financial information available which is needed to trigger the necessary action. The managements of these companies are not able to interpret the danger signals and select the options that might ensure survival. In other companies the warning signs are simply ignored. Sometimes creative accounting is employed to try to conceal those signs from those parties who may have an interest in the performance of the company.

SOLVENCY ANALYSIS

To remain solvent a company needs to have sufficient funds available to meet obligations as they fall due. A situation may arise where a company has substantial non-liquid assets and is trading profitably but, if it becomes unable to meet liabilities as they fall due, it may be forced into a hasty realization of assets. Such a situation may not be apparent from a casual reading of the accounts. Rising profits and the existence of substantial net assets may draw the reader's attention away from the indicators of potential insolvency. For this reason, solvency analysis is best understood within a framework of a funds flow model. Utilizing this model Beaver (1966) views the firm as a reservoir of liquid assets which is supplied by inflows and drained by outflows. The solvency of the firm can be defined in terms of the probability that the reservoir will be exhausted, at which point the firm will be unable to pay its obligations as they mature. From this Beaver derives four propositions:

(1) the larger the reservoir of liquid assets the smaller the probability of failure;
(2) the larger the funds flow from operations the smaller the probability of failure;
(3) the larger the amount of debt held by a company the greater the probability of failure;
(4) the larger the fund expenditures from operations, the greater the probability of failure.

TRADITIONAL RATIO ANALYSIS

The 'amount' of funds in the reservoir can be indirectly measured by financial performance indicators which reflect the firm's liquidity, gearing and profitability. This involves the computation of a series of financial ratios based on past profit and loss accounts and balance sheets. The ratios that are considered in this section are shown in Table 3.1.

Comparisons of data based on financial ratios need to be made with caution. There are several problems which may be encountered. One is the frequent use of absolute standards for making comparisons. For example, many textbooks state that companies should aim for a ratio of current assets to current liabilities of 2:1. It is dangerous to assume that there are hard and fast norms such as this. The process of deciding whether ratios are satisfactory or not depends on many circumstances which involve judgement. A second problem concerns extraneous factors which may invalidate comparisons if not taken into account. If comparisons of ratios are made through time it is important to identify (and if possible allow for) any changes which have taken place in the environment in which an organization operates, or in the accounting policies which it adopts. If the inflation rate has doubled, or if a government has introduced legal restraints on dividend payments by companies, accounting data will not be directly comparable. Likewise, if a company has altered its accounting treatment of important items, such as stock valuation or leases, comparisons will be invalid unless the items are adjusted to a common base. The same problem exists for inter-firm comparisons. If companies adopt different accounting policies comparisons are difficult. The accounting standards programme aims to ease this difficulty by standardizing accounting methods or ensuring that sufficient information is disclosed to enable users to identify material differences in accounting treatment.

Table 3.1 Financial performance indicators

Liquidity ratios

1 Current ratio: $\dfrac{\text{Current assets}}{\text{Current liabilities}}$

2 Quick ratio: $\dfrac{\text{Current assets} - \text{Stock}}{\text{Current liabilities}}$

3 Debtors turnover: $\dfrac{\text{Debtors}}{\text{Turnover}} \times 365$ days

4 Stock turnover: $\dfrac{\text{Turnover}}{\text{Stock}}$

Gearing ratios

5 Capital gearing: $\dfrac{\text{Fixed interest and fixed dividend capital}}{\text{Ordinary share capital and reserves}}$

6 Interest cover: $\dfrac{\text{Operating profit before interest and tax}}{\text{Interest payable}}$

Profitability

7 $\dfrac{\text{Profit before interest and tax}}{\text{Total assets employed}}$

Liquidity ratios

Liquidity ratios are concerned with an organization's current financial position, that is, its ability to meet its current financial obligations. Liquidity implies the ready ability to convert assets into cash. If an enterprise cannot meet its current obligations as they become due its continued existence becomes doubtful.

The current ratio is considered by many textbooks to be the most widely used measure of the firm's liquidity position because current liabilities are usually paid with funds generated by turning current assets into cash within the current operating period. The current ratio aims to provide a measure of the margin of safety in meeting obligations that will fall due during the current period. If a company's current assets are large in relation to the value of current liabilities, it is highly probable that the liabilities can be paid as they fall due. As stated earlier, it is dangerous to assume rules or norms for adequate liquidity. In a detailed study Ohlson (1980) found that the average current ratio of the failed businesses in his sample was above the mystical 2:1 standard in all five years preceding the ultimate failure. The current ratio is a static concept of what resources are available at a given time to meet the obligations of that moment, whereas future flows of funds depend on elements not included in the ratio, such as sales, profits and changes in business conditions.

Wright (1956) showed how changes in the current ratio are difficult to interpret.

> It would appear therefore that the interpretation of the current ratio is so ambiguous as to be almost worthless. An increase in the current ratio may indicate over-stocking, poor credit control, loss of sales or repayment of overdrafts; a decrease may reflect better stock and credit management, greater use of bank finance or overtrading and non-payment of creditors.

The quick ratio (see Table 3.1) is a more rigorous test of liquidity. However, it suffers from all the disadvantages of the current ratio and the widely held rule of 1:1 must be viewed with scepticism. Robertson (1983) researched the predictiveness of the quick ratio in forecasting failure and was able to show that many retail businesses could survive with quick ratios of only 0.5.

Figure 3.1 shows how cash flows within a firm begin in a cash reservoir and move to raw materials through purchases. Raw materials are placed into production and the funds representing finished goods are accumulated through costs and move on again to finished goods. Finally, as finished goods are sold the funds return to the cash reservoir, normally via debtors.

The debtors turnover ratio indicates how quickly debt is turned into cash. Similarly, the stock turnover ratio is a gauge of liquidity in that it conveys a measure of the speed with which stock can be converted into cash. Both ratios need to be interpreted with caution. For example, a low debtors balance may indicate that credit terms are too restrictive and the company is losing business, while a low inventory figure may result in high costs at a future date if the company runs out of stock.

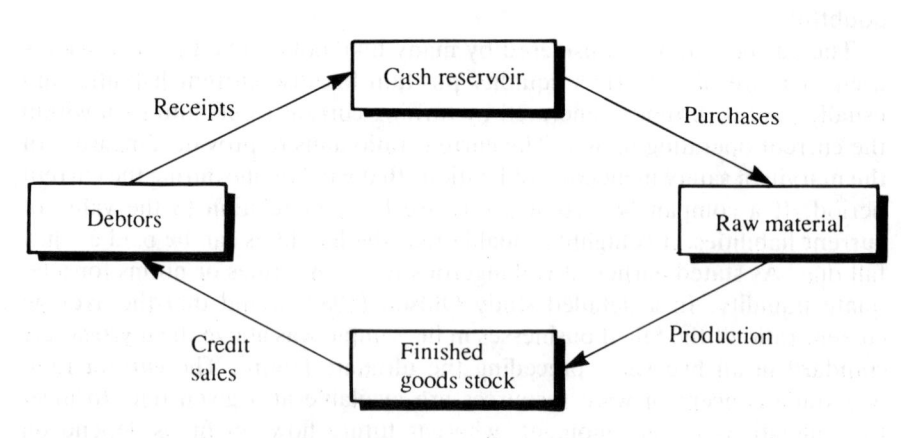

Figure 3.1 Flow of working capital

Gearing ratios

These ratios relate to an organization's ability to survive and operate in the long term. They give indications of the organization's fitness for future trading and are concerned with its long-term financial structure.

The chief indicator of long-term financial position is the capital gearing ratio (see Table 3.1), which shows the relationship between shareholders' funds and loan capital. This ratio may be calculated on either book values or market values of securities. Here, we consider book values only. Companies are considered highly geared if a relatively large proportion of capital is in forms which carry interest charges, and low geared if the reverse applies. The significance of gearing is that it introduces financial risk to both a company and its shareholders. One aspect of this is the risk of failure. Interest charges attaching to capital, for example interest on debentures, are contractual obligations which, if not met, could result in failure. This clearly presents a risk to both company and shareholders. The second aspect of financial risk is the extra variability in earnings to shareholders which results from gearing. Earnings to shareholders are the residue in the profit and loss account and their value depends upon earnings from operations and deductions therefrom, including fixed charges. To illustrate this, consider the example of a company which has £1 million of 10 per cent debentures as its only long-term fixed-charge capital and earnings net of non-interest expenses of £250,000. Assume that corporation tax is charged at 40 per cent.

The effect of this company's gearing is felt if operating earnings (represented by pre-tax earnings net of non-interest expenses) vary: earnings to shareholders will vary more. In Table 3.2 we illustrate the effects of the stated percentage changes in operating earnings on shareholders' income. Because of gearing, earnings to shareholders fall by 17 per cent when operating earnings fall by 10 per cent. This differential increases if gearing becomes higher. Gearing is not wholly disadvantageous as the examples of growing earnings show: shareholders benefit more than proportionately from growth.

An alternative way of indicating the effects of financial structure and its attendant risks is found by using figures from the profit and loss account to calculate the interest cover ratio:

$$\frac{\text{Operating profit before interest and tax}}{\text{Interest payable}}$$

Profitability

Our discussion in the previous section shows the importance of long-term profitability as an indicator of performance. Profits are one of the most desirable and reliable sources of funds for the longer-term payment of interest and the repayment of principal. As a source of funds generated by operations,

Table 3.2 The effects of gearing on operating earnings

	Decrease in operating earnings from base:		Base (£000)	Increase in operating earnings from base:	
	20%	10%		10%	20%
Pre-tax operating earnings	200	225	250	275	300
Interest	(100)	(100)	(100)	(100)	(100)
Pre-tax earnings	100	125	150	175	200
Corporation tax (at 40%)	(40)	(50)	(60)	(70)	(80)
Earnings to shareholders	60	75	90	105	120
% change in earnings to shareholders from base	−33	−17		+17	+33

profits are the yardstick against which the coverage of interest and other fixed charges is measured. Furthermore, a reliable and stable trend of profits is one of the best assurances of an enterprise's ability to borrow in times of funds shortage and its consequent ability to extricate itself from the very conditions that lead to insolvency.

Profitability is measured by the ratio:

$$\frac{\text{Profit before interest and tax}}{\text{Total assets employed}}$$

This ratio reflects the ability of management to generate profit on a given amount of total assets. Profit before interest and tax is used in order to eliminate the influence of differential tax treatment and different capital structure decisions on earnings performance. The use of total assets as a denominator rather than net assets is justified by Horngren (1970) as follows: 'The measurement of operating performance (i.e. how profitably assets are employed) should not be influenced by the management's financial decisions (i.e. how assets are obtained). Operating performance is best measured by the rate of return on total assets.'

The profitability ratio may be disaggregated into other ratios which represent different aspects of performance. In particular, it should be noted that two secondary ratios (representing two aspects of business performance) comprise the primary ratio, thus:

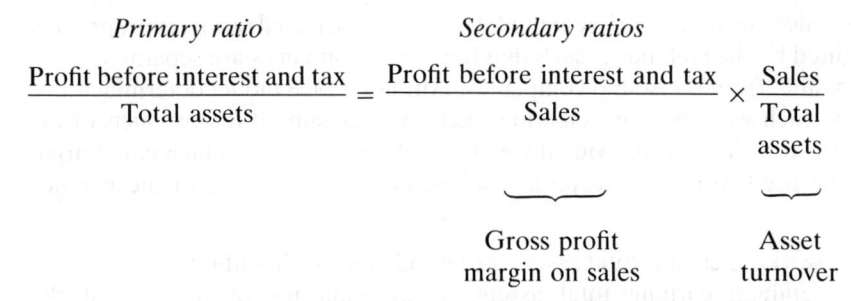

$$\underbrace{\frac{\text{Profit before interest and tax}}{\text{Total assets}}}_{\textit{Primary ratio}} = \underbrace{\frac{\text{Profit before interest and tax}}{\text{Sales}}}_{\substack{\text{Gross profit}\\\text{margin on sales}}} \times \underbrace{\frac{\text{Sales}}{\text{Total assets}}}_{\substack{\text{Asset}\\\text{turnover}}}$$

The gross profit margin assesses the profitability of sales, while the asset turnover ratio assesses the ability of the company's assets to generate sales.

PREDICTIVE MODELS

Using more powerful statistical techniques than his predecessors, Beaver (1966) found that financial ratios proved to be useful in the prediction of failure in that such failure could be predicted at least five years before the event. He concluded that ratios could be used to distinguish accurately companies that would fail from those that would not, with much more success than would be possible by random prediction. One of his significant conclusions was that the most effective predictor of failure was the ratio of both short-term and long-term cash flow to total debt. Beaver defined 'cash flow' as net profit plus depreciation; 'total debt' includes current and long-term liabilities. The next best ratio was the ratio of net income to total assets. One of Beaver's most surprising findings was that the current ratio was among the worst predictors of failure. Turnover ratios were found to be at the bottom of the list of effective predictors. Generally, Beaver found that 'mixed ratios' which had income or cash flows compared to assets or liabilities, out-performed short-term solvency ratios which had been believed traditionally to be the best predictors of failure.

In a later study, Beaver (1968) suggested that business failure tends to be determined by permanent factors. He argued that if the basic financial position of a company was sound and profit prospects were good it would recover from a temporary shortage of liquid assets, but that if the long-term prospects in these regards were not good, business failure could not be prevented by a good liquid position.

Altman (1968) extended Beaver's univariate (single variable) analysis to allow for multiple predictors of business failure using a statistical technique known as multiple discriminant analysis. His work set a new standard and was a turning point in research studies into predicting corporate failure. This technique is applied to two groups of financial ratios, one set derived from the last accounts of companies prior to failure and the other from the accounts of sound companies. The statistical procedure is then designed to select the set of measures that together best discriminate between the two groups of companies, and derives a linear model made up of selected ratios, appropriately weighted by the technique, such that the failed companies are separated as far as possible from the sound companies. Altman's 1968 model determined five ratios, each with its own weighting, such that the sum of the products of the individual ratios and individual weights yielded a Z score which could arguably be used to predict corporate failure or not. These five financial ratios were:

X_1 = working capital/total assets, as an indicator of liquidity;
X_2 = retained earnings/total assets, as an indicator of the age of the firm and its cumulative profitability;
X_3 = earnings before interest and tax/total assets, as an indicator of profitability;
X_4 = market value of the equity/book value of debt, as an indicator of financial structure;
X_5 = sales/total assets, as an indicator of capital turnover.

The discriminant function chosen after numerous computer runs was:

$$Z = 0.012X_1 + 0.014X_2 + 0.033X_3 + 0.006X_4 + 0.010X_5$$

The pass mark for Altman's Z score is 3.0. Companies scoring above that level should be safe, while companies scoring below 1.8 will be classified as potential failures. Altman's five-variable model correctly identified 95 per cent of the total sample of companies tested for failure. This percentage rate of success in predicting failure fell to 72 per cent when the data used was obtained two years prior to failure. As earlier data was used in testing the model, so its predictive ability became more unreliable.

Taffler (1983) has applied multiple discriminant analysis to companies in the United Kingdom. Although his Z score has not been published, the ratios and weightings given are as follows:

(1) income before tax/current liabilities (53 per cent);
(2) current assets/total liabilities (13 per cent);
(3) current liabilities/total assets (16 per cent);
(4) immediate assets (current liabilities/operating costs − depreciation) (16 per cent).

The major limitation of the research on corporate-distress prediction arises from the absence of a general theory of corporate failure with which to specify the variables to be included in the discriminant function. Furthermore, the research is of an *ex post* nature. To demonstrate that the results have direct applicability for auditors and others requires *ex ante* predictions about the failure, and its timing, of firms that currently have not failed. The wide range of error which is inherent in the studies seems to be underplayed by many researchers. For example, only 43 per cent of the 115 companies identified by Taffler as being at risk in a study in 1976 had failed in six years. This was in sharp contrast to the 98 per cent accuracy which was claimed at the development stage.

The importance of profitability

A large number of failure prediction models now exist (Jones, 1987). Overall, it is fairly clear that the major warning signal is low profitability measured over a period of years. This confirms our view of the development of insolvency as a long-term phenomenon. As we saw in Chapter 1, there is, over the longer term, a close relationship between the level of profits earned and the amount of cash generated. The effect of reduced profitability over a period of years is cumulative and can soon assume serious proportions. A fall in internally generated funds affects both working capital and the long-term investment vital for growth.

MEASURING FUNDS FLOW

The profit and loss account and the balance sheet are the two financial statements which traditionally have provided users of accounts with information concerning a company's activities. A major limitation of ratios derived from these statements is that they do not directly measure funds flow, a desirable characteristic for solvency analysis which we established at the beginning of this chapter. This is important in the short run where profitability and liquidity do not necessarily go together.

Profit and loss accounts emphasize the matching of revenues and costs, not the flows of resources, cash and otherwise, into and out of a company over a period of time. They concentrate only upon operating activities, not the effects of other important aspects of business activity, such as financing and investment decisions. Therefore, although the profit and loss account may show a favourable position, the company may have insufficient cash to meet its immediate needs. The balance sheet, although concentrating upon financing and investment, liabilities and assets, does so at particular points in time. One may make inferences about the investment and financing activities of a company by comparing the appropriate totals from opening and closing balance sheets for a period, but such information is not shown directly. Two statements, the cash-flow statement and the funds flow statement, attempt to deal with some of the deficiencies just noted.

Cash-flow statements

Cash is usually regarded as the most important resource possessed by any company. Cash gives a company command over resources and, perhaps of greater importance, allows a company to meet its commitments and thus remain in existence. Ultimately business transactions involve cash: wages and salaries are paid in cash, as are dividends, tax liabilities and creditors. Failure to meet contractual obligations, for example interest on borrowings or payments to creditors, may result in liquidation. Failure to make profits need not have the same result, at least in the short term.

Profitability and solvency are clearly related. Long-run solvency depends on long-run profitability. In the short run, however, profitability and solvency do not necessarily go together. First, accounting profit is determined by matching expenses with sales, rather than cash disbursements being matched with cash receipts. Revenue which accrues to a period may not involve the receipt of cash until later due to sales being made on credit. Similarly, expenses which are matched against those revenues may not involve cash outflows, e.g. depreciation or purchases on credit. Profit needs to be adjusted for such accruals if it is to be brought nearer to cash flow. Second, cash resources may have been affected by investment activities such as the acquisition or sale of fixed assets and investments and the making of loans. Third, cash may originate from sources other than the operations summarized in the profit and loss account, e.g. new issues of shares. Cash may be used for non-operating purposes such as the redemption of long-term debt and the payment of dividends. These are financing activities. A cash-flow statement is illustrated in Table 3.3.

Research shows that cash-flow statements provide useful information to users. Two studies have examined the collapse of W. T. Grant in the USA (Largay and Stickney, 1980) and Laker Airways in Britain (Lee, 1982). They concluded that cash-flow analysis would have indicated impending failure.

Table 3.3 Cash-flow statement

	£	£
Net cash flow from operating activities		
Net profit after tax	1,600	
Non-cash expenses, reserves, losses and gains included in profit:		
Depreciation	800	
Deferred tax	200	
Net increase in stock, debtors, creditors	(2,000)	
Increase in interest accrued but not paid	100	
Gain on sale of property	(600)	
Net cash flow from operating activities		100
Cash flows from investing activities		
Acquisition of plant and equipment	4,000	
Proceeds from disposal of property and plant	3,000	
Net cash used by investing activities		(1,000)
Cash flows from financing activities		
Increase in long-term debt	1,000	
Dividends paid	(500)	
Net cash provided by financing activities		500
Net decrease in cash		(400)

Table 3.4 Laker Airways: cash flow

	1976 £m	%	1977 £m	%	1978 £m	%
Operating cash flow	4.5	100	4.5	65	12.1	52
Additional borrowing	—	—	—	—	11.2	48
Decrease in cash assets	—	—	2.4	35	—	—
	4.5	100	6.9	100	23.3	100
Additional investment	0.5	11	3.5	51	19.1	82
Repayment of borrowing	2.1	47	3.4	49	—	—
Increase in cash assets	1.9	42	—	—	4.2	18
	4.5	100	6.9	100	23.3	100

	1979 £m	%	1980 £m	%	Total £m	%
Operating cash flow	10.7	27	17.6	25	49.4	34
Additional borrowing	27.3	68	52.0	74	90.5	62
Decrease in cash assets	2.0	5	0.8	1	5.2	4
	40.0	100	70.4	100	145.1	100
Additional investment	40.0	100	70.4	100	133.5	92
Repayment of borrowing	—	—	—	—	5.5	4
Increase in cash assets	—	—	—	—	6.1	4
	40.0	100	70.4	100	145.1	100

Lee (1982) compares the reported profit figures of Laker Airways from 1976 to 1980 with analysis of the cash flow, as shown in Table 3.4.

According to Lee, 'the full and stark picture of impending failure can only be seen in the cash flow analysis'. From 100 per cent contribution of cash inflow from operations in 1976, the figure falls steadily to 25 per cent by 1980, and averages 34 per cent over the five years. Borrowing, on the other hand, increased in an opposite direction with equivalent speed – 47 per cent of cash outflow was committed to borrowing repayment in 1976, deteriorating rapidly to a position where 74 per cent of cash inflow was received from net borrowings in 1980. Over the five years 62 per cent of the total inflow came from borrowings. Lee concludes, 'if cash flow analysis techniques had been used by the bankers responsible for the Laker Airways account, they ought to have become worried in 1978, and taken action after the 1979 reporting'.

Funds flow statements

For most people 'funds' are synonymous with cash and hence a common view of the funds of a business is that they are represented by its cash resources.

An alternative is to consider funds as working capital which is the focus of business activity. Together with fixed assets, working capital provides a business's operating capability. An expansion of business activity may require additional working capital which, in turn, requires either the investment of additional funds or the reallocation of existing funds. Cash may be the medium of exchange to obtain or support operating capability but it is only one part of the operating cycle. In contrast, working capital is at the centre of business operations.

This wider concept of funds includes all current assets and current liabilities and therefore a funds flow statement will explain the changes in net working capital during an accounting period. Figure 3.1 (see page 36) illustrates the flow of working capital throughout a business. This is the approach used in Statement of Standard Accounting Practice No. 10 (SSAP 10), which indicates that the following items would normally be included:

(1) *Sources*
   (a) profit for the period before taxation;
   (b) extraordinary items;
   (c) adjustments for items not involving the movement of funds;
   (d) issues of share capital;
   (e) funds raised by medium- or long-term loans;
   (f) proceeds from the sale of fixed and non-current assets.
(2) *Applications*
   (a) dividends paid;
   (b) taxation paid;
   (c) acquisitions of fixed and non-current assets;
   (d) repayment of medium- or long-term loans;
   (e) redemptions of issued share capital.
(3) *Change in working capital*, subdivided into
   (a) stocks;
   (b) debtors;
   (c) creditors;
   (d) net liquid funds (defined as cash at bank and in hand, with cash equivalents, less bank overdrafts and other borrowings repayable within one year).

Although SSAP 10 implies a working capital view of funds, the list of items above excludes proposed dividends and tax payable in favour of dividends paid and taxation paid, suggesting a cash concept of funds.

Usefulness of funds statements

At the beginning of this section we considered some of the deficiencies of balance sheets and profit and loss accounts in aiding users of financial statements in their evaluation of companies. Cash-flow and funds flow statements provide more information on company activities and the decisions of management over the relevant accounting period. We may conclude that the funds statement, whether in its cash or working capital form, can answer, *inter alia*, the following questions.

(1) Did the funds generated from ordinary trading activities cover payment of tax and dividends?
(2) How dependent is the company on external sources of financing, such as borrowing and new equity?
(3) Were the funds to pay taxation and dividend obligations raised by long-term borrowing or asset disposals?
(4) Are temporary loans or other short-term liabilities being used to finance long-term investments?
(5) How were loans repaid?
(6) How was the increase in working capital financed?

Over a number of years a series of funds statements may provide the analyst with valuable information on liquidity trends which assists his estimates of the future.

In common with other financial statements, the funds statement can reveal what has happened but cannot tell us why. For example, it may show an increase in stocks but it cannot tell us whether this occurred because of deliberate policy, poor stock control or an inability to sell the product. Similarly, an increase in share capital does not tell us whether this was the best method of raising the finance or whether the action could have been avoided by better asset control.

IMPROVING THE PREDICTABILITY OF ACCOUNTS

Two recommendations for improving the predictive ability of published company accounts are the introduction of future-orientated disclosure and the improvement of accounting standards.

Future-orientated information

Company accounts paint a picture of the past whereas users are usually more interested in the future. 'Making corporate reports valuable', a discussion document issued by the Research Committee of the Institute of Chartered Accountants of Scotland in 1988, recommends that company accounts disclose the following:

(1) a summary of the corporate financial plan for the next three years and the assumptions on which the plan is based; in addition, management should provide a discussion of the differences between the financial plan disclosed in last year's report and the actual results for the year;
(2) a forecast of future cash flows for the next three years.

Improving accounting standards

Earlier in this chapter we examined some of the problems that may be encountered in comparing company accounts. One such problem is the use of creative accounting, by which companies manipulate the figures reported in their annual accounts. This is a result of the flexibility of accounting rules which govern how financial statements should be prepared and presented. Creative accounting can be used to hide the true financial position of a failing company. Research shows that ailing companies are more likely than successful companies to make accounting changes that increase profits (Lilien, Mellman and Pastera, 1988). For example, in the 1960s Rolls-Royce was having difficulties in reporting a profit. Instead of charging research and development expenditure against income as they had in the past, the directors carried part of the expenditure forward as an asset in the 1967 balance sheet. In that year Rolls-Royce had a trading profit after interest of £17.5 million; it spent £9.6 million on research and development (of which only £5.7 million was charged against income) and £4.2 million was provided for tax. That left funds of £3.7 million in a year when the company paid out £6.1 million in dividends. At the time of the company's collapse in 1971 it was argued that this new policy had disguised the serious financial position of the company. The Rolls-Royce case had an important influence on the deliberations of the Accounting Standards Committee, which concluded initially that on the grounds of prudence, uniformity and the avoidance of subjectivity, expenditure on research and development should be written off in the years in which it is incurred.

In 1988 the Dearing Committee, which was set up to review current procedures for developing and enforcing accounting standards in Great Britain, published its findings and conclusions in a report (Dearing, 1988). The report paid tribute to the work of the Accounting Standards Committee during the eighteen years since its foundation but concluded that there is a consensus for change to respond to the needs of the present time. The report emphasized that compliance with accounting standards is best achieved by ensuring that standards are of high quality and command support throughout the financial and commercial community. It proposed that the Accounting Standards Committee should be replaced with an Accounting Standards Board under the guidance of a Financial Reporting Council and supported by a Review Panel. Furthermore, it proposed that the standard-setting process be speeded up and that new standards be more tightly drawn. These proposals should improve the quality of company accounts and therefore assist the external user better to evaluate the performance of companies. They are currently in the process of being implemented.

QUALITATIVE ANALYSIS

In addition to the accounting information so far considered in this chapter, qualitative sources of information exist which may have predictive content with respect to corporate failure. In this section we consider three types of qualitative information: the behaviour of directors, the timeliness of financial reporting, and going concern qualifications.

Behaviour of directors

Two aspects of the behaviour of directors warrant attention. First, are board resignations and appointments affected by directors' inside knowledge of impending corporate failure although this situation is not necessarily reflected in financial ratios? Second, do changes in directors' shareholdings correlate with impending good or bad news not necessarily reflected in financial ratios? These questions were considered by Peel, Peel and Pope (1985). They sampled seventy-eight companies (thirty-four failed and forty-four non-failed), all quoted on the London Stock Exchange. They concluded that failing companies are typified

> by a declining proportion of directors' holdings of beneficial shares as a proportion of total issued equity capital, by a higher frequency of resignations than appointments as a proportion of the total board (therefore, a net fall in the size of the board), and finally by an increasing frequency of resignations over the period of last accounts compared to previous year's published accounts.

Timeliness of financial reporting

The timing of corporate disclosures and variables associated with differential timing has attracted the attention of a number of researchers in recent years. The finding that bad news takes longer to reach the market has been fairly consistently documented (Whittred and Zimmer, 1984). These studies support the proposition that failing companies take longer to produce their annual financial statements than do healthy companies. Therefore, a long lag in the publication of these statements and an increase in this lag may be signals indicating impending company failure.

Going concern qualifications

According to SSAP 2, going concern is identified in terms 'that the enterprise will continue in operational existence for the foreseeable future. This means in particular that the profit and loss account and the balance sheet assume no intention or necessity to liquidate or curtail significantly the scale of operation.' 'Foreseeable future' is defined in the auditing guideline as extending to a minimum of six months following the date of the audit report or one year after the balance sheet date. The question arises: to what extent are failing companies qualified by auditors on going concern grounds? Taffler and Tseung (1984) examined a sample of eighty-six quoted industrial and distribution companies in the United Kingdom that were involved in insolvency proceedings in the seven-year period 1977 to 1983. Of these, only twenty-one were qualified on a going concern basis in their last accounts prior to failure. Therefore, audit qualifications are poor predictions of failure. Clearly auditors are reluctant to provide going concern qualifications for troubled companies in case they become self-fulfilling prophecies.

REFERENCES AND FURTHER READING

Altman, E. I. (1968) Financial ratios, discriminant analysis and the prediction of corporate bankruptcy, *Journal of Finance*, September.

Beaver, W. H. (1966) Financial ratios as predictors of failure, *Empirical Research in Accounting: Selected Studies*, supplement to *Journal of Accounting Research*.

Beaver, W. H. (1968) Alternative accounting measures as predictors of failure, *Accounting Review*, January.

Dearing Report (1988) *The Making of Accounting Standards*, Report of the Review Committee, ICAEW, London.

Horngren, C. T. (1970) *Accounting for Management Control – an Introduction*, 2nd ed, Prentice-Hall, Englewood Cliffs, New Jersey.

Jones, F. L. (1987) Current techniques in bankruptcy prediction, *Journal of Accounting Literature*, Vol. 6.

Largay, J. A. and Stickney, C. P. (1980) Cash flows, ratio analysis and the W. T. Grant Company bankruptcy, *Financial Analysts Journal*, July–August.

Lee, T. A. (1982) Laker Airways – the cash flow truth, *Accountancy*, June.

Lilien, S., Mellman, M. and Pastera, V. (1988) Accounting changes: successful versus unsuccessful firms, *Accounting Review*, October.

Ohlson, J. A. (1980) Financial ratios and the probabilistic prediction of bankruptcy, *Journal of Accounting Research*, Spring.

Peel, M. J., Peel, D. A. and Pope, P. F. (1985) Some evidence on corporate failure and the behaviour of non-financial ratios, *Investment Analyst*, January.

Robertson, J. (1983) Company failure: measuring changes in financial health through ratio analysis, *Management Accounting*, November.

Taffler, R. J. (1983) The assessment of company solvency and performance using a statistical model, *Accounting and Business Research*, Autumn.

Taffler, R. J. and Tseung, M. (1984) The audit going concern qualification in practice – exploding some myths, *Accountant's Magazine*, July.

Whittred, G. and Zimmer, I. (1984) Timeliness of financial reporting and financial distress, *Accountancy Review*, April.

Wright, F. K. (1956) An examination of the working capital ratio, *Australian Accountant*, March.

4
Aspects of Liquidity Management

Companies generally become insolvent because of poor trading performance leading to lower profits and a subsequent cash crisis. However, a surprising number of companies that have been generating satisfactory profits fail because they run out of cash. The objective of this chapter is to examine the policies that management can adopt to ensure that this does not happen.

Liquidity (or working capital) management refers to the management of short-term assets – cash, trade debtors, stock and short-term investments – and their financing by bank overdrafts and credit received from suppliers. The objective of liquidity management is to ensure both that proper control is exercised over the assets of the company and that sufficient liquid funds are available when required. In the absence of a sufficient supply of working capital a company finds itself unable to continue to survive in much the same way as the human body does without an adequate supply of blood.

Working capital is required for two main reasons: first, business takes place on credit, which causes a lag in the inflow of cash to the company; second, money may be tied up in stocks to ensure a continuous supply of raw materials and finished goods. The volatile nature of working capital imposes a strain on the company's financing (Firth, 1976). Fluctuations can result from seasonal factors or can relate to fiscal and monetary policies imposed by the government, or to changes in policies of management aimed at stimulating business or meeting competitive pressures.

PRINCIPLES OF WORKING CAPITAL MANAGEMENT

Before dealing with the management of the main current assets we examine some general principles for the management of these assets as a group.

Minimize investment

The need to hold sufficient working capital in order to allow the smooth running of a profitable company is costly. First, working capital ties up a company's funds and prevents their use for other purposes, such as buying plant and equipment. Second, a company's return on investment in assets can be maximized if the minimum necessary level of capital is maintained. This can be seen from the following relationship:

$$\text{Return on investment} = \frac{\text{Profit}}{\text{Current assets} + \text{Fixed assets}}$$

Clearly, the lower the amount of current assets for given levels of profit and fixed assets, the higher will be the return on investment achieved.

Relationship with sales level

The relationship between the level of a company's sales and the level of its working capital is an important one for management to understand and control. When a company decides to increase its level of sales, there must be an asset base consisting of current and fixed assets sufficient to support this sales growth. Although the existing facilities of plant and equipment may be adequate for several years, there will certainly have to be increased commitments to the cash, trade debtors and stock accounts. Similarly, when a company experiences a permanent sales decline, the asset base should be decreased because it is too large to support the lower level of sales. Asset reduction strategies are discussed in Chapter 5.

Managing working capital efficiently

In addition to minimizing the level of working capital, funds should be managed efficiently by adopting the following strategies.

(1) Pay trade creditors as late as possible without damaging the company's credit rating, but take advantage of favourable cash discounts, which are an enticement to pay accounts early in order to reduce the purchase price of goods.
(2) Turn over stock as quickly as possible, avoiding stockouts (i.e. running short of stock) that might result in shutting down the production line or a loss of sales.
(3) Collect trade debtors' accounts as quickly as possible without losing future sales due to high-pressure collection techniques. Cash discounts may be used to accomplish this objective.

Working capital must be kept circulating or turning over by ensuring that the cycle from stock to debtors to cash is kept moving. In fact, the greater the speed of this cycle, the lower the amount of working capital needed for a given level of sales in a particular type of business.

CASH MANAGEMENT

Since the other major current assets (stocks and trade debtors) will eventually be converted into cash through receipts and sales, cash is the denomination to which all liquid assets can be reduced. The aim of cash management is to minimize the investment in cash while at the same time protecting the company against sudden, unforeseen cash drains.

Given that cash balances do not earn money, why does the company hold them? The two most important motives commonly advanced are the transactions motive and the precautionary motive. Transaction balances are kept in order to meet routine cash needs such as the purchase of raw materials and to meet payroll commitments. Precautionary balances are kept to meet unexpected drains on the company's cash caused by such things as steep increases in raw material costs, shifts in consumer demand and unexpected slow-downs in the collection of trade debtors.

The main determinants of the amount of cash a company should hold are the regularity and predictability of its cash inflows and outflows. The greater the uncertainty, the more cash must be held as a buffer against unforeseen demands. The question of balance is of central importance. A balance must be achieved between the liquidity and profitability objectives of financial management which, in this case, are opposed to each other. By holding large cash balances the company is able to meet debts and reduce the risk of insolvency. However, because cash does not earn interest, the greater the amount of resources kept as cash balances, the less the profit-earning potential of the company.

CASH BUDGETING

It is generally agreed that the most effective tool for planning and controlling a business's liquidity is a cash budget which shows the receipts and payments and the estimated cash balances for each interval of the budget period. The preparation of a cash budget was described in the case study in Chapter 2: 'Budgetary planning at Jay plc'. In that study the cash budget is divided into quarterly intervals, which implies a stable level of cash flows. The more seasonal and uncertain a company's cash flows, the greater the number of intervals. Usually a monthly or weekly analysis will be required.

The major purpose of the cash budget is to co-ordinate the timing of the company's cash need. It identifies those times when the company will be short of cash so that arrangements can be made early and without undue pressure. The cash budget would identify such seasonal or abnormally large cash requirements as repayment of a bank loan. Also, it identifies those times when the company will have a temporary excess of cash, so it can invest the funds in short-term securities and earn additional income. The cash budget also allows the company to plan ahead so that it has sufficient cash on hand to take advantage of cash discounts available from its creditors, to pay obligations when due, to formulate dividend policy, to plan financing of capital expansion, and to help unify the production schedule during the year so that the company can smooth out costly seasonal fluctuations.

The first reaction to budgeted cash shortages should be: are they really necessary? If cash shortages are a result of the problems that cause company failure and which were dealt with in Chapter 2 – overtrading, poor credit control, excessive drawings, etc. – then an improvement in financial control is required. If they seem inevitable as a result of the company's expansion, the task is to decide how best to finance them from the various sources available. As we saw in Chapter 3, if the cash shortages arise from seasonal fluctuations which even out over time, then a short-term, self-liquidating source of funds like a bank overdraft should be used. If the shortages arise from a permanent need to increase working capital, or from investments in fixed assets, then long-term or permanent sources are more appropriate.

In addition to exercising care in the preparation of sales forecasts and other estimates in the cash budget, there are two ways of reducing the uncertainty of the cash budget. One is by preparing several cash budgets, based on optimistic, pessimistic and the most likely forecasts. This provides an idea of the best, worst and most likely cash balances that can be expected and allows management to determine the amount of financing necessary to cover the most adverse situation. It will also provide some indication of relative risks of various alternatives so that more intelligent short-term financial decisions are made. A second and more sophisticated way of reducing uncertainty in the cash budget is by computer simulations. By simulating the occurrence of sales and other uncertain events, a probability distribution of the company's closing cash balances for each week can be developed. Management can then determine the amount of financing necessary to provide a certain degree of protection against a cash shortage (Gallinger and Healey, 1989).

INCREASING THE EFFICIENCY OF CASH MANAGEMENT

The efficiency of cash management can be increased by accelerating receipts and slowing down payments. The objective is to maintain the same level of activity and profitability with less cash.

Accelerating receipts

Four ways of accelerating receipts and thereby lessening the need for cash are:

(1) *Prompt invoicing:* one of the simplest methods of accelerating receipts is to invoice promptly and accurately.
(2) *Trade discounts:* the objective of offering a trade discount for early payment is to speed up collection.

(3) *Concentration banking:* this a banking service whereby all accounts with one bank, irrespective of which branch they are held at, are consolidated for the purpose of interest calculation. This system minimizes overall interest expense and maximizes investable funds (Johnson and Aggarwal, 1988).

(4) *Lock-box services:* this is another method of reducing the amount of time that elapses between customers paying their bills and the company actually having the funds available for disbursement. The lock-box system differs from concentration banking in that, instead of mailing payments to a collection centre, customers send them to a post office box. This is emptied by the company's bank, which opens the payment envelopes, deposits the cheques in the company's account and sends a deposit slip indicating the payments received, along with any enclosures, to the company. The lock-box system eliminates one step in the collection process since the payments are received and deposited by the bank. This allows the company to use the funds as quickly as possible for disbursing payments (Stancil, 1968).

Slowing payments

Two actions which slow the payment of funds thereby lessening the need for cash balances are:

(1) *Delaying payment:* if advantage is not taken of any trade discounts for early payment, it is well to delay payment as long as possible provided this does not sacrifice trade relationships with suppliers.

(2) *Playing the float:* a company can have a negative or zero cash balance on its books but still have a positive balance in the bank. This arises because at any given time there are payments made by companies that have not been cleared through the banking system. If the amount of the float can be determined accurately the firm can utilize this technique to maintain smaller bank balances. Care should be taken in using this technique because a bad credit reputation can be developed if a company is frequently in an overdraft position with a bank.

MANAGING TRADE DEBTORS

The level of trade debtors which a company carries is a function of the level of credit sales, the credit terms, the riskiness of individual customers given credit and any seasonal influences. Although management can increase sales turnover by making credit terms more attractive, granting credit also involves costs in the build-up in trade debtors, increased administrative expenses and the probability of bad debts. Therefore, managing trade debtors is primarily concerned with the trade-off between profits from increased sales generated by credit policies and the costs of such policies. As a general rule, a company should expand credit facilities as long as the profitability of sales generated exceeds the cost of maintaining trade debtors.

The major policy variables that are associated with managing debtors include determining credit terms, evaluating credit applicants, and monitoring trade debtors. These are discussed below.

Credit terms

These are included in a company's credit policy, which must be clearly communicated to customers before they buy. Among the terms specified should be (1) the length of time for which credit is extended, and (2) the amount of discount to be allowed for prompt payment, and the time allowed.

To take the first of these, assume a company changes its terms from net payment within thirty days to net within sixty days and the average debtors for the year rise from £200,000 to £500,000. The increase would be caused partly by the larger credit terms and partly by the larger volume of sales. With a cost of capital needed to finance the investment in trade debtors of 10 per cent, the marginal cost of lengthening the credit period is £30,000 (i.e. £300,000 × 10 per cent). If the profit from the increased sales exceeds £30,000, the change in credit policy is profitable.

Cash discounts (for example, 2 per cent discount for payment within ten days of invoice) are a powerful stimulant to quick payment of bills. Unfortunately, they represent a cost in the form of reduced receipts from sales. Assume a company has monthly sales of £180,000. Half its customers pay their accounts in the month of invoicing, a third in the following month and the remainder during the second month after invoicing. It has been decided to offer 1 per cent discount for payment in the month of invoicing. During the first six months of the new policy receipts are improved so that on average three-quarters of the customers pay in the first month, this improvement coming entirely from those customers who had previously paid in the month after invoicing. The current cost of capital is 15 per cent a year. Ignoring any changes in clerical costs which arise from the new policy, the following calculations show that the change in policy is not financially justified:

Receipts:	*Month 1*	*Month 2*	*Month 3*
Old policy	£90,000	£60,000	£30,000
New policy	£135,000	£15,000	£30,000
Discount (1% × £135,000)	£1,350		
Interest saved (£45,000 × 15/12%)	£562.50		

The cost to the company in the form of reduced receipts from sales is greater than the saving in interest.

An important factor in determining the success of a company's policy on credit terms will be management's knowledge about the elasticity of demand for the company's products. This will indicate the impact on the sales quantities of the company and the resulting impact on profitability of adopting various policies.

Finally, it should be noted that individual companies may have only limited choice as to the credit terms they offer because customers will expect the company to adopt those terms usual to the industry. Furthermore, any major deviation from the industry norms may create retaliatory measures from competitors.

Financing trade debtors

There are various other ways in which a company can speed up its collection of cash without requiring the customer to pay any earlier. The most common examples are:

(1) *Bills of exchange* – which are drawn by the purchaser promising to pay for the goods at a specific future date, often as far ahead as three or six months. The supplier is willing to take the bill in settlement if it has been 'accepted' or if the purchaser is completely creditworthy, and can then sell the bill in the money market. This is known as 'discounting the bill'. The rate of discount will depend on the status of the customer. Bills of exchange are used to a small extent in domestic trade, but are very common in export business.

(2) *Factoring of debtors*: in its simplest form this means selling the debts to a finance house (the factor), which will then be responsible for the administration and collection procedures. The factor will, if required, advance up to about 80 per cent of the value of the debts immediately they are invoiced, at a financing charge of about 3 per cent above the clearing banks' base rate. The service charge for sales accounting and debt collection may be up to 2.5 per cent on sales value.

The total cost of factoring can be quite heavy, particularly in times of high interest rates. However, if a company uses a factor for all its credit sales it will have no direct collection charges of its own. The criterion is the cost to the company of its own credit and collection department for the year.

(3) *Invoice discounting* – by which a company can convert invoices into cash by discounting them through specialized finance companies. The company agrees to guarantee payment of any debts that are purchased. The finance company will advance up to 80 per cent of approved invoices against a bill of exchange given by the buyer. The company is responsible for collecting the debt and for returning the amount advanced, whether the debt is collected or not.

Evaluating credit applicants

Credit evaluation involves the credit investigation of the customer or potential customer to determine whether credit will be granted and, if so, how much. It may also be used to review outstanding accounts or infrequent customers.

The decision to extend credit to an individual customer depends in large part on an evaluation of what are termed the 'five Cs' of credit management (Bolton, 1976): character, capacity, capital, collateral and conditions of the potential customer. The 'character' of a credit applicant refers to the probability that the applicant will make every effort to honour the contract, that is, pay for the purchase. This in effect reflects the moral character of the individual. 'Capacity' to pay is based on the supplier's evaluation of the customer's ability to pay. 'Capital' examines the financial statements to determine the tangible net worth of the company. This can be accomplished by the use of ratio analysis. 'Collateral' represents the availability of assets that can be mortgaged or pledged as security for extended credit. 'Condition' refers to the general level of the economy and whether there is a forecast of a down-swing – the economy that may affect the potential customer and his future ability to pay.

The five Cs are the basis of credit evaluation, but require information to be collected and evaluated before a general credit picture of a customer can be drawn. Investigations of creditworthiness can be made by obtaining references and reports from various institutions, with the agreement of the debtor, and from independent agencies, without such consent. The major sources are:

(1) *Trade references:* a customer can be asked to provide one or two references from other suppliers. The standard of the references and the standing of the companies which supplied them will indicate the creditworthiness of the customer.
(2) *Bank references:* a customer's bank may be asked to comment on the financial standing of its client. This is of limited use, however, because the manager of a bank may be reluctant to report unfavourably on one of its own customers.
(3) *Credit agencies:* a number of independent credit agencies, such as Dun and Bradstreet, provide reports on potential customers for a fee. A credit report is a fairly comprehensive analysis of the company, containing financial information, records of poor account-keeping with other creditors and possibly a credit rating.
(4) *Financial statements:* by requiring the credit applicant to provide financial statements for the past few years the company can analyse the applicant's financial stability, profitability and debt capacity. If a customer is unwilling to submit these financial statements, the supplier can rightfully assume that the financial position of the potential customer is weak.
(5) *Salesmen's opinions:* the opinions and impressions formed by salesmen when visiting a customer can be useful additional information.

Monitoring trade debtors

It is important to monitor trade debtors continually for indications of deterioration in their ability to pay. A useful way of monitoring the overall position is to see that the trade debtor's turnover ratio (see Chapter 3) remains within acceptable limits. If, for example, the average collecting period approaches thirty-five days when the supplier extends a maximum of thirty days' credit, there is clearly a deterioration and a problem with the trade debtor's policy or screening process which requires immediate attention. Similarly, a turnover ratio which is significantly lower than the industrial average is a clear indication of a trade debtor's problem.

Another monitoring indication is the age of trade debtors, which is categorized by the number of days they have been outstanding, as shown in Table 4.1.

From the analysis management can take action on accounts that have been outstanding beyond the average period of credit.

Table 4.1 Analysis of age of debts

Number of days the debt has been outstanding	Percentage of total debtors	Number of accounts
Under 30	70	800
31–60	20	500
61–90	7	200
Over 90	3	50

STOCK

Stock represents a large portion of a company's assets. A stock of both raw materials and work in progress is required to ensure that required items are available when needed. Finished goods stocks must be available to provide a buffer stock that will enable the company to satisfy sales demands as they arise. As we saw in Chapter 1, poor stock management is a major cause of financial failure.

Determining stock levels

The amount of stock a company maintains will depend upon such factors as the level of sales, the length of the production cycle and the degree of durability of the product. Although it is essential for a company to maintain stocks for the reasons mentioned above, there are costs associated with stock accumulation. Therefore, management has to balance the costs of having too little stock with the costs of holding too much.

The cost of stock to a company is usually divided into three categories: costs associated with ordering stock, costs associated with carrying the stock, and the cost of being out of stock. Ordering costs include the administrative paperwork in ordering goods and the physical work involved in unloading, inspecting and storing the goods. Carrying costs include storage costs, insurance costs, interest costs on funds tied up and costs of spoilage and obsolescence.

58 Corporate Insolvency in Practice

The third category of costs, running short of stock, is difficult to measure but would include the costs involved in sales lost due to stockouts, the loss of customer goodwill, and potential disruption in production schedules.

Figure 4.1 uses the foregoing as a foundation for determining optimal investment in stocks. As one might expect, 'carrying costs', as shown in the diagram, are upward sloping. As stock balances increase, warehousing costs, interest on funds tied up in stocks, obsolescence, etc., rise sharply. On the other hand, ordering costs decline as the amount of stock increases. Adding together the two gives us our total cost curve. The minimum point on the total cost curve would be our desired average stock balance.

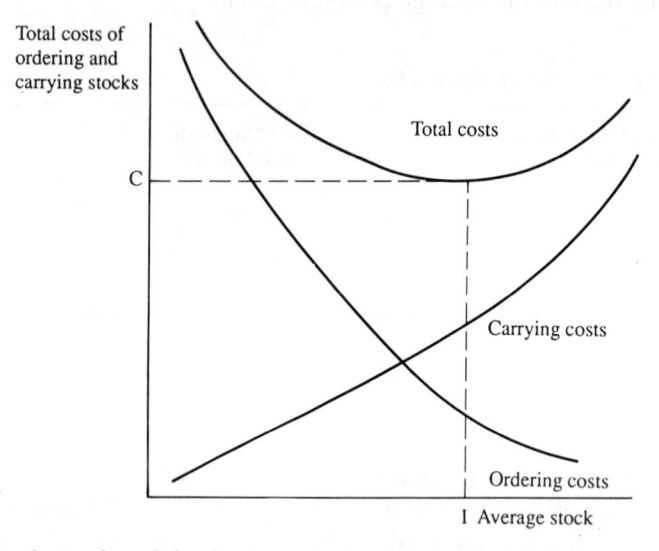

Figure 4.1 Optimal stock level

Stock control models

Many stock control models exist that incorporate the costs outlined above. A model commonly cited for determining the optimal order quantity is the economic order quantity (EOQ) model, which can be found by the following equation:

$$\text{EOQ} = \sqrt{\frac{2FU}{CP}}$$

where F = fixed costs of placing and receiving an order
 U = annual usage in units
 C = carrying cost, expressed as a percentage of stock value
 P = purchase price per unit of stock

The number of orders that must be placed each year can be found by dividing U by EOQ. The average stock on hand (i.e. average balance sheet stock figure) will be:

$$\text{Average stock level} = \frac{\text{EOQ}}{2}$$

The EOQ model assumes that usage is at a constant rate and that delivery times are constant. In fact, for most companies usage is likely to vary considerably due to unexpected changes in demand and delivery lead times, which will vary depending on weather conditions, strikes, demand in the suppliers' industries, etc. Because of these factors, companies add safety stocks to their stock levels, and the average becomes:

$$\text{Average stock} = \frac{\text{EOQ}}{2} + \text{Safety stock}$$

Although EOQ is only the basic stock decision model it is still widely used in practice. Another model, which has gained acceptance in Japan and is finding acceptance with some large companies in other parts of the world, is the just-in-time (JIT) technique. This technique removes the safety stock requirement and shifts stockholding costs on to the suppliers and carriers (Cocker, 1989). Unfortunately, the characteristics that make the system successful in Japan are not easily transferred to Western cultures.

Reorder point

Having established the economic order quantity and the stock level, we now are interested in determining when to reorder. To accomplish this it is necessary to know the lead time, or time required to obtain delivery after an order has been placed. This, of course, varies with the location of the suppliers and the complexity of the product. For example, assume that the lead time is established at one month and that average usage per month is 1,900 units. If a desired stock of 500 units is required the reorder point may be calculated as:

	Units
Desired stock level	500
Average demand during lead time	1,900
Reorder point	2,400

SUMMARY

This chapter has examined the policies management can adopt to control liquidity, thereby ensuring that the company does not run out of cash. Efficient liquidity management is based on three strategies:

(1) paying invoices as late as possible without damaging the company's credit rating;
(2) managing the stock-production cycle in order to maximize the stock turnover ratio; and
(3) collecting debtors' accounts quickly.

Additional refinements such as concentration banking, lock-box services and playing the float in the banking system can further increase the efficiency of liquidity management. The cash budget co-ordinates the timing of the company's cash need. It allows the company to plan ahead so that it has sufficient cash on hand to pay obligations when due.

REFERENCES

Bolton, S. E. (1976) *Managerial Finance*, Houghton Mifflin, Boston, Mass.
Cocker, M. (1989) Financial management and just-in-time, *Management Accounting*, March.
Firth, M. (1976) *Management of Working Capital*, Macmillan, London.
Gallinger, G. W. and Healey, P. B. (1989) *Liquidity Analysis and Management*, Addison-Wesley, Wokingham.
Johnson, C. and Aggarwal, A. (1988) Cash management comes to the ball, *Accountancy*, December.
Stancil, J. M. (1968) A lock-box model, *Management Science*, October.

5
Company Turnaround

In this chapter we consider the steps necessary to reverse the causes of failure which were examined in Chapter 2. Unless these defects are corrected, the company may sink deeper into a crisis situation. Both academic commentators and those with practical experience of devising corporate turnaround strategies have indicated that a number of critical ingredients are required if a turnaround is to be successfully planned and implemented. First, regardless of the quality of the rescue plan, it will not succeed without the existence, or if necessary the introduction, of good management to motivate, design and monitor the implementation of the rescue plan. Second, management must think strategically and act decisively. Third, it is possible at a very early stage to form an opinion as to whether the company has a viable core that can serve as a foundation for rebuilding the company. Fourth, the rescue will generally take longer than anticipated and initial assessments will frequently underestimate the degree of change required (Murphy, 1986).

These critical ingredients have important implications for the insolvency practitioner. As we saw in Chapter 1, the main purpose of the appointment of an administrator or administrative receiver will be to save the company or part of its undertaking by restoring it to financial viability or to sell the business as a going concern, thus achieving the best possible return for creditors generally or the debenture holders in particular. The Insolvency Act 1986 requires that administrators must be licensed insolvency practitioners and that they will be appointed by and operate under the guidance of the court. The limitation imposed by the licensing does not apply to those turnaround specialists who restrict their activities to companies not yet defined as insolvent – potentially the time when managements are most vulnerable to undue influence and in need of protection from unethical conduct.

The steps in a company turnaround are:

(1) evaluation stage;
(2) change of top management;
(3) emergency action stage;
(4) developing corporate recovery strategies;
(5) implementing and monitoring the plan.

EVALUATION STAGE

During this stage a detailed analysis is undertaken of the many factors surrounding the company. The time available to make such an analysis varies from company to company. A small but seriously troubled company may require immediate turnaround action, which reduces the evaluation process to several days. On the other hand, larger, reasonably stable companies may require months of detailed analysis before the scope and the nature of the solutions to their problems are known. The analysis would include:

(1) the reasons for the company's decline;
(2) the severity of the problem;
(3) an identification of the viable core of the business;
(4) a financial review of the whole company;
(5) a review of human resources;
(6) a review of the market position;
(7) auditing each remaining function of the company.

The reasons for the company's decline

The insolvency practitioner will analyse and attempt to identify the causes of the company's decline. As we saw in Chapter 2, these could include inadequate sales, improper pricing, excessive overhead costs and operating costs, excessive interest charges on long-term debt, over-investment in fixed assets and stocks, insufficient working capital and an unbalanced capital structure. Usually more than one cause is involved.

The severity of the problem

A 'turnaround' can refer either to a company that faces financial disaster or action taken to prevent the occurrence of that financial disaster. In the first situation, turnaround is required as an immediate response to a situation where a company has run out of cash and it may, technically speaking, be insolvent (using the test given by section 123 of the 1986 Act). The second situation could refer to a company which suffers an erosion of profits but has no immediate cash-flow shortage. The severity of the problem determines the time available to accomplish a turnaround. In a crisis situation it is necessary to assess the severity of the down-turn, forecast existing cash flow and programme the required cash flow if the company is to become stabilized and remain solvent. The insolvency practitioner is concerned with crisis situations.

Identification of the viable core

Usually companies in a severe financial crisis will need to look at recovery as a two-stage process. The first stage is survival, which entails contracting and rationalizing the business back to a viable core (Nelson and Clutterbuck,

1988). This is that nucleus of activity that is both a cash generator and a profit generator and can serve as the foundation for rebuilding the company. Peripheral operations that do not contribute significantly to the main business should be divested, both to raise cash and to prevent management wasting time on issues that do not directly relate to the health of the core. The company can then move towards more growth-orientated strategies to build a sustained recovery. These latter strategies are implemented only once survival is assured.

In some cases the viable core may not exist. These occur where companies have depleted assets to the point where the viable core is destroyed and cannot be recreated.

A financial review of the whole company

The primary objective of a company turnaround is to regain financial strength. Therefore, an analysis of the company's financial statements which identifies strengths and weaknesses should be the first step in the assessment process. Trends over the past five years should be evaluated. There are two reasons for giving top priority to this analysis of financial statements: first, it will reveal the company's cash-flow situation; second, some authorities believe that 'turnarounds are most successful when they are aimed solely at improving return on investment. This target demands an accurate, high-powered rifle with its sights always trained on the bull's-eye' (Finkin, 1987). Such reasoning illustrates the importance of performance indicators not merely as symptoms of failure as discussed in Chapter 3, but also as essential ingredients in the corporate recovery process.

A review of human resources

A company must have the right people to achieve a successful turnaround. The strategy adopted for the revitalized company and its complementary business plan – including its manufacturing, engineering, purchasing, marketing, cash-raising plans and the like – will conceptually establish the types and numbers of employees needed. The troubled company, at the outset, may have a mix of people who are not matched to the needs identified by these plans. Therefore, an early but continuing task is to identify and justify the need for recruiting people with missing skills. The gaps may exist at all levels. Looking first towards the top, the heads of manufacturing, finance or, say, purchasing may occupy these positions for historical reasons and not be sufficiently knowledgeable, experienced, or capable of handling these duties in the manner now required. If so, replacements will need to be recruited. A similar evaluation of middle management and salaried staff will take place; significant reductions in middle management and salaried staff, once decided on, should be quickly carried out and be done at one time, if practical. A slow, drawn-out process of continual firings debilitates an organization. Also, termination benefits should be carefully thought out and consistently applied.

A review of the market position

The turnaround leader will conduct an analysis to uncover the reasons for slumping sales or decreased market share, whether segmented by product, channel or distribution, end-user group or geographical area.

Audit each remaining function of the company

It is necessary to evaluate systematically the current performance level of each remaining function of the company. The objectives of this analysis are twofold: first, it assures a comprehensive search for problem areas; second, it provides the foundations for the turnaround strategies, including the establishment of short- and long-range objectives. The corporate strengths that this process identifies should be exploited and the weaknesses corrected.

CHANGE OF TOP MANAGEMENT

It is unlikely that a chief executive who has led a company into a serious financial crisis will be capable of restructuring the forces to reverse the situation. For large businesses, therefore, it is generally recognized that a new chief executive is necessary to effect a turnaround. Additionally, the introduction of a new chief executive is a signal to outsiders and company staff alike that positive steps are being taken.

The success of a small company turnaround inevitably rests on the ability of the owner. He or she may have to delegate responsibility to more capable employees or rely heavily on outside professionals to bolster the management effort. In these situations turnaround strategies may often be based on what the owner can tolerate and achieve rather than the best strategy for the company. The small entrepreneur must face squarely fundamental questions regarding his or her reasons for wanting the company to survive. If, irrespective of managerial abilities, he or she does not have the motivation and enthusiasm to face the challenge of a turnaround, he or she may instead settle for a sale or liquidation.

EMERGENCY ACTION STAGE

The two most serious threats to the troubled company are cash-flow problems and threatened action by creditors. The company needs to ascertain its current and immediate cash position and the extent to which internal and external sources of financing exist to cover a negative cash flow. With regard to the second threat, gaining the co-operation of creditors is never easy because they want payment before the company collapses and may take legal action or require their debt to be secured.

From our discussion in Chapter 3, it is apparent that there are many reasons for a negative cash flow, including lower sales volume, poor debtors-collection policy and increased costs and expenses. A company must achieve a positive cash flow if time is to be made available for a successful turnaround. The disposal of slow or obsolete stock will provide some cash and reduce stock carrying costs. In critical cases stock may have to be marked down and dumped on the market to raise cash immediately. Where poor control over debtors' accounts exists, procedures for improving the collection of debts should be established immediately. Also, as we saw in Chapter 4, invoices may be factored to provide ready cash. Buildings and machinery can be turned into cash in a sale and lease-back arrangement. This action may provide significant cash now, when it is needed, thereby possibly overcoming an immediate crisis.

Once the cash drain has been stopped the company must impose strong centralized financial control in order to rebuild its cash reserves. Typically this necessitates preparing short-term cash budgets and reviewing all manufacturing and overhead expenditures. In a turnaround situation effective systems in these areas need to be operational within weeks if control and direction are to be established.

DEVELOPING CORPORATE RECOVERY STRATEGIES

The first stage in developing strategies is to set objectives that define the direction of the firm. These must be achievable from both a financial and operational viewpoint. They should represent a consensus view of all key managers within the organization. Furthermore, they should be supported by creditors and other groups outside the organization whose support is essential.

Strategies define how the company will achieve its objectives. In the following sections individual strategies will be discussed separately, but it should be borne in mind that to maximize the prospects of success the overall rescue plan may incorporate a combination of the strategies outlined. Additionally, the strategies employed may change as the company progresses through the various stages of the turnaround. For example, during the emergency stage the company will necessarily focus on strategies most closely related to cash flow, such as asset-reduction, cost-reduction and debt-restructuring strategies. As the company becomes more stabilized the strategies will centre more on profit improvement. At this stage the company may focus on improving operations, reshaping its product mix and improving organizational structure. Once the company reaches the return-to-growth stage, the strategies may focus on acquisitions, new product development, or increased market penetration – to name but a few possibilities. Further details of the strategies discussed in this section can be found in Slatter (1984).

Asset-reduction strategy

In seeking to reverse a financial crisis a company will generally have two short-term financial goals: to return to profitability as soon as possible, and to generate immediately cash flow to improve its position with bankers and other creditors.

As discussed at the evaluation stage, one of the strategies to obtain profitability is to contract activities back to a profitable core by eliminating marginal or unprofitable activities (products, branches, customers, divisions). To generate the necessary cash flows such a plan is often utilized in conjunction with an asset-reduction strategy whereby assets that are poorly utilized or not required for the remaining profitable core business are converted into cash.

An asset-reduction strategy could include the elimination of product lines which are unprofitable or are unnecessary due to a proliferation of models, sizes or colours. It could include the elimination of unprofitable customers, distribution channels and regions; the sale of subsidiaries or branches which do not meet profitability requirements; the sale of under-utilized or surplus fixed assets; and reducing working capital requirements by improved stocks and debtors performance.

An asset-reduction strategy could take the form of a management buy-out (MBO). This is a misleading name: managers usually put up only a small slice of the cash to take their company over, most of the money coming from institutional investors as equity capital. MBOs usually occur when a large organization decides to close or sell a subsidiary whose activities have become peripheral to its mainstream business and no longer fit into its strategic plans. This could assist the company to contract back to a viable core. In 1988 there were 256 MBOs in the United Kingdom.

Asset-reduction strategies which involve the sale of assets or parts of a company are not always easy to implement. Porter (1976) identifies several problems, including the existence of specialized assets – both fixed and current – for which there are no ready purchasers. Second, costs are associated with these strategies – such as redundancy costs, contract cancellations, divestment costs, etc. Third, the interrelatedness with other product-market segments (as, for example, in a vertically integrated business) ensures that unprofitable activities should not be considered in isolation.

Cost-reduction strategies

An integral part of any overall recovery package will be a systematic review of all company activities to reduce costs. The results of this analysis may either improve an organization's cost position relative to competitors or internally improve efficiency to bring expenses more in line with existing sales volume.

The initial efforts should be concentrated in areas where management suspect there are current inefficiencies or potential savings. For example, if it is critical for a given organization to lower raw material costs, management should systematically investigate possibilities of improving purchasing, making better use of materials and using substitute materials.

An effective turnaround also includes control of the size of the workforce. Management must reduce staff numbers to the absolute minimum consistent with continued operations.

Debt restructuring and other financial strategies

As was explained in Chapter 3, companies in financial crisis are generally over-geared. This can have a crippling effect particularly when interest rates are high. Debt restructuring and other financial strategies can form part of the overall rescue plan. For example, the use of asset-reduction strategies can assist in the reduction of borrowing levels. The success of any debt restructuring and other financial strategies will depend on the insolvency practitioner's (or new management's) ability to convince financiers and other interested parties that the appropriate rescue plan has been actioned and prospects of recovery are sound. A number of options that can be considered include:

(1) consolidation of funding – the company in crisis will often have a proliferation of funding arrangements with a number of financiers. Substantial benefits may be obtained by consolidating borrowings with one financier. In negotiating this package it may be able to reduce the overall cost of borrowing, convert short-term debt to a longer-term facility, include currently outstanding interest in a new loan facility and arrange the sale and lease-back of property or equipment;
(2) raising additional loans or converting existing loans to equity;
(3) raising additional capital;
(4) informal or formal schemes of arrangement with creditors. Such schemes are examined in Chapter 6.

Improved organizational structure

The appropriate organizational structure is a widely debated area in the management literature. There are also arguments within companies about whether they are too centralized or decentralized, and whether they should retain a purely functional structure or adopt a divisional approach. Decentralizing places authority to make decisions at points as near as possible to where events take place. Advantages of decentralizing include greater economies of supervision, improved morale, better development of managers, and in general more awareness of the contribution that decentralized units make to the whole. Divisionalization (or breaking the company up into operating units, each under the profit and loss responsibility of a general manager) may accompany or precede decentralization. Divisionalization of operations may be necessary in order to facilitate divesting parts of the business under an asset-reduction strategy.

Improved marketing

After deciding the profitable products and markets in which to concentrate activities, this strategy seeks to improve profitability further in those selected areas by improving marketing effectiveness.

Many successful turnarounds have been characterized by immediate price increases, but this requires an understanding of the competitive situation and price elasticity of demand for the product range. Most troubled firms do not possess this information. In a mature market, where the number of competitors and buyers is reasonably small, it is possible to develop an understanding of the competitors' costs and likely pricing behaviour. Not having this market information has frequently led to serious underpricing for fear of losing the business. The direct consequence is often sales volume without profit. The marketing function should refocus on the most profitable product–customer segments. This entails selling a small range of profitable products, in volume, to a small number of profitable customers.

Acquisition and sale strategy

Provided that the troubled company has access to a new source of capital financing, an acquisition may be one of the best strategic means of achieving a turnaround. If shareholders or financiers are willing to commit additional funds to protect their current investment, such a move may be very advantageous if a suitable target can be identified. The acquisition target would need to be a competitor in the same industry whose current performance is also poor. The rationale of the strategy is that the increased volume, new distribution channels, economies of scale and rationalized expense levels obtained by the acquisition would bring increased levels of profitability and restore financial strength (Stallworthy and Kharbanda, 1988).

The sale strategy, by which parts of a company are sold off, has already received attention in this chapter. In other cases, the ailing business as a whole may be sold to an outside buyer on a going concern basis. An advantage of this strategy is that any goodwill which attaches to the company is received in the selling price. The role of goodwill in insolvency strategies is discussed in Chapter 7. One method of achieving a beneficial sale is through a 'hive down' company, where the valuable assets of the company are transferred by administrators or receivers to a newly formed company. 'Hive downs' are discussed in Chapter 9.

Investment strategy

An investment strategy can be adopted if the company is still not lacking financial resources. Such investment may include the introduction of new production facilities to restore the company's competitive edge in the marketplace. This investment may also take the form of increased funding for new product development and marketing.

IMPLEMENTING AND MONITORING THE PLAN

Implementing the turnaround plan is largely a matter of management control. It involves communicating the plan to all levels of management and delegating responsibility for all aspects of the plan. Once the plan is put into action, effective management control depends on being able to compare actual performance against planned results. A turnaround plan will fail unless actual progress is measured and its impact on corporate recovery carefully monitored.

We have seen that part of the cause of decline is associated with the fact that employees do not have a sense of direction being taken by the company and morale is low. Therefore, it is necessary to create shared vision and values that lead the company to success. Moreover, where the nature of the business needs to change radically, a new culture may be essential to break old patterns of beliefs, values and methods of operation within the company.

TURNAROUND SPECIALISTS' SKILLS AND EXPERIENCE

Turnaround is potentially more commercially orientated than traditional insolvency activities and relies less on the detail of many of the provisions of insolvency legislation and practice than would be the case in liquidations and receiverships. This is because its aim is ongoing commercial viability rather than maximization of proceeds for the various classes of creditors in a strict sequence. Corporate recovery strategies involved in the turnaround of an insolvent company concentrate on the commercial aspects of the business – marketing, manufacturing, product development and general management/leadership – in addition to commercial and legal issues.

According to Miles (1988) an experienced turnaround specialist introduced to a problem company may import into the situation certain intangible benefits that existing management cannot bring to bear. The most important of these are:

(1) psychological leverage in management/leadership terms;
(2) independence of decision;
(3) clarity of thought;
(4) previous experience.

In particular, the turnaround specialist must be able to reinstate a sense of purpose and motivate people within the organization with the assurance that success can be achieved. To turn a company around he must have the co-operation and confidence of others.

Case Study
Northern Manufacturing Ltd.

Northern Manufacturing was founded in 1918, in Sheffield, to manufacture products used in the machine tool industries. Over the years the company expanded its range of products in order to lessen its dependence on one sector. In 1965 the company became a holding company, having diversified into a range of activities including forgings and stampings and domestic products. Adamson and Young, a company making heavy hydraulic presses and sheet-bending equipment, was acquired in 1978.

In 1980 the company had a turnover of over £20 million, with profits before taxation of £1 million on capital employed (i.e. net assets) of nearly £15 million. In 1981 there was a recession in manufacturing industry; in that year Northern Manufacturing suffered a loss after taxation of nearly £1.6 million. By the spring of 1982 the company was in a severe cash crisis and the group's bankers decided to take action. Their intervention resulted in the appointment of Alex Murray and James Drummond as managing director and financial director respectively. What followed was a remarkable turnaround. Key financial data for this period are shown in Table 5.1.

Table 5.1 Northern Manufacturing financial data

£ million	1980	1981	1982	1983	1984	1985
Turnover	20.4	14.8	12.2	14.5	18.9	24.1
Profit (loss) after tax	1.0	(1.6)	(4.4)	1.2	3.5	4.6
Capital employed	14.8	11.6	11.4	11.7	12.8	16.2
Return on capital employed	6.8%	(13.8%)	(38.6%)	10.3%	27.3%	28.4%
Profit as a % of sales	5.0%	(10.8%)	(36.1%)	8.3%	18.5%	19.1%

Causes of decline

Poor management

Many of the group's problems stemmed from weak top management. The group had a high reputation for design flair and consequent product engineering but suffered from a lack of professional management. Management information systems were poor, there was little management structure and reporting frameworks were limited. The subsidiaries operated on a completely autonomous basis, lacking direction or common controls. The whole group reflected this lack of direction, especially where profits were concerned.

Inadequate financial control

There was evidence, especially at the beginning of 1981, that working capital was out of control. For example, huge stocks were built up, especially at later production stages. Similarly, little attention was given to cost control.

Poor acquisition

Adamson and Young, the company acquired in 1978, was a poorly run company which faced marketing and technical difficulties. The company was acquired at a high price financed from borrowings.

Changes in the environment

In common with most manufacturing companies, the company suffered from the general economic recession which began in 1979. Also, foreign competition in the machine tool industry was becoming intense. Penetration of the United Kingdom market by Japanese products, particularly in computer numerically controlled machining centres and lathes had been spectacular. The Japanese share of imports rose overall from 4 per cent in 1976 to 13 per cent in 1982.

Emergency action

The immediate problem facing Northern Manufacturing's new management team in spring 1982 was to improve cash flow. Therefore, the first job of James Drummond, the new financial director, was to reduce working capital – trade debtors and stock levels. Control of trade debtors had been slack. Drummond investigated the debtor situation and then pressed outstanding debtors for payment. At the same time, optimal stock levels were established and vigorously enforced. Within six months group working capital had been reduced by over £3 million.

Recovery strategies

The financial crisis forced Northern Manufacturing into a far more critical analysis of the firm's strategy and organization. The following steps were taken.

Asset reduction

Adamson and Young was quickly disposed of and the machine tool group was rationalized. Two of the companies which produced machine tools were closed and the production was moved to the Sheffield plant.

Stronger financial control and corporate planning

A tight system of financial control and planning was established. Each subsidiary was required to prepare a detailed plan for the following year and another, in less detail, covering three years ahead. These plans were discussed with the central executive team and were sometimes revised in the light of the issues raised at such meetings. Monthly operating reports comparing actual performance with budget were prepared by each subsidiary.

Cost reduction

The new management team aimed to achieve product cost reductions of 10 per cent through product engineering cost savings, better purchasing and improved manufacturing management.

Growth strategy

Once Northern Manufacturing had been jolted out of its declining position, top management began to spend an increasing proportion of their time on developing growth opportunities. This was reflected in the purchase of several companies in 1984 and 1985.

REFERENCES

Finkin, E. F. (1987) *Successful Corporate Turnarounds*, Quorum Books, Westport, Connecticut.
Miles, K. (1988) Practical corporate recovery: psychiatric, medical and surgical solutions, *Management Accounting*, May.
Murphy, J. (1986) First aid for unhealthy companies, *Australian Accountant*, May.
Nelson, R. and Clutterbuck, D. (1988) *Turnaround*, Mercury Business Books, London.
Porter, M. (1976) Please note location of nearest exit: exit barriers and planning, *California Management Review*, Vol. XIX, Winter.
Slatter, S. (1984) *Corporate Recovery*, Penguin, Harmondsworth.
Stallworthy, E. A. and Kharbanda, O. P. (1988) *Takeovers, Acquisitions and Mergers: Strategies for Rescuing Companies in Distress*, Kogan Page, London.

6
Procedures for Dealing with Insolvency

In this chapter we examine the procedures which the directors and their advisers can utilize to achieve a turnaround or to liquidate the company's assets. As we have emphasized in previous chapters, it is important that as soon as the directors perceive a problem, either through information derived from monitoring the company's cash-flow predictions and its budgets and forecasts, or through being alerted to potential problems by its bankers or auditors, they seek advice from an accountant or insolvency practitioner.[1] The various mechanisms for dealing with the insolvency or potential insolvency can then be considered in order to determine the most appropriate response to the company's financial crisis. These are:

(1) *Informal procedures*
    (a) informal agreements or compositions with creditors;
    (b) unofficial receivership.
(2) *Formal procedures*
    (a) schemes of arrangement;
    (b) voluntary arrangements;
    (c) administration;
    (d) administrative receivership;
    (e) creditors' voluntary liquidation;
    (f) compulsory liquidation.

INFORMAL PROCEDURES

There are a number of procedures that do not necessarily involve the intervention of an insolvency practitioner in the capacity of an 'office-holder' under a legally regulated procedure and, consequently, these procedures are of an informal nature.

Informal agreements or compositions with creditors

As we saw in Chapter 4, a debt-restructuring strategy may enable directors to reach agreement with individual creditors to defer or release their claims against the company or to convert their lending into an equity holding. If successful, an agreement with creditors may at least 'buy some time' in which the directors can seek more secure financing. Creditors whose own businesses depend on the continued existence of the company which is in financial difficulties may be willing to agree to such a compromise to ensure the long-term survival of their customer.

The disadvantage of an informal agreement with creditors is that it does not bind dissenting creditors and thus the rescue plans can be upset by any dissenting creditor petitioning to wind up the company. Also, from the point of view of the directors, if the informal arrangements fail, trading during the period of agreement with creditors, when they clearly knew of the risks of insolvency, may well be wrongful and this will provide ammunition against the directors in any later proceedings for wrongful trading brought by the liquidator.[2]

'Unofficial receivership'

One of the first external creditors to recognize the risk of impending insolvency will be the company's bank, which can strongly recommend that the directors call in an independent accountant to investigate the company's financial position with a view to diagnosing the problems and recommending solutions. From the bank's point of view, such an investigation may well have the effect of improving management information systems and budgetary control and may avert the need to appoint an administrative receiver. The directors will probably have little option but to accept the results of such an investigation. However, this is an informal procedure with the investigating accountant having none of the formal powers of an administrative receiver and no obligation to investigate and report on the directors' conduct.

Such informal investigations are limited in nature in that the accountant has no legal powers to ensure that his recommendations are implemented because managerial powers remain vested in the board of directors. Furthermore, the accountant should exercise some caution in framing his recommendations, particularly if he suggests continued trading by the company. There is just the remote possibility that he may become potentially liable in any subsequent insolvency for wrongful trading on the basis that in giving directions or instructions to the directors he has become a 'shadow director' of the company.[3]

FORMAL PROCEDURES WITHOUT THE NEED TO INVOLVE AN INSOLVENCY PRACTITIONER

Schemes of arrangement under section 425 of the Companies Act 1985

Under section 425 of the Companies Act a company, acting through the board of directors, may institute a rescue plan by means of a compromise or arrangement with its creditors or any class of creditors. The essence of such a scheme is that, at a class meeting, the creditors agree, for example, to the company paying them a lesser amount in full satisfaction of their debt; the conversion of some of their unsecured debt into secured long-term debt; or a scheme may even be proposed that the whole or part of the undertaking of one company is transferred to another company. In return creditors agree to hold off from any legal action to recover their debts or agree not to petition for winding up. If a three-quarters majority in value of the creditors or classes of creditors who are present and vote at the meeting agree to the arrangement, then, once the scheme has been sanctioned by the court, it becomes binding on all creditors or classes of creditors and on the company.[4]

The advantage of such a scheme as a mechanism for corporate rescue is that the majority required depends only on those present and voting. Thus, creditors who are absent from the meeting or those who do not vote will not be counted and the decision binds dissenters.

However, schemes under section 425 of the Companies Act are rarely used because of their disadvantages. The procedure is complex, cumbersome and expensive to operate, involving an initial application to court;[5] the calling of meetings of creditors involving a careful determination of the different classes of creditors[6] affected by the scheme, and the provision of information in the form of an explanatory memorandum detailing the purposes and effects of the scheme;[7] the passing of resolutions by a three-quarters majority in value of the creditors or classes of creditors or members or classes of members and, finally, an application to court to sanction the scheme.[8] Furthermore, a crucial disadvantage is that there is no power to prevent action by creditors against the company to recover their debts or to petition for winding up until the scheme has been sanctioned by the court. This defect can be overcome by petitioning for an administration order and specifying that one of the purposes of such an order is the implementation of a scheme of arrangement under section 425.[9] If successful, the administration order will enable the scheme to be put into effect under the full protection of the moratorium.[10]

FORMAL PROCEDURES NECESSITATING THE INVOLVEMENT OF AN INSOLVENCY PRACTITIONER

The remaining procedures described in this chapter must be supervised or implemented by an insolvency practitioner. Before embarking on a formal procedure, an insolvency practitioner must ensure that there is in force security for the proper performance of his functions, in the form of a professional indemnity bond.

Voluntary arrangements

Part I of the Insolvency Act 1986 provides a framework in which the directors may propose an agreement with creditors. Although the procedure is formal in that the supervisor of the arrangement must be a qualified insolvency practitioner,[11] and the procedure involves the preparation of a report to the court, it is not as complex a procedure as the scheme of arrangement under section 425 of the Companies Act 1985. The involvement of the court in a voluntary arrangement is minimal and the procedure is flexible enough to accommodate all types of schemes of reconstruction or compromise with creditors. Once the proposal is approved by creditors, it is binding on every person who had notice of and was entitled to vote at the creditors' meeting.[12]

The procedure under Part I is that the directors propose a scheme to the company's creditors,[13] the implementation of which is to be supervised by the insolvency practitioner, who at this stage is designated the 'nominee'. Where the nominee is not the company's administrator or liquidator, he must, within twenty-eight days of receiving the proposal, submit a report to the court stating whether meetings of creditors should be called and proposing the date, time and place of such meetings.[14]

In addition to creditors' meetings which may be held, a shareholders' meeting must also be summoned to consider and agree to any proposals so that the scheme becomes binding on the company and its members.[15] The proposals, together with such other information as the nominee thinks desirable, will be put to the creditors and the shareholders and, in the case of the creditors, the meeting will decide – by a three-quarters majority in value of the creditors present in person or by proxy and voting on the resolution – whether to accept the proposals.[16] However, there is an important provision in the Insolvency Rules to the effect that a resolution will be invalid if those voting against it include more than half in value of those creditors who are not connected with the company.[17] It is for the chairman of the meeting to decide whether any person is a 'connected person', but, for example, directors who are owed substantial amounts on their loan account may well have their votes on a voluntary arrangement discounted. Once agreed, the scheme is implemented by the supervisor.

There are two major limitations on the scope of any proposal put forward either by the directors or by the company's administrator or liquidator. First, no proposal can affect the rights of secured creditors to enforce their security without the concurrence of the creditors concerned;[18] this effectively gives the secured creditors a veto on a scheme if it involves their rights. Second, a meeting may not approve a scheme under which a preferential debt of the company is to be paid otherwise than in priority to the non-preferential debts, unless the preferential creditor consents to such a change in priorities.[19]

Once agreed, a scheme can be challenged, but only within a twenty-eight-day period commencing with the date on which the report of the meeting is presented to the court. The grounds upon which there may be a challenge are either that there has been a procedural irregularity in the summoning or conduct of the creditors' or shareholders' meetings or that the voluntary arrangement unfairly prejudices the interests of the petitioning creditors or members.[20]

Two main overriding disadvantages are associated with the voluntary arrangement. First, because there is no moratorium while the scheme is being considered, a recalcitrant creditor can easily upset the turnaround proposals by entering judgment against the company or petitioning for winding up. Second, because the scheme is binding only on creditors who receive notice of the meeting, there could be creditors left out of the scheme who might subsequently disturb the agreed rescue plans.

Administration

As we saw in Chapter 1, administration is a new insolvency procedure first introduced in the Insolvency Act 1985. It is now governed by sections 8–27 of the Insolvency Act 1986.

The procedure for obtaining an administration order is formal, involving an application to court. The court has a discretion whether to grant the order provided it is satisfied that one of the purposes of an administration order is capable of being achieved.[21]

The main advantage of the administration procedure is that there is provision for an immediate moratorium – that is, a 'freezing' – on all legal actions which could otherwise be taken by creditors. This moratorium begins with the presentation of the petition for the administration order and lasts, in the first instance, until the hearing of the petition.[22] If the order is granted, the moratorium is then continued until the termination of the administration.[23] It provides a breathing space and a relief against creditors' pressure, during which the administrator can explore all the options for a rescue. If the purposes of the administration order include either the proposal of a voluntary arrangement under Part I of the Insolvency Act or a scheme of arrangement under section 425 of the Companies Act, the moratorium provided by the administration order enables such schemes to be proposed and adopted without the danger of their being undermined by dissenting creditors petitioning for liquidation.

A second major advantage of administration is that administrators are endowed with extensive powers in relation to their trading activities, in their dealings with corporate management and in their ability to sell or otherwise dispose of charged property belonging to the company or property held under hire-purchase agreements or subject to retention of title clauses.[24] Additionally, some contracts, which are expressed to terminate automatically upon certain types of insolvency proceedings, will not so terminate on the appointment of an administrator. The administrator's powers are discussed further in Chapters 7 and 9.

There are a number of drawbacks which may limit the usefulness of this potentially valuable rescue procedure. First, a petitioner must give notice of his intention to apply for an administration order to any person who is or who may be entitled to appoint an administrative receiver.[25] If that person decides to appoint his own administrative receiver, the court has no option but to dismiss the petition for an administrator to be appointed.[26] Thus, the debenture holder with power to appoint an administrative receiver effectively has a veto over the appointment of an administrator. Since both an administrator and an administrative receiver could put into effect a rescue scheme for the company, it would appear that there is no reason why one insolvency procedure should be preferred to the other – but an administrative receiver does not have the same broad scope for achieving a rescue as does an administrator: he may not sell property in the possession of the company under a hire-purchase agreement or subject to a retention of title clause, and his position may be subordinate to that of other security interest holders in the company.

Second, the appointment of an administrative receiver does not prevent any creditor who has grounds for so doing, petitioning for compulsory winding up of the company,[27] or the company going into voluntary liquidation.[28] Indeed, because the company will in all probability be insolvent, a receivership is frequently followed by a liquidation. Liquidation, however, does not terminate administrative receivership – the two insolvency procedures can and sometimes do co-exist. Once the company is in liquidation, however, the status and powers of the administrative receiver are significantly affected, with the result that his chances of achieving a turnaround are minimal. Upon liquidation, the administrative receiver ceases to enjoy the status he previously had as an agent for the company,[29] and so he incurs personal liability if he continues to trade. Consequently, if part of his rescue plans involved trading prior to sale of the business as a going concern, these plans will be brought to an end by the appointment of a liquidator. This position should be contrasted with that of an administrator, because, once an administration order has been made and remains undischarged, no resolution may be passed or order made for the winding up of the company.[30]

Above all, though, the administrative receiver's primary loyalty and responsibility are to act in the interests of the charge holder (often a bank) which appointed him. Thus, if a rescue plan is not in the interests of such a secured creditor, the administrative receiver need not, indeed should not, pursue it even though this might be contrary to the interests of the unsecured creditors, the shareholders and the employees.[31]

Administrative receivership

Whereas the other insolvency procedures so far described in this chapter have involved a consideration of the interests of the creditors as a whole (or certain classes of them), administrative receivership is primarily a recovery mechanism for an individual creditor (or group of creditors) having a particular security interest, namely a floating charge, over corporate property. The secured creditor decides, in accordance with the terms of his security, when and how to appoint 'his' administrative receiver.

Only a floating charge holder may appoint an administrative receiver. The nature of a floating charge will be examined in Chapter 8; suffice it to say here that such a charge, although it creates a present interest over corporate property, 'hovers' over all the assets described in the charge, but it is not until crystallization that it attaches to any particular asset. The subject matter of the charge will usually be items of corporate property whose nature is constantly changing, for example stock in trade, book debts or work in progress. The hallmark of the floating charge is that, until the moment when it crystallizes, the company is free to deal with its assets, including those described in the charge, as if they were not subject to the charge. The time at which the charge crystallizes is crucial, because from that moment it becomes a fixed equitable charge and the company cannot thereafter deal with any assets comprised in the charge without the prior consent of the charge holder.

Upon the crystallization of the floating charge, the debenture holder may appoint an administrative receiver. His position is defined in section 29(2) as:

> a receiver or manager of the whole (or substantially the whole) of a company's property appointed by or on behalf of the holders of any debentures of the company secured by a charge which, as created was a floating charge, or by such a charge and one or more other securities.

The main advantage of the security from the point of view of the holder of a floating charge is his ability to appoint an administrative receiver when he wishes, for example by providing for crystallizing events in the instrument of charge.[32] If he wishes to pre-empt the possibility of the unsecured creditors or the directors petitioning for an administration order and thereby being able to take the initiative as to the insolvency procedure, the floating charge holder has only to provide that the presentation of a petition for an administration order will be an event causing the crystallization of his charge.

The appointment of an administrative receiver can be made speedily with no court action and few formal procedures to observe and because of this it is a much quicker and cheaper procedure than a petition for an administration order.[33] The administrative receiver can immediately start work on any rescue plans if these are considered appropriate in the secured creditor's interests and need not observe the formalities of putting proposals before a meeting of creditors for their consent. In common with administrators, the powers of administrative receivers are defined in Schedule 1 of the Insolvency Act and are as extensive, giving full managerial competence to the receiver. Additionally, as the appointee of the secured creditor, which will usually be the company's bank, the administrative receiver may well be able to call on bank funds to assist in the financing of any viable rescue plan. The administrator, as a court appointee whose responsibilities extend to all creditors, may well find the financing of any rescue an insurmountable stumbling block.

The disadvantages of the appointment of an administrative receiver have already been touched on. The administrative receiver does not have the benefit of the moratorium provisions and this may limit his scope of action in relation to a corporate rescue. Likewise, he becomes personally liable on trading contracts that he enters into once liquidation supervenes. He is also liable on employment contracts adopted by him in carrying out his functions.[34] Finally, even after the appointment of an administrative receiver, the validity of the debenture under which the appointment was made may be challenged either on the hearing of the petition for the appointment of an administrator[35] or in any subsequent liquidation.[36]

Creditors' voluntary liquidation

This procedure is still the most commercially effective and consequently the most used corporate insolvency procedure.[37] A voluntary winding up is initiated by a resolution of the company in general meeting. After the shareholders have passed the requisite extraordinary resolution,[38] the creditors then control the remainder of the procedure. They appoint the liquidator, who will proceed to realize the company's assets; investigate the conduct of the directors and the affairs of the company; examine transactions entered into in the period prior to the commencement of winding up; and, finally, distribute such final dividend as may be made according to the order of priority laid down by statute.

The overwhelming advantage of a creditors' voluntary liquidation is that it is a relatively informal, well-established and well-tried procedure. No application to court is necessary, and although the liquidator must be a licensed insolvency practitioner, the procedure in itself will be less expensive than an administration. If there is no possibility of rescuing the business and a sale of its assets on a break-up basis would be the best plan, commercially speaking (because, for example, there is no going concern business), a creditors' voluntary liquidation is likely to yield the best return for creditors. This should thus be the preferred course of action.

However, liquidation is an admission that the company is insolvent and must cease to carry on its business except in so far as continued trading is necessary for its beneficial winding up.[39] In this respect, the liquidator has only limited powers of trading and he will utilize these simply to run the business down and convert assets into cash or perhaps negotiate the sale of a business as a going concern.[40] Because the company is in liquidation, this will inevitably be a forced sale at a price which reflects this state.

This limitation on trading can be contrasted with the more extensive powers of an administrator, who may continue the business with a view to its sale as a going concern. Since he will, in part, be in control of the timing of the sale, he is likely to achieve a better realization price than could have been obtained in a liquidation.

Compulsory liquidation

A company may be wound up by the court following the presentation of a petition by a creditor or creditors or by one or more shareholders. This is an apt procedure either:

(1) where the members refuse to pass the necessary resolution to commence a voluntary winding up, perhaps because they deny the company's insolvency; or

(2) where creditors have failed to achieve recovery of their debts in any other way, as, for example, where creditors have obtained judgment against the company which is returned unsatisfied; or
(3) where the creditors believe that there has been some impropriety or wrongful trading in the conduct of the company's business in the period leading up to the insolvency, which requires investigation by the Official Receiver.

Compulsory liquidation is an expensive procedure because of the involvement of the Official Receiver, an employee of the Department of Trade, and because it involves application to and supervision by the court. It is useful, however, if serious malpractice is suspected, because the court-appointed liquidator or the Official Receiver may undertake either a private[41] or, in a serious case, a public examination[42] of the conduct of the directors. The results of these inquiries may be used in subsequent actions against the directors,[43] either for various criminal offences which may have been committed prior to or during the liquidation or as evidence to be used in civil actions designed to compel the directors to compensate the company for their wrongful trading.

REFERENCES AND FURTHER READING

Frieze, S. A. (1987) *Compulsory Winding Up Procedure*, 2nd edn, Longman, London.
Grier, I. S. and Floyd, R. E. (1987) *Voluntary Liquidation, Receivership and Administration*, 2nd edn, Longman, London.
Grier, I. S. and Floyd, R. E. (1988) *Company Administration Orders and Voluntary Arrangements*, Longman, London.
Lingard, J. R. (1989) *Corporate Rescues and Insolvencies*, 2nd Edn, Butterworth, London.
Milman, D. and Durrant, C. (1987) *Corporate Insolvency: Law and Practice*, Sweet and Maxwell, London.
Pennington, R. R. (1987a) *Company Liquidations: The Substantive Law*, Jordans, Bristol.
Pennington, R. R. (1987b) *Company Liquidations: The Procedure*, Jordans, Bristol.
Stewart, G. (1987) *Administrative Receivers and Administrators*, C. C. H. Editions, Bicester.
Wooldridge, F. (1987) *Administration Procedure*, Jordans, Bristol.

NOTES

1 See Chap. 1, p. 11.
2 See Chap. 10, p. 172–3.
3 However, s. 251 makes it clear that a person is not deemed to be a shadow director by reason only that the directors act on advice given by him in a professional capacity.
4 CA 1985, s. 425(2); the scheme becomes binding when it has been registered with the Registrar of Companies, s. 425(3).

82 Corporate Insolvency in Practice

5 CA 1985, s. 425(1).
6 The difficulties in determining the different classes of creditors who will need to be consulted on the scheme are discussed in Lingard (1989), paras. 5.29–5.31.
7 CA 1985, s. 426.
8 As to the factors which will be taken into account in sanctioning a scheme, see *Re Anglo-Continental Supply Co. Ltd* [1922] 2 Ch 723.
9 IA 1986, s. 8(3)(c).
10 See Chap. 7, p. 88–9.
11 S. 1(2).
12 S. 5(2).
13 S. 1(1).
14 S. 2.
15 As to the summoning of meetings, the proceedings thereat and voting rights and necessary majorities, see IR, rr. 1.13–1.21.
16 IR, r. 19(1).
17 IR, r. 19(4)(c).
18 S. 4(3).
19 S. 4(4).
20 S. 6.
21 S. 8(1); the court has complete discretion as to whether to make an order, even if all the conditions are satisfactorily made out, see *Re Consumer & Industrial Press Ltd* (1988) 4 BCC 68; *Re Harris Simons Construction Ltd* [1989] BCLC 202.
22 S. 10(1).
23 S. 11(3).
24 Ss. 14 and 15 and Sched. 1 (this latter is reproduced in the case study appended to Chap. 9).
25 S. 9(2).
26 S. 9(3); a secured creditor may appoint an administrative receiver at any time before the making of an administration order and does not require the leave of the court to do so, s. 10(2)(b).
27 S. 122(1).
28 S. 84.
29 S. 44(1).
30 S. 11(3)(a). By s. 11(1) any pending petition for the winding up of the company must be dismissed.
31 See Chap. 9, p. 140.
32 *Re Woodroffes (Musical Instruments) Ltd* [1986] Ch 366; *Re Brightlife Ltd* [1987] Ch 200. Note that the actual decision in this latter case would now be different in the light of IA 1986, s. 40.
33 For an example of a deed of appointment, see case study appended to Chap. 8.
34 S. 44(1)(b).
35 S. 9(3)(b).
36 Ss. 239 and 245, see Chap. 10, p. 166–8, 170–1.
37 See Chap. 1, Table 1.2.
38 S. 84.
39 Sched. 4 – Powers of Liquidators, para. 13 (Sched. 4 is reproduced in the case study appended to Chap. 10).
40 *Re Great Eastern Electric Co. Ltd* [1941] Ch 241.
41 S. 132.
42 S. 133.
43 S. 132(2).

7
Administration: Purposes and Procedures

INTRODUCTION

The Cork Committee, having reviewed the success of receiverships as a vehicle for turnarounds, recommended that a procedure be introduced to facilitate the rescue and rehabilitation of companies in financial difficulties particularly where no creditor had a charge permitting the appointment of an administrative receiver.[1] The administration procedure was put into effect by the Insolvency Act 1986. In the circumstances specified in section 8 of that Act, the company,[2] its directors[3] or any of its creditors may apply to the court for an order that the affairs of the company be put under the control of an administrator, who must be a licensed insolvency practitioner, who will examine its business and the circumstances leading to its decline and make proposals designed either to achieve a turnaround, with the survival of the company and its business, or to come to an arrangement with the company's creditors and shareholders reorganizing its affairs or make plans to achieve a better realization of the company's assets than would be achieved on a winding up.[4]

Administration, unlike its closest alternatives – creditors' voluntary winding up and the appointment of an administrative receiver by a secured creditor – is a formal, court-driven procedure. It is defined in section 8(2) of the Insolvency Act as: 'an order directing that during the period for which the order is in force, the affairs, business and property of the company shall be managed by a person (the administrator) appointed for the purpose by the court'.

The court has power to make an administration order if it is satisfied that the company is, or is likely to become, unable to pay its debts and the court considers that the making of the order would be likely to achieve one or more of the purposes set out in section 8(3). These are:

(a) the survival of the company and the whole or any part of its undertaking as a going concern;
(b) the approval of a voluntary arrangement under Part I of the Act;

(c) the sanctioning of a compromise or arrangement under section 425 of the Companies Act 1985;
(d) a more advantageous realisation of the company's assets than would be effected on a winding up.

In *Re Charnley Davies Business Services Ltd*[5] the court held that these purposes are not mutually exclusive – a combination of purposes may be specified in the petition.

CIRCUMSTANCES IN WHICH ADMINISTRATION WILL BE AN APPROPRIATE REMEDY

An independent accountant, usually a licensed insolvency practitioner who will ultimately be proposed as the company's administrator, will normally prepare a report indicating why administration is the most appropriate insolvency procedure in the light of the company's circumstances.[6]

He will take into account the skills of the current management; the financial information prepared by the directors (or auditors); his cash forecasts relating to trading and/or sale of the business; the extent to which creditors are pressing for payment; and the existence and attitudes of any secured creditors having the power to appoint an administrative receiver.

Administration might be considered to be the preferred option for achieving a rescue of the company or an advantageous sale of the business in the following cases.

First, where the company currently has a healthy balance sheet but is experiencing a cash-flow crisis leading to an inability to pay debts as they fall due: normally, it would be expected that an extension of the company's overdraft facilities would suffice in this situation, but perhaps adequate security is not available to sustain the additional borrowing or creditors could be pressing for an immediate winding up. In this eventuality, a turnaround in administration might be achieved by the administrator negotiating sources of finance, coupled with the use of his power to charge any uncharged assets or to sell assets subject to a charge, and perhaps also utilizing the voluntary arrangement procedure to negotiate deferred payment of debts. It may be that in a company of this type, where financial backing cannot readily be obtained by the existing management, the presence of a respected insolvency practitioner may give added confidence to the banks and other financial institutions and encourage them to provide working capital for the company. The protection against pressing creditors gained through the moratorium provisions[7] may be particularly significant where a bank or other provider of venture capital might be willing to inject funds subject to a protection against such funds simply being funnelled into payment of creditor's claims.

Second, administration might also prove a useful route to a turnaround where, upon an investigation of the trading background of the company and its product base, the insolvency practitioner forms the view that, though the business is basically sound, failure in management decision-making with regard to marketing strategy or financial and liquidity control lies at the root of the current financial difficulties. The administration procedure permits a short-term breathing space during which the administrator might consider exercising his power to dismiss the incumbent directors[8] and/or place future decision-making in the hands of a more experienced management team.

Third, administration may be useful as a holding operation prior to the sale of the business as a going concern so as to achieve a better realization of assets for the benefit of creditors than would otherwise be available on a winding up. This presupposes the existence of a viable business capable of sale on a going concern basis and the need to continue trading to maintain existing contractual rights, to fulfil existing profitable contractual obligations or to complete work in progress. All these activities may be more difficult to achieve in liquidation.[9] Similarly, administration may be the technically preferred route where, despite its costs, there are profitable realizable assets in the form of licences, contracts or intellectual property rights whose terms include a proviso for termination, repudiation or reversion of rights in the event of any other form of insolvency procedure.

Finally, administration might also be considered where the business is in need of rationalization to curtail excessive overheads, and this might involve staff redundancies. When a company is not in insolvency proceedings, the closure and redundancy costs involved in rationalizing an ongoing business could be prohibitively expensive, whereas, if the administration procedure is utilized, part of the redundancy costs will be borne by the state.[10] Shorn of these costs, a viable business might be capable of being 'hived off' to a clean subsidiary for sale to a third party.[11]

CONDITIONS FOR MAKING AN ADMINISTRATION ORDER

The court has jurisdiction to make an administration order if it is satisfied, first, that the company is, or is likely to become, unable to pay its debts.[12] In assessing whether a company is insolvent, the court may take into account any of the various alternative tests defined in section 123.[13]

Second, the court must be satisfied, on the evidence presented to it, that an administration order would achieve one or more of the purposes specified in section 8(3).[14] The petitioner bears the onus of proving that there is a real prospect that one or more of these purposes will be achieved – thus, the candidates for an administration order tend to be self-selecting. Hence the necessity of obtaining the advice of an insolvency practitioner who will devise credible plans to achieve either the survival of the company and the whole or part of its undertaking (this purpose will not be achieved if the undertaking and business are sold, leaving the company as a dormant shell with no undertaking) or to ensure that administration will bring about a better realization of assets than would be achieved in a winding up. For the latter to be presented cogently, the insolvency practitioner will prepare valuation figures indicating that the business, after a period of trading or shorn of some of the more complex security interests held in relation to its assets, is capable of being sold as a going concern at a price which would be in excess of that which would be likely to be achieved by a liquidator.

PROCEDURE ON APPLICATION FOR AN ADMINISTRATION ORDER

An application for an administration order may be made by petition presented in either the High Court or in a county court having jurisdiction to wind up the company.[15] The application may be presented by the company; the directors (indeed, because of the pressure to avoid claims for wrongful trading and possible disqualification proceedings, most applications are brought by directors); by a creditor or creditors, including contingent or prospective creditors; or by all or any of these parties together or separately. Additionally, an application for an administration order may be made by a recognized self-regulatory body or by the Secretary of State for Trade and Industry.[16] Not only may petitions be presented by unsecured creditors, but also by secured creditors as an alternative to the appointment of a receiver. However, when the court is exercising its discretion whether to make an administration order, the interests of secured creditors will weigh less in the balance than the interests of unsecured creditors since the former can have recourse to their security interest as a protection against the company's insolvency.[17]

The petition must be accompanied by an affidavit containing a statement of the company's financial position,[18] specifying its assets and liabilities, including its contingent and prospective liabilities and details of any security known or believed to be held by the company's creditors. The affidavit should also specify whether any winding-up petition has been presented.[19] Additionally, exhibited to the affidavit should be the written consent of the proposed administrator to accept appointment and the report prepared by an independent person showing that on the information revealed to him, and with regard to the proposed future conduct of the business, the appointment of an administrator is expedient.[20]

This report is a very significant document as it will form the basis upon which the court will exercise its discretion to appoint an administrator. An example of such a report prepared in support of the directors' petition is reproduced in the case study later in this chapter. The report will outline the purposes which may be achieved in making the administration order; in the case study, for example, the independent accountant indicates that the objective of the order will be for the business (in this case a loan brokerage business) to continue trading for a short time pending negotiations for its sale as a going concern. The report will also deal with the funding of any administrator's trading activities – whether he will trade from current receipts or arrange other sources of working capital. In the case study the proposal indicates that the sources of funding will be receipts from commissions paid by lenders and the effects of such receipts will be enhanced by a substantial reduction in overheads. Part of the success of the trading plans in the case study flowed from the fact that the administrator did not have to seek external sources of working capital. The report should also deal with the proposed administrator's plans with regard to any voluntary arrangement with creditors, any financial restructuring or the introduction of better management information systems, etc. Any additional information which will assist the court to determine whether administration has a real prospect of success should be included, for example cash-flow forecasts, budgets and comparative valuations of assets on a break-up and sale as a going concern basis. Although such a report is not mandatory, its absence must be explained in the affidavit[21] and it will be crucial to the success or failure of the application.

The petition for an administration order must be served on any person who has appointed or is entitled to appoint an administrative receiver.[22] Although there are strict limits on the actions which can be taken by creditors during the moratorium immediately following the presentation of the administration petition, an administrative receiver can be appointed during this time,[23] and if such an appointment is made the court is obliged to dismiss the administration petition unless the person by whom the administrative receiver was appointed consents to the making of the administration order, or the security by virtue of which the appointment was made could be challenged as being invalid.[24]

Consequently, the attitude of banks holding security interests in the form of floating charges enabling them to appoint administrative receivers is a crucial consideration for any insolvency practitioner considering recommending administration as a method of dealing with insolvency. In as much as an administrative receiver will be the bank's appointee (though his legal position will be that of agent for the company),[25] banks will normally tend to favour this route to achieve a turnaround or a sale of the business.

However, there are circumstances in which an insolvency practitioner might successfully negotiate the consent of a floating charge holder to the appointment of an administrator. Clearly, if the security under which an appointment might be made could be challenged as being either a transaction at an undervalue[26] or a preference,[27] it may not be worth the risk of litigation to defend a challenge to the security and better to acquiesce in the appointment of an administrator. Also, if the directors petition for an administration order and they have provided personal guarantees in relation to the company's debts which, if called in, would effectively cover the bank's lending, then agreement to the appointment of an administrator might not only be perceived as a positive move in encouraging a corporate rescue, but also, in the event of the sale of the business would ensure that the bank did not run the risk of liability towards guarantors of the company's debts.[28] A greater degree of persuasion will be necessary if the insolvency practitioner prepares a rescue plan whose terms could equally well be implemented by an administrative receiver appointed by the security holder. Here, he might stress that continued trading, completion of contracts[29] and re-stocking or refurbishing the undertaking could offer a better chance of the secured creditor being paid, without the possible risks of an administrative receiver trading with personal liability and the possible indemnity risks which could be incurred if winding up co-exists with administrative receivership.[30] Additionally, a technical consideration – which may well have a bearing on the bank's attitude – will be the extent to which the subject matter potentially included in a floating charge is subject to the prior claims of those with retention of title clauses, chattel-leasing agreements and hire purchase agreements.[31]

Even where a creditor with power to appoint an administrative receiver consents or would be prepared to consent to the making of an administration order, the final decision about appointment remains with the court, and even where all the circumstances under which an appointment could be made are fulfilled, there may be situations, such as deadlock or breakdown of trust and confidence between the corporators, which are more suited to final resolution through liquidation proceedings than the appointment of an administrator.[32]

The petition must also be served on any person who has petitioned for the winding up of the company.[33]

Normally, the petition will be served not less than five days before the date fixed for the hearing but, in appropriate circumstances, the court can abridge the time for service.[34] If the petition has been presented by a creditor or creditors, notice of it must be served on the company.[35] Furthermore, so that those who may have an interest in distraining on the company's goods know of the existence of administration proceedings, notice must also be served on any sheriff or other officer charged with execution or other proceeding against the company or its property and any person who has distrained against the company or its property.[36]

THE CONSEQUENCES OF AN ADMINISTRATION PETITION

The idea behind the administration procedure is that it permits a breathing space during which plans for a rescue can be finalized or the sale of the business as a going concern can be negotiated. Therefore, to free the administrator from the pressing claims of creditors, which might hinder these plans from coming to fruition, the Insolvency Act introduces a new idea: a moratorium immediately upon the presentation of the petition, providing relief against creditors' claims until the hearing of the petition.

Pre-hearing moratorium

The immediate consequence of the presentation of a petition is that, from that time until the hearing of the administration order, a moratorium is placed on all enforcement actions by creditors. Section 10 provides that:

(a) no resolution may be passed or order made for the winding up of the company;
(b) no steps may be taken to enforce any security over the company's property, or to repossess goods in the company's possession under any hire-purchase agreement, except with the leave of the court and subject to such terms as the court may impose; and

(c) no other proceedings and no execution or other legal process may be commenced or continued, and no distress may be levied, against the company or its property except with the leave of the court and subject to such terms as aforesaid.

Nothing in the pre-hearing moratorium requires the leave of the court for certain types of actions, including the presentation of a petition for the winding up of the company[37] (though the court may restrain advertisement of the petition until the hearing of the administration petition).[38] Similarly, nothing in the pre-hearing moratorium provision prevents the appointment of an administrative receiver.[39] The effect of this moratorium is to safeguard the status quo of the corporate assets thus enabling the administrator to put into operation the best rescue plan that he can devise. This considerable degree of protection accorded to corporate assets may be compared with the comparative lack of security when an administrative receiver is appointed. In this latter event, holders of property subject to retention of title agreements, those with prior security interests over corporate assets and those exercising their rights of execution and distress against corporate property may, by exercising their diverse rights, undermine any potential rescue plan for the business or effectively prevent its sale as a going concern.

The post-hearing moratorium

At the hearing an administration order may be made leading to the moratorium detailed in section 11 or the petition may be dismissed, in which case the company will almost always then be subject to some alternative insolvency procedure. The court also has a wide discretion to adjourn the hearing conditionally or unconditionally or to make an interim order or any other order that it thinks fit.[40] Although it has been held that the court does not have jurisdiction to appoint an interim administrator,[41] it can appoint an insolvency practitioner to take control of the company's assets and manage its affairs until the time of the adjourned hearing.[42]

During the post-hearing moratorium, which lasts for the duration of the administration order, no resolution may be passed or order made for the winding up of the company;[43] no administrative receiver may be appointed[44] and no other steps may be taken to enforce any security over the company's property or repossess goods in the company's possession except with the consent of the administrator or leave of the court – and subject, where the court gives leave, to such terms as the court may impose.[45] Finally, no other proceedings and no execution or legal process may be commenced or continued[46] and no distress levied against the company or its property without the consent of the administrator or leave of the court, subject (where the court gives leave) to such terms as it may impose.[47]

Thus, the post-hearing moratorium vests considerable discretion in the administrator, who may lift its effect in favour of particular creditors on such terms as he thinks fit. His decisions will be subject to some redress if their effect is unfairly to prejudice one group of creditors as against another.[48]

DUTIES OF ADMINISTRATORS

Duties upon the making of the administration order

Prior to the acceptance of his proposals by the creditors' meeting, the administrator is under an obligation to manage the affairs of the company in accordance with any directions given by the court.[49]

Within three months of the making of the order, the administrator must send to the Registrar of Companies, and to all creditors, a statement of his proposals for achieving the purposes specified in the order.[50] He cannot begin to implement these plans until they have been approved by the creditors' meeting called for that purpose. Since effectively he cannot begin to act positively (as opposed to acting to preserve the status quo) until his rescue plans have been approved, it is in the administrator's interests to lay his proposals, even if they are in a general or conditional form, before creditors at the earliest convenient date.

An example of a proposal put by an administrator to creditors is contained in the case study. It reveals that because the administrator had been able to continue trading and elicit offers for the purchase of the business as a going concern, he estimated that he would be able to realize some £20,000 for the goodwill of the business (there would be no goodwill on the sale of the assets on a break-up basis in liquidation) and he estimated that he would generate £53,260 from trading during the three months he was in office. The total deficiency in the insolvency proceeding was £303,747 in the administration as opposed to £390,177 in a liquidation. The administrator indicated that he intended to continue trading and, having already received several offers for the business, to sell the business to the highest bidder. He further proposed that, after the sale, the company be placed in a creditors' voluntary liquidation to enable dividends to be paid to creditors.

The difficulty of acting before the creditors' approval of the administrator's proposals was highlighted in the *Charnley Davies* case.[51] The administrator, who was appointed to a group of companies, quickly formed the view that he could not achieve a rescue or turnaround and proceeded to sell corporate assets without calling a creditors' meeting as required by section 23. The administrator defended his actions on the basis that a rapid sale was necessary in the best interests of the creditors and both time and expense could be saved by not calling a meeting whose purpose would simply be to receive a report on the results of the sale, as there were now no 'proposals' for the meeting to consider.

The court, in agreeing to discharge the administration order, indicated, in a judgment that was critical of the administrator's actions, that creditors were entitled to be told what the administrator proposed and, in a situation which necessitated a rapid sale, it would be desirable for him to send a copy of his proposals for the sale to the Registrar of Companies and the creditors. Since it was pointless to hold a meeting simply to report on the completion of the sale, the court discharged the administration order without a creditors' meeting.

The creditors' meeting has the power to approve the proposals with or without modifications, but if changes to the administrator's plans are put forward, the administrator must consent to each modification.[52] Of course, it is open to the creditors to refuse to accept the administrator's proposals, in which case the court may discharge the order and make such consequential provision as it thinks fit.

Duty to act in accordance with the proposals

After approval of the proposals, it is the administrator's duty to act in accordance with the proposals and with any revisions agreed to by a specially convened creditors' meeting.[53] To assist the administrator in executing his plans, the creditors' meeting may, if it thinks fit, establish a creditors' committee.[54] The role of this committee is primarily advisory, but it is given a power to require the administrator to attend before it and furnish it with such information relating to the conduct of the administration as it may reasonably require.[55] It is fundamental to the concept of administration that creditors be consulted and agree to the administrator's plans, and the courts have on several occasions underlined the obligation on administrators to lay proposals before creditors, whether or not those creditors will receive a dividend at the conclusion of the administration.[56]

However, it may be the case that the administrator cannot carry out the proposals in the exact terms in which they have been agreed by the creditors. In such a case, an administrator has power to apply to the court for directions,[57] and the court may, in exceptional circumstances, sanction an action which differs from that approved by the creditors' meeting. For example, in *Re Smallman Construction Ltd*[58] a scheme relating to the sale of the company's business had been agreed by the creditors' meeting but it could not be implemented owing to a disagreement with an outside party. An alternative scheme was proposed, which the administrators considered was in the best interests of the company and its creditors. The court was prepared to sanction the sale following the alternative scheme as it was not commercially practical to call a further meeting of creditors.

In carrying out his proposals, the administrator will incur other obligations. For example, if the purpose of the proposals is the approval of a voluntary arrangement, the administrator will have to call a separate creditors' meeting to deal with the arrangement.[59] Additionally, he will have to call a shareholders' meeting to consider the arrangement. And, if the administrator is appointed as the supervisor of the arrangement, as will almost always be the case, he will be under a duty to report the result of the meetings to the court and to implement the arrangement in accordance with its terms.[60] There are similar procedural obligations if the purpose of the administration is to sanction a compromise under section 425 of the Companies Act.

TERMINATION OF THE ADMINISTRATION

The administration comes to an end upon discharge of the order under section 18. The administrator is under a duty to apply for a discharge of the order if it appears to him that the purpose or each of the purposes specified in the order has been achieved or, alternatively, is incapable of achievement.[61] Also, an administrator is under a duty to apply for a discharge of the order if required to do so by the creditors' meeting summoned to consider the proposals.[62]

As will often be the case when the purpose was that specified in section 8(3)(d), the company will be destined for winding up after the successful sale of the business to a purchaser. However, as was held in *Re Brooke Marine Ltd*,[63] the court has no jurisdiction under section 18 to make a winding-up order unless the administrator, as agent for the company, has presented a petition for winding up. Such petition can be heard at the same time as the application for the discharge of the administration order, and the court has the power to abridge the time for the advertisement and hearing of the winding-up petition.[64] Where a winding-up order is made upon the discharge of an administration order, the court may appoint as liquidator the ex-administrator. However, such appointment should be carefully considered to avoid the possibility of any conflict of interest, in that one of the duties of the liquidator is to investigate the conduct of management of the company prior to the liquidation and this may include an examination of the administrator's conduct.

In accordance with the Insolvency (Amendment) Rules 1987, where a winding-up petition is filed by an administrator and it contains a request for the appointment of the administrator as liquidator, the administrator must, not less than two days before the hearing of the petition, file at court a report indicating that he has notified creditors in writing of his intention to seek appointment as the liquidator, and he must also file any responses to his notice, including any objections thereto. The recognized professional bodies, such as the Insolvency Practitioners Association, have issued ethical guidance notes to assist practitioners who face potential conflict of interest situations.[65]

Where an administrator applies for discharge of the order, he will also apply for his release from liability. The effects of such release are detailed in section 20(2):

> Where a person has his release under this section, he is, with effect from the time specified above, discharged from all liability both in respect of acts or omissions of his in the administration and otherwise in relation to his conduct as administrator.

The administrator's release takes place at such time as the court may determine, and for this purpose the court may specify a release date after the discharge of the order.[66] Release may be delayed so that a liquidator can investigate the conduct of an administrator and/or take action against him for negligence. However, the fact that an administrator has had his release does not prevent action being taken against him for misfeasance, breach of fiduciary duty or to compel him to account for corporate property retained or misapplied, but in this case action after his release can be commenced only with leave of the court.[67]

Case Study
Northern Loans Ltd

This case study gives examples of the formal documents and reports prepared in relation to an administration order whose purpose was to secure a more advantageous realization of the company's assets than would be achieved on a winding up.

The documents included here are not, of course, the full set of documentation associated with such an administration. Technical and legal details of the documentation may be found in practitioners' works such as Totty and Jordan (1987) and Kerr (1989).

The materials are:

(1) report by an independent accountant pursuant to rule 2.2 of the Insolvency Rules 1986;
(2) report by the administrator pursuant to section 23 of the Insolvency Act – being a statement of the administrator's proposals.

Document 1: Report pursuant to rule 2.2(1) of the Insolvency Rules 1986 in support of the petition of the directors for the grant of an administration order in respect of Northern Loans Limited

1. Introduction
   [*There follows a brief introduction indicating the status of the independent accountant and the circumstances in which he came to be instructed for the purposes of preparing the report.*]
2. My brief was the following;
   (a) to advise and assist with the application to the court for the appointment of an administrator under the provisions of the Insolvency Act 1986.
   (b) to prepare a short report on the current financial position of the company with a view to its being exhibited to the affidavit in support of the petition for an administration order.
3. My investigation, report and advice have been based upon information presented to me by directors of the company. I have not performed an audit, or carried out any checks, test or verification work.

Statutory information

Company Number	000000
Date of incorporation:	19——
Directors:	X
Company secretary:	Y
Share capital:	
Authorized	2,000 ordinary shares of £1 each
Issued and fully paid	2,000 ordinary shares of £1 each
Shareholders:	X 1,950
	Z 50
	2,000
Registered office:	Any Street, Any Town
Secured creditors:	The premises at Any Street are owned by the company subject to a fixed charge thereover held by Anybank plc.
	There are also three vehicles which are subject to hire-purchase contracts.

Company history and business

4. The business began as a sole tradership in 1970 under the name of 'X'. It was incorporated as 'Northern Loans Ltd' in February 1973.
5. The company trades as a broker for loans based on secondary mortgages. It acts as an intermediary between borrowers and merchant banks.
6. The majority of the company's business is gained by advertising in both national and local newspapers, which leads to telephone or written inquiries to the company. These are followed up by a salesman visiting each potential client's home.
7. Until early 1986 adverts were predominantly in local newspapers in the north of England. It became apparent during 1986 that this approach needed to be changed due to the excessive cost of advertising required to generate sales leads.
8. From 1986 the company extended to advertising in national newspapers. However, the concentration of its sales force in northern England only, meant that many sales leads were lost.
9. Both local and national advertising continued at a high level until the end of 1988.
10. Late in 1988 the level of local advertising was reduced and some of the northern sales force removed. National advertising was increased and further administration staff were employed to handle the expected upturn in sales leads.
11. In summer 1989 a drop in the number of sales leads led to cash-flow

problems. Slow payment of advertising creditors led to a stop on further credit and hence fewer advertisements being published.
12. On 1 September 1989 director X placed funds of £35,000 into the company's bank account to ease the company's financial position. On 19 October 1989 a meeting was held at the offices of [*the named accountants*] at which director X and his auditors were present. At that meeting financial information was presented which showed that the company was insolvent.

Financial history

13. The company made profits through the late 1970s, and in the early 1980s the company's net profit before tax was as follows:

1982/3	£29,776
1983/4	£56,737
1984/5	£74,950
1985/6	£35,665

14. The last set of completed accounts for the company were for the year ended 5 April 1986.
15. The current auditors are finalizing the 1986/7 accounts, later periods have yet to be prepared. The latest accounts filed at Companies House were for the year 1983/4.
16. The company does not employ an in-house accountant and does not produce its own management or statutory accounts.
17. In 1984/5 turnover had been £741,035 from which a net profit before tax of £74,950 had been achieved. Taxable profits in 1985/6 were £35,665 on a turnover of £1,065,000. The balance sheet as at 5 April 1986 showed the company was solvent to the sum of £146,968.
18. Accounts for the year 1986/7 have not yet been finalized. You have been informed by your auditors that there will probably be a loss of £20,000 in that year.
19. You have confirmed that the pattern of trading since 1986 will have resulted in continual losses from then to date.
20. Current turnover is estimated to be in the region of £750,000 per annum.

Commentary on estimated statement of affairs

21. The estimated statement of affairs as at 23 October 1989 is shown at Appendix A. This has been prepared on two bases: (1) break-up on liquidation, and (2) administration assuming a short period of trading and a going concern sale of certain assets. These figures have been prepared in conjunction with Anyname Chartered Surveyors.
22. There may be some equity in the freehold premises of the company, especially if sold on a going concern/existing use basis. My agents

believe that such a sale may be achieved giving an increased realization of some £10,000 over an open market sale.

23. My agents advise that the fixtures and fittings, if sold *in situ* as part of a business, have a value of some £2,500 more than would be achieved at auction.

24. The figure shown as a debtor is a loan to an employee, which should realize its full value.

25. If the business is sold as a going concern a premium for goodwill of up to £20,000 may be achieved.

26. Motor vehicles are unlikely to be included in a going concern sale and will probably achieve the same realization under either basis.

27. Preferential liabilities include PAYE and NIC for approximately two and a half months. At 20 October 1989 all weekly paid staff were paid up to date, although salaried staff have been paid only up to the end of September 1989. The company is exempt from VAT on its turnover and therefore not registered for VAT purposes.

28. The directors' loan account is in favour of director X. This had a negative balance until 1 September 1989 when the sum of £35,000 was paid to alleviate what was then seen as a cash-flow problem.

The Inland Revenue is owed some £60,000–70,000 in corporation tax for the financial years 1980/1 to 1985/6, estimated on trading profits for those years. However, it is likely that accrued interest and penalties on unpaid tax will be substantial and I have therefore estimated a total liability of £100,000, although this may vary significantly.

Funding of future trading

Receipts

29. Commissions from lenders have recently been averaging £15,000 per week. It is estimated that this will continue for the next four weeks, after which they will fall to approximately £10,000 per week. This fall will be due to cessation of advertising during the administration period.

30. The company has previously traded at a loss. However, it is believed that a profit can be achieved in an administration period through a substantial reduction in overheads.

Payments

31. It will be necessary to reduce staff levels. Anticipated savings are in the region of £3,700 per month.

32. I anticipate that income generated from commissions receivable will finance the administrator's trading.

33. A reduction in sales staff will allow the return of some vehicles to leasing companies, reducing lease payments by an estimated £5,000 over two months. It is also estimated that vehicle running expenses will be halved to £2,000 per month during the administration period.

34. Sales commissions to the remaining salesmen will be made on a cash basis, monthly in arrear.

Profit from trading

35. Appendix B includes a profit and loss account for the anticipated trading period of November and December 1989. This indicates that commissions receivable of £110,000 will be achieved, generating a profit of £53,260.

Reasons for seeking an administration order

36. In my opinion an administration is likely to produce a more advantageous realization of the company's assets than would be effected on a winding up, for the following reasons.
    (a) While the company continues to trade the administrator can market the business for sale as a going concern and commence negotiations with the existing management team, who have already expressed an interest.
    (b) The company has previously traded at a loss for the reasons stated in paragraphs 7 to 11 above. However, I believe an administrator could achieve a profit as set out in the budgeted profit forecast at Appendix B. The commissions becoming receivable during the next two months have already, to some extent, been paid for in terms of recent advertising. It will not be necessary to spend on any further advertising to achieve the estimated turnover. The administrator also intends to reduce overheads by reducing staff levels and lease costs.
    (c) Our agents, Messrs Anyname, believe that the freehold building, together with fixtures and fittings, will realize more if sold as part of a going concern. It may be possible to generate a payment for goodwill, which would not arise on a liquidation.
    (d) If the administrator can achieve a sale of the freehold property, or goodwill, any capital gains can be offset against the trading losses in the same year, as administration is not a cessation for corporation tax purposes. If the company was liquidated immediately, a set-off would not be possible and sale of such assets may lead to a capital gains tax liability.
    (e) If the business can be sold as a going concern, then the employment of most of the employees may be safeguarded. Following the decision in *Litster* v. *Forth Dry Dock and Engineering Company Limited (In Receivership)*[68], any employees who have contracts transferred in a going concern situation will not have claims against the insolvent company. This will reduce preferential creditors by an estimated £6,000 and unsecured creditors by an estimated £13,850.
37. If the company continues to trade, it is anticipated that the difference in realizations would be at least £33,000. Further, a trading profit is foreseen of some £53,000 giving a total improved realization of some £86,000 over the liquidation route.

38. If the company were to go into liquidation and I was appointed liquidator, I would not be prepared to continue trading the business even if leave of the court could be obtained, as I would be personally liable for any contract which the company entered into. Similarly, I do not believe that any other licensed insolvency practitioner will be prepared to carry on the trade in a liquidation.
39. Therefore, if the company is to achieve the enhanced realization predicted as a result of continuing to trade, this would have to be under an administrator. In an administration the likely dividend to unsecured creditors would be 24.5p in the £ as opposed to 2.9p in the £ in a liquidation, both before costs.

Conclusion and recommendations

40. An administrator has greater trading ability than a liquidator. A short period of trading would allow the company to be marketed and the costs thereof would be recovered from the realization of commissions on current loan applications. If a buyer could be found, asset realizations should be substantially greater than under liquidation. We do not anticipate requiring any additional sources of funding and I would not expect the period of trading to exceed two months.
41. In our opinion the grant of an administration order will enable the company to achieve a more advantageous realization of the company's assets than would be effected on a winding up.
42. The grant of an administration order is expedient for the purposes set out in section 8(3)(d) of the Insolvency Act 1986.

Appendix A: Estimated statement of affairs as at 23 October 1989

	Estimated realizable value	
	Administration 'going concern'	Liquidation 'break-up'
	£	£
Assets specifically pledged		
Freehold premises	100,640	90,000
Due to Northern Bank plc	86,000	86,000
Surplus for other creditors	14,660	4,000
Motor vehicles	14,000	14,000
Due to HP creditors	16,013	16,013
Shortfall to HP creditors	2,013	2,013
Assets not specifically pledged		
Cash in hands of accountant	2,900	2,900
Fixtures/fittings/equipment	5,530	3,020
Debtors	3,400	3,400
Goodwill	20,000	–
Motor vehicles	11,500	11,500
Profit generated from trading	53,260	–
	96,590	20,820
Total assets available	111,250	24,820
Preferential creditors		
PAYE/NIC	7,372	7,372
Wages and holiday pay	6,000	6,000
	13,372	13,372
Surplus as regards pref. creditors	97,878	11,448
Unsecured creditors		
Shortfall to HP creditors	2,013	2,013
Director's loan a/c	19,892	19,892
Redundancy/pay in lieu	13,850	13,850
Salesmen's commissions	13,000	13,000
Trade creditors	250,870	250,870
Inland Revenue (est.)	100,000	100,000
	399,625	399,625
Deficiency as regards unsecured creditors	301,747	388,177
Share capital	2,000	2,000
Total deficiency	303,747	390,177

Appendix B: Budgeted profit and loss account

	£	£
Sales commissions receivable		110,000
Less costs:		
Wages (administration staff)	20,000	
Commissions (salesmen)	15,000	
Equipment lease costs	5,350	
Property valuations	5,750	
Building society questionnaires	4,600	
Heat, light, telephone, etc.	2,140	
Sundry expenses	4,000	56,840
Estimated net profit from trading		53,160

Document 2: Report pursuant to section 23 of the Insolvency Act 1986 – statement of administrator's proposals: Northern Loans Limited

[*Much of this document is a reiteration of the details contained in the report in Document 1. The following headings are included.*]

1. Introduction

2. Statutory information

3. Company history and business

4. Recent financial history

5. Reasons for seeking an administration order
   17. The reason for seeking an administration order is that an administration is likely to produce more advantageous realizations of the company's assets than would be effected on a winding up. This is for the following reasons.
       (a) While the company continues to trade, the administrator can market the business for sale as a going concern. To that end the business has been advertised in *The Financial Times* and I have distributed a business profile to in excess of forty interested parties. This has produced considerable interest and a number of those are seeking further details and visiting the company's premises.
       (b) It is likely that the freehold building, together with fixtures and fittings, will realize a greater sum if sold as part of a going concern. It may be possible to generate a payment for goodwill, which would not arise on a liquidation.

(c) Any capital gains arising on the sale of the freehold property or goodwill can be offset against the trading losses arising in the same year in an administration as this is not a cessation for corporation tax purposes. If the company had been liquidated, a set-off would not be possible and sale of such assets would have led to a capital gains tax liability as a cost of liquidation.

(d) If the business is sold as a going concern, then the employment of most of the employees may be safeguarded. In this case, the employee's contracts would be transferred to a new purchaser and this would effectively reduce both preferential and unsecured creditors by an estimated £19,850.

(e) By continuing to trade in administration, the company is likely to realize a trading profit and take full advantage of the previous press advertising carried out by the company. There are also likely to be substantial enhanced realizations of assets in an administration. It is unlikely that a liquidator would have been prepared to continue trading the business as this would involve personal liability for contracts which the company had entered into.

(f) The administration is being funded by continuing commissions received from the banks. Just prior to administration, these were averaging £15,000 per week and it is estimated that this level will continue for the first month after which it will fall to approximately £10,000 per week due to the cessation of advertising.

(g) The staff levels have been reduced by approximately 50 per cent, creating savings in the region of £3,700 per month. The reduction in sales staff has allowed the return of some of the leased vehicles, reducing leasing payments by approximately £2,500 per month. There is also likely to be a corresponding decrease in the vehicle running expenses, of approximately £2,000 per month. Sales commissions to the remaining salesmen will be made on a commissions received basis only.

6. Administrator's proposals

18. My marketing of the business has resulted in several offers being made for the business and I propose to continue trading the business until early January and then sell the business to the person making the highest offer, subject to confirmation of the valuations from my agents.

19. I further propose that the administrator's fees be paid on a time basis.

20. The company is insolvent and upon completion of my administration I propose that the company be placed in creditors' voluntary liquidation to enable dividends to be paid to creditors, and that the administrator be allowed to seek appointment as liquidator.

REFERENCES AND FURTHER READING

Anderson, H. (1987) *Administrators: Part II of the Insolvency Act 1986*, Sweet and Maxwell, London.
Goldring, J. (1989) Administrations – practical lessons of the first two years, *Insolvency Law & Practice*, Vol. 5, pp. 2–8.
Grier, I. S. and Floyd, R. E. (1987) *Voluntary Liquidation, Receivership and Administration*, 2nd edn, Longman, Harlow.
Grier, I. S. and Floyd, R. E. (1988) *Company Administration Orders and Voluntary Arrangements*, Longman, Harlow.
Homan, M. (1989) *A Survey of Administrations under the Insolvency Act 1986*, report for the Research Board of the Institute of Chartered Accountants of England and Wales, ICAEW, London.
Kerr, W. W. (1989) *The Law and Practice as to Receivers and Administrators*, 17th edn, Sweet and Maxwell, London.
Phillips, M. (1987) Administration orders – the first few months, *Company Lawyer*, Vol. 8, pp. 273–77.
Stewart, G. (1987) *Administrative Receivers and Administrators*, CCH Editions, Bicester.
Totty, P. and Jordan, M. (1987) *Insolvency*, Longman, Harlow.

NOTES

1. Insolvency Review Committee, *Insolvency Law and Practice*, Cmnd. 8558, esp. Chap. 9, Administration.
2. S. 9(1). A petition by the company will require the approval or ratification of the members in general meeting.
3. S. 9(1). The directors must act as a board either unanimously or by the required majority as specified in the company's articles of association, see *Re Equiticorp International plc* (1989) 5 BCC 599. Thus, it is not possible for an individual director (unless he is the sole director) to present a petition.
4. S. 8(3).
5. (1987) 3 BCC 408.
6. IR, r. 2.2.
7. See pp. 88–9.
8. S. 14(2).
9. As to the limited powers of liquidators, see Chap. 10.
10. See Employment Protection (Consolidation) Act 1978.
11. See Chap. 9, p. 141.
12. S. 8(1)(a).
13. See Chap. 1, p. 11.
14. S. 8(1)(a). There has been some disagreement as to the standard required to show that an administration order would be 'likely' to achieve its purposes. In *Re Consumer & Industrial Press Ltd* (1988) 4 BCC 68, it was said that it should be 'more likely than not' to achieve the purposes, but in *Re Harris Simons Construction Ltd* [1989] BCLC 202, it was suggested that the court ought to be satisfied that there was a 'real prospect that one or more of the stated purposes would be achieved'. A similar standard was adopted in *Re Primlaks (UK) Ltd* (1989) 5 BCC 710.
15. S. 117.
16. This is where the company involved is authorized as a member of a recognized self-regulatory organization or professional body; Financial Services Act 1986, S. 74.
17. *Re Imperial Motors (UK) Ltd* (1989) 5 BCC 214.

18 IR, rr. 2.1 and 2.3.
19 Ibid.
20 IR, r. 2.2.
21 IR, r. 2.3(6).
22 S. 9(2) and IR, r. 2.6(2).
23 S. 10(2)(b).
24 S. 9(3).
25 S. 44(1)(a); see Chap. 8, p. 116.
26 S. 238; see Chap. 10, pp. 168–9.
27 S. 239.
28 *Standard Chartered Bank* v. *Walker* [1982] 3 All ER 938; *American Express Banking Corp.* v. *Hurley* [1985] 3 All ER 564.
29 *Re Harris Simons Construction Ltd* [1989] BCLC 202.
30 Before liquidation, the administrative receiver has a statutory right of indemnity out of the assets of the company in respect of any personal liability he incurs on contracts entered into in the course of his management of the business, s. 44(1)(c). After liquidation, he will rely for an indemnity on the debenture deed (if this contains such an indemnity clause).
31 For a discussion of the implication of these rights see Chap. 9, pp. 133–5.
32 *Re Business Properties Ltd* (1988) 4 BCC 684.
33 IR, r. 2.6(2)(c).
34 *Re A Company (No. 00175 of 1987)* (1987) 3 BCC 125.
35 IR, r. 2.6(3).
36 IR, r. 2.6A (inserted by the Insolvency (Amendment) Rules 1987 S.I. 1987 No. 1919).
37 S. 10(2)(a).
38 *Re A Company (No. 001992 of 1988)* [1989] BCLC 9.
39 S. 10(2)(b) and (c).
40 S. 9(4).
41 *Re A Company (No. 00175 of 1987)* (1987) 3 BCC 125.
42 S. 9(5).
43 S. 10(1)(a). Any petition for winding up the company which is currently pending must be dismissed, s. 11(1)(a).
44 S. 11.
45 S. 11(3)(c).
46 This has been interpreted to cover 'creditor' remedies which require the assistance of the court and does not cover 'self-help' remedies, e.g. the right of set-off (see Chap. 9, p. 136) or the forfeiture of leases. Also, the pre- and post-hearing moratoria will not prevent other legal actions, for example actions commenced by a competitor relating to trade practices, licences, etc., see *Air Écosse* v. *Civil Aviation Authority* (1987) 3 BCC 492.
47 S. 11(3)(d).
48 S. 27.
49 S. 17(2)(a).
50 S. 23. As to statements which must be annexed to the proposals, see IR, r. 2.16.
51 *Re Charnley Davies Business Services Ltd* (1987) 3 BCC 408.
52 S. 24(2).
53 S. 25.
54 S. 26. As to the structure of the committee and its rules of procedure, see IR, rr. 2.32 *et seq*.
55 S. 26(2).
56 See the comments of Harman J in *Re Charnley Davies Business Services Ltd* (see note 51) and also *Re Consumer & Industrial Press Ltd (No. 2)* (1988) 4 BCC 72.
57 S. 14(3).
58 [1989] BCLC 420.

59 S. 3(2).
60 S. 4(6). IR, r. 1.24.
61 S. 18(2)(a).
62 S. 18(2)(b).
63 [1988] BCLC 546.
64 Steven Frieze (1988) Converting administrations to liquidations, Vol. 1, *Insolvency Intelligence*, 11.
65 Helpful guidance is given in the *Guide to Professional Conduct and Ethics*, published by the Insolvency Practitioners Association.
66 S. 20(1).
67 S. 20(3); s. 212 (see Chap. 10, p. 173).
68 [1989] 2 WLR 634.

8
Administrative Receivers: Purposes and Procedures

Before examining the purposes for which administrative receivers are appointed, the procedure for their appointment and their status, it is important to be aware of the different types of receivers who may take possession of corporate assets for the benefit of secured creditors, and the nature of the security interests under which appointments may be made. Important consequences flow from the origin of the appointment, that is, from whether the appointment was made by the court or was a contractual appointment made under the terms of a fixed or a floating charge.

The High Court may appoint a receiver in any case where it would be just and equitable to do so, as, for example, where the company ceases to trade or where the assets over which a creditor's security extends are in jeopardy.[1] Such a receiver is an officer of the court and not an agent for either the company or the creditor who requested his appointment.[2] The receiver's powers are limited to those expressed in the court order and he will not normally be given powers of management unless these are necessary to sell the business as a going concern.[3] The nature and powers of court-appointed receivers are outside the scope of this book.

Receivers appointed out of court derive their status and powers both from the contract between the company and the lender that creates a security interest over the company's property and from statutory powers detailed in the Insolvency Act 1986.[4] The exact nature of the receiver's status and powers will depend upon whether he is appointed under a fixed or a floating charge.[5]

FIXED AND FLOATING CHARGES

Commercial companies which have power to borrow money to finance trading will also have an express or implied power to give security for such loans by way of mortgage or charge over their assets. The types of security interest which can be given are many and varied; for example, legal or equitable mortgages over land and buildings, charges over specific assets and charges over changing assets such as stock in trade and book debts. Such charges may stand alone, as single security interests, but it is common practice for the loan contract (the debenture) to create several types of charge covering a wide range of corporate property in a single instrument.

Fixed charges

In essence, a fixed charge relates to a specific, identifiable item of corporate property, for example its freehold or leasehold property or its book debts. The instrument of charge creates for the lender an immediate proprietary interest over the property comprised in the charge, the effect of which is to prevent the company from dealing with that asset without the consent of the chargee. Both presently owned assets and those to be acquired in the future may be the subject of a fixed charge; in the case of future assets, the lender will acquire a proprietary interest as soon as the assets come into the possession of the company.

The most significant feature of the fixed charge is the limitation it places on the company's dealings with the assets comprised in it. This can best be illustrated by the fixed charge over the company's book debts created in the *Siebe Gorman* v. *Barclays Bank Ltd*[6] case. Prior to the case, it had been thought that because future book debts were not presently identified, ascertained items of property, they could not be subject to a fixed charge. However, the instrument of charge in the case specified that all book debts should be paid into a special account with the lending bank and that the company had no power to dispose of, charge or assign the book debts without the consent of the bank. The court held that this instrument created a fixed charge on the proceeds of the book debts as soon as they were received.

The debenture coupled with a fixed charge will usually give the chargee the power to appoint a receiver if the company defaults in payment of the principal or interest due under the loan or if it breaches any other obligation contained in the debenture instrument. If the instrument of charge does not contain an express or implied power of appointment, such a power will be implied under section 101 of the Law of Property Act 1925, though a receiver appointed under such authority has only limited powers.[7] The receiver's role will be to take possession of and sell the assets comprised in the charge, and to repay the lender before any other corporate creditor is paid. This priority of payment is in marked contrast with the position of a floating charge holder. The lender with the latter type of security interest may be repaid only after the preferential creditors have been paid[8] (even though the company is not in liquidation). This low priority position weakens the status of a floating charge holder in the case of an insolvent company with extensive debts in respect of statutorily preferred creditors, e.g. national insurance contributions, PAYE payments, VAT and employees' remuneration.[9]

In addition to its strong and unassailable priority position, another advantage of a fixed charge is that, because it creates an immediate proprietary interest for the chargee, it will take in priority to all later charges created over company property.[10] Again, the position may be contrasted with that of the floating charge which, because of its characteristics (which will be explained later), allows the creation of other charges, particularly fixed charges which, although created after the floating charge, will rank as to payment in priority to the floating charge. There are, however, techniques whereby the floating charge holder can try to preserve his priority position and prevent the creation of other security interests ranking in priority to or equally with his interest.[11]

Finally, although there are circumstances in which a registered fixed charge may be challenged as being invalid, the provisions under which such a challenge may be made are much more difficult for a liquidator or administrator to prove than the corresponding provisions for challenging floating charges. In brief, a liquidator or administrator may challenge the security created in either a fixed or a floating charge, as being a preference caught within the definition given in section 239.[12] The period during which the security can be challenged under this section is six months prior to the onset of insolvency or, in the case of charges given to connected persons,[13] two years prior to that date. The liquidator or administrator bears the heavy onus of proving that in giving the charge the company was influenced by the desire to prefer that particular creditor.[14]

In contrast, a floating charge may be avoided under section 245 if it is created within twelve months of the onset of insolvency,[15] except to the extent of money paid or goods supplied to the company at the same time as, or after the creation of the charge. There is no onus on the liquidator or administrator to show that the charge was given in order to prefer the charge holder.

The major drawback of the fixed charge, when it stands alone, uncoupled with a floating charge, is that the receiver appointed by the chargee will be an ordinary receiver having powers limited simply to taking possession of the property covered by the charge and selling those assets; he will not be an administrative receiver with all the extended statutory powers which such a receiver possesses by virtue of Schedule 1 to the Insolvency Act. Thus, he cannot manage the business, sell or otherwise deal with property not included in the charge, or devise and implement a turnaround or rescue plan. An ordinary receiver is not an 'office-holder' within the meaning of section 234 of the Insolvency Act and will not enjoy the benefits relating to trading which office-holders possess, nor will he have the reporting obligation in connection with the conduct of the directors. An ordinary receiver need not be an insolvency practitioner.[16]

The statutory provisions governing the status of 'ordinary' receivers are sections 33–38 of the Insolvency Act. In particular, section 37 governs the liability of such receivers when entering into contracts in the course of their receivership; they will incur personal liability on such contracts, unless the contracts themselves provide otherwise, and they will be liable on any contract of employment adopted in the performance of the receivership, but they will be entitled to an indemnity in respect of this liability out of the assets comprised in the charge.

Floating charges

A floating charge is an equitable charge over assets of the company which are changing in nature and not specifically identified. Such a charge could cover, for example, goods in the process of manufacture, stock and materials and book debts. The floating charge provides the ideal way in which the company can extend the range of its security interests to include items which are constantly in a state of flux or which have not yet come into existence and which could not have been the subject of a fixed charge. The nature of a floating charge was well explained by Lord MacNaghten in the case of *Illingworth v. Houldsworth*:[17]

> A specific charge, I think, is one that [...] fastens on ascertained and identified property or property capable of being ascertained and identified; a floating charge, on the other hand, is ambulatory and shifting in nature, hovering over and so to speak floating with the property which it is intended to affect, until some event occurs or some act is done which causes it to settle and fasten on the subject of the charge within its reach and grasp.

The essential characteristic of a floating charge is that the company remains free to deal with the assets in the ordinary course of its business as if they were not affected by the charge. It can sell assets or create charges over its property without the consent of the floating charge holder unless there is some contractual agreement to the contrary.[18]

Since the floating charge is vulnerable to the creation of other charges over specific items (i.e. fixed charges), which would rank for payment in priority to the floating charge, it has become commonplace for lenders to insert contractual restrictions in the instrument of charge to prevent the company from creating prior-ranking security interests. These are so-called 'negative pledge' or 'prohibition' clauses. Though they are effective as between the lender and the company, there is some doubt as to their effectiveness with regard to subsequent lenders who may not have notice of the negative pledge in the debenture. This is because, although all floating charges have to be registered with the Registrar of Companies,[19] and the register of charges may contain a notice that there is a negative pledge in the instrument of charge, it is not legally required to register such pledges, and thus, although subsequent lenders who have actually inspected the register of charges will have actual notice of the limitation on the creation of later charges ranking in priority, those who have not inspected will not have constructive notice of the existence of any negative pledge.[20]

The company's licence to deal with property subject to a floating charge comes to an end when the charge crystallizes. It then becomes a fixed equitable charge attaching to all those items encompassed within the charge then in the ownership of the company and to all after-acquired property. After crystallization the company may not deal with the assets comprised in the charge without the consent of the charge holder.

Crystallization will occur:

(a) on the appointment of an administrative receiver by the charge holder[21] (the power of appointment will usually arise where the company has defaulted on the obligations set out in the debenture instrument, e.g. it has failed to make principal or interest payments on the loan and a demand for such payments has been made by the lender);
(b) on the commencement of winding up, either through the presentation of a petition to wind up the company or the passing of a resolution for voluntary winding up;[22]
(c) on the company ceasing to do business;[23]
(d) if the debenture specifies that on the happening of a certain event the floating charge will crystallize, then upon the occurrence of that event;[24]
(e) if the debenture specifies that the floating charge holder can cause the charge to crystallize by the giving of notice to the company, then upon such notice being served.[25]

Circumstances (d) and (e), that is, 'automatic crystallization' and crystallization on notice, have been a matter of controversy in legal circles over the past ten years or so. The advantage of an 'event' causing crystallization is that, without the intervention of the lender or the appointment of an administrative receiver, the occurrence of the event causes the charge to become a fixed equitable charge, thereby immediately ending the company's licence to deal with its property and preserving the chargee's priority position in relation to other security holders in any insolvency proceedings. The disadvantage of an automatically crystallizing event is that there may be no way in which persons dealing with the company or other charge holders can know whether a triggering event has occurred. Also, from the points of view of the charge holder and the company, the occurrence of the event may bring about an unwanted crystallization with, perhaps, irreversible results.[26]

The legality and effectiveness of such clauses were recognized in the case of *Re Brightlife Ltd*,[27] where the court affirmed the contractual freedom of the parties to insert such clauses into their debenture agreements. However, the actual result of the case, which reversed the order of priority of payment of preferred creditors and floating charge holders, has been statutorily reversed by section 251 of the Insolvency Act, which defines a floating charge as a charge which 'as created' is a floating charge. This section, combined with section 40, ensures that preferred creditors are *always* paid first – ahead of floating charge holders even where the floating charge has crystallized to become a fixed charge.

As already indicated, the operation of automatic crystallization clauses creates problems for subsequent lenders and security interest holders. Currently, there is no way in which the event causing crystallization can be notified to the Registrar of Companies and, through this public register, to those dealing with the company or holders of other charges over the company's property. So, for example, if a company has two floating charges over its property, the later in time may crystallize upon an event specified in the instrument of charge and, unless the first also has an automatic crystallization clause drawn in careful terms, the later charge may take in priority to the earlier created charge.

The Companies Act 1989 makes provision for regulations to require the registration of automatic crystallization clauses, crystallization on notice to the company and negative pledge clauses. This part of the Companies Act is not yet in force and is in many respects vague and unsatisfactory. Section 100 of the Companies Act 1989 (which would add a new section 410 to the Companies Act 1985) provides that the Secretary of State may by regulation require notice to be given to the Registrar of Companies of:

(1) the occurrence of such events as may be prescribed affecting the nature of the security under a floating charge of which particulars have been delivered for registration, and
(2) the taking of such action in exercise of powers conferred by a fixed or floating charge of which particulars have been delivered for registration, or conferred in relation to such a charge by an order of the court, as may be prescribed.

The regulations, as yet unpublished, may make provision as to the persons by whom notice may be given and the consequences of failure to give notice. Some indication of the effect of failure is to be gleaned from section 410(3), whereby the regulations, when enacted, may provide that crystallization shall be treated as ineffective until the particulars are delivered, and if they are delivered after the expiry of a prescribed period, they may continue to be ineffective against certain persons – probably other chargees whose crystallization notices have been delivered to the Registrar.

Similarly, section 103 of the Companies Act 1989 – which inserts a new section 415 to the Companies Act 1985 – provides that the forthcoming regulations may include, as one of the 'prescribed particulars' relating to a charge which must be delivered to the Registrar of Companies, 'whether the company has undertaken not to create other charges ranking in priority to or *pari passu* with the charge'.

While the floating charge is of advantage to the company enabling it to tap hitherto unavailable assets as a source of security for a loan, it is also of advantage for the lending institution or individual. This is because, if the company defaults on its obligations under the loan agreement, an administrative receiver can be appointed with extensive powers to manage and perhaps rescue the business and restore it to commercial viability, or to hive down the profitable parts to a subsidiary for sale as a going concern thus achieving a much better price than would be achieved on a forced sale of assets on a break-up basis. The sale of the business as a going concern may also preserve some jobs for the company's employees and may prevent the loss of economically important goods and services.

Though some advantages and disadvantages of floating charges have already been mentioned, it is appropriate to restate them at this point.

(1) *Advantages*
   (a) The floating charge holder can appoint an administrative receiver with extensive powers of management and sale. He has adequate powers to achieve a turnaround.
   (b) The range of property that can be included in a floating charge is very extensive, including assets in the process of manufacture and after-acquired property.
(2) *Disadvantages*
   (a) The priority position is weak because the company can create other, later fixed charges and floating charges over a more limited range of assets which will rank before a general floating charge in payment.
   There are ways of trying to prevent this loss of priority but the effectiveness of some of these methods is doubtful.
   (b) The administrative receiver must set aside an amount from any realization of assets covered by the charge to pay preferential creditors, even though the company is not in liquidation. This obligation is imposed by section 40(1) of the Insolvency Act and preserves the priority of the statutorily preferred creditors even where the floating charge has crystallized into a fixed charge.[28] The need to provide for the statutorily preferred creditors is, from the lender's point of view, perhaps the greatest weakness of the floating charge.
   (c) The security comprised in a general floating charge is usually expressed in all-embracing language to cover all the assets and undertaking of the company not already charged. However, the charge can cover only property which the company already owns or later acquires. Thus, property which the company hires under a hire-purchase agreement; property, such as vehicles and machinery, which the company leases from a commercial leasing company; property which is subject to retention of title clauses[29] and property which the company holds on trust[30] for other people will not be covered by the floating charge.
   (d) A floating charge created within twelve months of the onset of the insolvency could be invalidated under section 245.[31]

In view of these quite severe disadvantages attached to the floating charge, banks and other lending institutions have preferred to rely on fixed charges and have tried to extend the scope of such charges to cover items of property previously thought not to be capable of being the subject of such a charge, for example book debts, fixtures and fixed plant and machinery.[32] This trend may have an unfortunate effect so far as corporate rescue plans in receivership are concerned. This is because an ordinary receiver appointed under the terms of a fixed charge has only limited powers in comparison with those of an administrative receiver appointed under a floating charge.

What is the situation if, in a composite charge, many items of corporate property are covered by a fixed charge and this is coupled with a floating charge over anything that remains and is not capable of being caught within the definition of a fixed charge? Can an administrative receiver be appointed over what is, in effect, the rump of the company's property?

The answer to this depends on the definition of an 'administrative receiver' in section 29(2):

> (a) a receiver or manager of the whole (or substantially the whole) of a company's property appointed by or on behalf of the holders of any debentures of the company secured by a charge which, as created, was a floating charge, or by such a charge and one or more other securities; or
>
> (b) a person who would be such a receiver but for the appointment of some other person as the receiver of part of the company's property.

There is no statutory definition as to what is 'substantially' the whole of the company's property, and it may be that if most – in terms of value – of the property is covered by fixed charges, there is little left for the administrative receivership to 'bite' on. The alternative definition in paragraph (b) may come to the rescue, because it implies that an appointee can still be an administrative receiver even if a receiver has been appointed to so much of the property that what remains cannot be regarded as 'substantially the whole of the company's property' under paragraph (a).

From now on we will deal only with administrative receivers appointed under the terms of a floating charge.

PROCEDURE FOR APPOINTMENT

The circumstances under which an administrative receiver may be appointed and the procedure to be followed in making the appointment will be set out in the instrument of charge. The first thing a lending institution should do is to ensure that the security is valid, because if it is subsequently successfully challenged and found to be invalid, any appointment made will be void and the administrative receiver is at risk of personal actions for damages by the company for trespass to property, and by third parties in respect of the receiver's personal liability on contracts entered into in purported exercise of his powers.

Grounds for invalidity

Three grounds for invalidity have to be considered.

Section 245 of the Insolvency Act

Section 245 invalidates floating charges created within twelve months of the onset of insolvency, or, if the floating charge is in favour of a person connected with the company,[33] within two years of the onset of insolvency. The charge will always be valid, however, to the extent of any money paid or goods supplied to the company at the same time as, or after the creation of the charge.[34]

Thus, a charge which secures past lending will be invalid provided that at the time when the charge was created the company was unable to pay its debts or became unable so to do as a result of the transaction under which the charge was created.[35] In the case of a charge granted to a connected person there is a presumption that the company was insolvent at the time when the charge was created.

However, the case of *Mace Builders (Glasgow) Ltd. v. Lunn*[36] is authority for the point that if the receiver has sold the assets comprised in the charge and repaid the debenture holders and, subsequently, the liquidator successfully challenges the validity of the charge, the sale of assets prior to liquidation will remain valid and money that has been paid to the chargee is irrecoverable.

Section 239 of the Insolvency Act

Under section 239 a liquidator or administrator may apply to the court to set aside any transaction (including the grant of a floating charge) with a creditor if the effect of that transaction has been to put that creditor in a better position in liquidation than he would have been in had the transaction not been entered into. The period in which a transaction can be scrutinized to see whether it may be declared void as a preference is six months prior to the onset of insolvency or, in the case of a transaction with connected persons, twelve months prior to insolvency.

It is quite difficult to challenge a transaction as a preference, because the liquidator or administrator has to show that the company giving the preference was influenced by a desire to prefer that creditor.[37]

Non-registration

The third ground of invalidity is that the charge has not been registered with the Registrar of Companies within twenty-one days of its creation, as required by section 395 of the Companies Act 1985. If a charge is not registered within the prescribed period, it is void against the liquidator and any creditor of the company even if the creditor had notice of the existence of the unregistered charge. However, the charge is not void against the company, and the lender who has, pursuant to a power contained in the charge, seized goods covered by the charge will be entitled to retain any proceeds of sale notwithstanding non-registration.[38]

Under regulations to be prescribed under section 93 of the Companies Act 1989, an instrument creating a floating charge (and many other types of security interest) must be registered within twenty-one days of the creation of the security. The sanction for non-registration under the new regulations is that the charge will be void against the administrator or liquidator and also against any person who for value acquires a right or interest over the property which is subject to the charge. Under section 95 of the Companies Act 1989, it will be possible to register a charge more than twenty-one days after its creation, where the particulars have been delivered late to the Registrar.

However, where, after late delivery of the particulars of charge, the company is unable to pay its debts and insolvency proceedings commence within two years (in the case of a floating charge created in favour of a connected person), within one year (in the case of any other floating charge) or six months in the case of a late registered fixed charge, the charge will be void against the administrator or liquidator.

Circumstances in which an appointment may be made

Assuming that the charge is valid, the debenture holder can usually appoint an administrative receiver in the following circumstances.

(1) Where the company has defaulted in payment of the principal and/or interest on the loan: frequently, the principal money is made payable on demand and power to appoint an administrative receiver will arise if the demand is not met.

It is clear from the case law relating to demands for payment under debentures that, although sufficient time should be allowed to enable the company to put into effect procedures for repayment, its directors cannot expect or feel entitled to any time in which to raise further capital or negotiate with other parties to service the loan repayments.[39] Lightman and Moss[40] (1986) cite the case of a manufacturing company given ninety minutes to repay a loan of £585,000. This deadline was extended to a week after negotiations, but then a receiver was appointed. Directors would be well advised to examine the instrument containing the security to ensure that such precipitate demands, resulting in the immediate right to appoint an administrative receiver, could not be made. A demand for repayment is satisfactory and effective if it makes it clear that the creditor requires to be paid a sum which is in fact due, even if the amount is not specified in detail[41] and even if an offer has been made to accept instalment payments.[42]

(2) In the absence of default in repayment of the loan, the debenture holder may wish to appoint an administrative receiver where the company has become, or is in grave danger of becoming, insolvent within the meaning of section 123 of the Insolvency Act. Provided that there is an express term in the security instrument which refers to the company's insolvency, the chargee can take the immediate step of appointing an administrative receiver to protect its interests.[43] In the absence of an express term, the court will not imply a power to appoint an administrative receiver where the company is insolvent and yet maintaining its payments to the debenture holder.[44] The only recourse in this case is for the lender to apply to the court for the appointment of a receiver on the ground that the assets comprised in the security are in jeopardy.[45]

(3) The right to appoint an administrative receiver arises on the presentation of a winding-up petition by any creditor or the passing of a resolution for voluntary winding up.

(4) The right to appoint arises where a company ceases to trade.[46]
(5) If an administration petition is presented, notice must be given to any person entitled to appoint an administrative receiver, and if such appointment is then made, the court must dismiss the administration petition.[47] It is usual in floating charges created after 1986 to provide that upon presentation of petition for an administration order, the charge holder may immediately appoint an administrative receiver.

Even if the wrong reason for the appointment is given by the secured creditor, provided that grounds exist on which a proper appointment could have been made, there can be no objection to the validity of the appointment.[48] If an appointment is defective because the correct procedure has not been followed, section 232 will operate to validate the acts of the office-holder.[49].

Once the conditions for the appointment of an administrative receiver have arisen, the creditor owes no duty of care towards the company or the guarantor of the company's debts in exercising his power of appointment. For example, in *Shamji* v. *Johnson Matthey Bankers Ltd*[50] the Gomba group of companies, which was indebted to its bankers in the sum of £21 million, was actively involved in arranging alternative sources of finance and had negotiated for an extension of time and the making of instalment payments. The bank, despite its knowledge of the refinancing negotiations, appointed a receiver, and when this appointment was contested as being in breach of duty towards the company and its guarantors, the court affirmed that the bank, as appointor of a receiver, did not owe the company or guarantors of its indebtedness such a duty in deciding whether and when to exercise its contractual right to appoint a receiver.

The actual appointment is made in writing (usually in the form of a deed of appointment)[51] but it does not become effective unless it is accepted by the proposed receiver before the end of the business day next following that on which the instrument of appointment is received by him.[52] The person selected to be the administrative receiver by the creditor must be a licensed insolvency practitioner.[53] The appointment commences at the time when the instrument is received by the administrative receiver. Once an appointment is made, several formalities have to be complied with.

(1) The administrative receiver must forthwith send to the company notice of his appointment and cause a notice of his appointment to be published in the *London Gazette*.[54]
(2) The receiver, who will normally take immediate possession of the property comprised in the charge, must give notice of his appointment to the company and, within twenty-eight days, must send notices to all the company's creditors indicating that he has been appointed.[55] He will also ensure that the fact of his appointment appears on all corporate correspondence and notices.

THE STATUS OF THE ADMINISTRATIVE RECEIVER

Upon his appointment, the administrative receiver is deemed to be the agent of the company; the agency terminates when the company goes into liquidation.

Section 44, which regulates the status of the administrative receiver, provides:

(1) The administrative receiver of a company—
   (a) is deemed to be the company's agent, unless and until the company goes into liquidation;
   (b) is personally liable on any contract entered into by him in the carrying out of his functions (except in so far as the contract otherwise provides) and on any contract of employment adopted by him in the carrying out of those functions; and
   (c) is entitled in respect of that liability to an indemnity out of the assets of the company.
(2) For the purposes of subsection (1)(b) the administrative receiver is not to be taken to have adopted a contract of employment by reason of anything done or omitted to be done within 14 days after his appointment.
(3) This section does not limit any right to indemnity which the administrative receiver would have apart from it, nor limit his liability on contracts entered into or adopted by him without authority, nor confer any right to indemnity in respect of that liability.

The significance of this 'deemed' agency is that, so far as continuing contracts, continuing leases and continuing occupation of premises are concerned, the appointment of an administrative receiver has no effect on the continuity of these contracts between the company and third parties.[56]

However, as agent for the company the administrative receiver is in an unusual legal position and, practically speaking, he is in an extremely powerful position. Though normally an agent will receive instructions from his principal, an administrative receiver is insulated from instruction or interference from the corporate management. As was observed in *Gomba Holdings UK Ltd v. Homan*,[57] the receiver has power to carry on the 'day to day process of realisation and management of the company's property without interference from the board'. Also, the agency is unusual because, although normally an agent's decisions will be taken in the best interests of his principal, in the case of a receivership, the administrative receiver's stewardship of the corporate assets is primarily designed to protect the interests of the person who appointed him. It is this ability to take decisions with a view to maximizing the return for the secured creditors, rather than considering the best interests of the company as a whole, which enables the receiver to decide whether to continue performance of contracts the company has with outsiders. The power of the receiver to repudiate existing contracts, thus making the company liable in damages to the other contracting party (an action which is likely to be worthless in the case of an insolvent company) was recognized in the leading case of *Airline Airspares Ltd v. Handley Page Ltd*,[58] where the receiver, arranging a classic hive down (that is, a transfer of the company's valuable and saleable assets to a 'clean subsidiary' prior to sale of the subsidiary to the highest bidder), repudiated a contract by which Handley Page had agreed to make commission payments to the plaintiff company. The court held that the receiver was under no obligation to adopt existing contracts and was free, provided that he did not act in bad faith, to cause the company to repudiate or ignore existing contracts. This ability, which is extremely important in conducting hive downs prior to sale of the business as a going concern, has recently been confirmed[59] and, moreover, aggrieved parties have no right to bring a personal action against the receiver for interference with contractual relations, provided that he acts, as he normally does, as agent for the company.[60]

Although the administrative receiver's primary responsibility will be to protect the interests of the secured creditor who appointed him, he does owe some general duties to the company and unsecured creditors. For example, he must, within three months of his appointment, send to the Registrar of Companies, and trustees for the secured creditors and all unsecured creditors (so far as he is aware of their addresses) a report on the company's affairs.[61] This will detail his actions or proposed actions in relation to the assets under his control, whether he has or intends to continue to run the business, whether he has made any plans for sale of the business as a going concern, and the amounts that he has paid or intends to pay to the statutorily preferred creditors.

The status of the administrative receiver will radically change if the receivership is followed by or concurrent with a liquidation. The administrative receiver will cease to be agent for the company.[62] Thereafter, if he continues to trade – entering into new contracts or continuing those which he started in receivership – he is in danger of incurring personal liability and, consequently, upon the appointment of a liquidator, the administrative receiver will usually close down the business and this will bring to an end any rescue plans.

In as much as an administrative receiver cannot prevent, by means of injunction, an ordinary unsecured creditor from petitioning for winding up, where he fears that such a petition could interfere with maturing plans for rescue or sale of the business the administrative receiver could take the drastic step of causing the company to petition for an administration order.[63] This would prevent the grant of a winding-up order and enable the administrator to carry the rescue or sale plans into effect. If the court were to be satisfied that the purposes of an administration order would be likely to be achieved, and the administrative receiver were to be willing to vacate office,[64] then the administration order could be well used to ensure that carefully prepared plans are not wasted.

RESIGNATION AND REMOVAL OF ADMINISTRATIVE RECEIVERS

The receivership will come to an end once all possible realizations by way of sale of the assets or restoration of the business have taken place and the secured creditor has been paid. It must be remembered that the administrative receiver is obliged to pay the preferred creditors before making any distribution to the secured creditors, and if he fails to do so he will be personally liable for damages for breach of statutory duty in the sums he should have paid to them.[65] If the receiver has surplus funds after the realization then, if the company is not in liquidation, these should be returned to the directors; if liquidation supervenes, any surplus gained from the sale of assets covered by the receivership must be paid to the liquidator for distribution to the unsecured creditors.

If the company is insolvent at the time when the administrative receiver has finished his realizations, but no winding-up petition has been presented, the administrative receiver himself has power to petition for the winding up of the company.[66] He would thereby be enabled to hand over any surplus to the liquidator and permit a liquidator to take over the conduct of any investigation into the company's affairs or directors' conduct which may need to be continued after the termination of the receivership.

An administrative receiver may resign at any time and must in so doing give seven days' notice to his appointor and to the company or its liquidator.[67] He must also send a notice of his resignation to the Registrar of Companies within fourteen days of the vacation of his office.[68]

A significant change introduced by the Insolvency Act, designed to protect the independence of the administrative receiver, is that, under section 45, an administrative receiver may be removed from office only by a court order, whereas previously a receiver appointed by the secured creditor could be removed at any time by his appointor.

Case Study
Any Windows Ltd.

This case study comprises an example of a viability study prepared for presentation to a bank which was considering whether to appoint an administrative receiver under the terms of its fixed and floating charge security.

After examining the figures, which indicated the cash flow required for the trading period under review and the profits which could be generated from current and potential contracts, as well as reviewing the production and costing systems operated by the company, the bank decided to appoint a receiver. Document 2 is an example of the clauses in a typical deed of appointment: Schedule 1 to the Insolvency Act (which is reproduced at the end of Chapter 9) is also relevant in the context of the powers of an administrative receiver.

Document 3 in the case study is the estimated statement of affairs, indicating the realizations made by the administrative receiver.

Shortly after the successful sale of this business, in which the receiver managed to realize a good value for the secured creditor, preserve the business – which was transferred to a large company – and save a number of jobs for the workforce, the company was placed into a creditors' voluntary winding up.

The documents are:

(1) extracts from viability study of Any Windows Limited;
(2) extracts from deed of appointment of administrative receiver;
(3) estimated statement of affairs at the termination of the administrative receivership.

Document 1: Viability report on Any Windows Limited prepared by A.N. (a licensed insolvency practitioner)

Introduction

1.1 In accordance with the directors' instructions, we have carried out an investigation into the affairs of Any Windows Limited. With permission we have passed a copy of this report to the Goodbank plc for their consideration.

1.2 The purpose of the investigation was:

(a) to assist in the preparation of cash-flow forecasts and to review these forecasts;
(b) to assist in the preparation of budgeted profit forecasts for the period to 31 March 1987;
(c) to examine the current and potential order book in order to determine the amount of business that can be generated in the period to 31 March 1987;
(d) to examine briefly the production and costings systems in order to determine their accuracy;
(e) to consider the immediate viability of the company and to advise on the level of finance necessary to support turnover, to product cost recovery and profits.

1.3 Any Windows Limited was incorporated on 1980 to commence manufacture of UPVC-framed windows. The company trades from leased premises. The factory is held on a twenty-four-year lease commencing in 1980 at an annual rent of £16,000. There are additional premises in Lightvale at an annual rent of £8,000.

1.4 Any Windows has fifty-two employees [*details of their employment are given*].

Summary and conclusions

2.1 The company is likely to experience severe financial pressure during the period January–March 1987. The cash requirement at February 1987 amounts to £212,000 and falls to £156,000 in March 1987. The current overdraft facilities amount to £130,000. In the absence of additional finance, the trade creditor payment period will have to be extended by approximately three to four weeks. The extension of credit payment period is at a time when the company will be requiring significantly increased purchases to meet its production schedules.

2.2 The company has significantly expanded its trading activities in recent weeks and is budgeted to sell 6,607 units in the next three months to March 1987. In the three months to 30 September 1986 sales amounted to 3,393 units. In our view this expansion has taken place without adequate financial support to finance the company's working capital requirements.

2.3 The directors acknowledge that there has been inadequate managerial control which has resulted in major errors being made, poor profitability, and has contributed to the current financial position.

2.4 There are many areas of uncertainty which we have encountered while reviewing the management accounts and budgets of the company. These are as follows.

(a) The company has recently increased its production and introduced two shifts. Current output is in the region of 400–450 units per week. The budget for January–March 1987 requires an output of 500 units per week. While management believe these units of production can be achieved we believe this to be optimistic.
(b) The sales mix has traditionally been to supply trade, contract and retail markets. The production schedule for January–March 1987 is almost wholly (85 per cent) to the contract market. These are in the main confirmed orders.
(c) There has been little control, if any, in respect of ordering goods from suppliers. This has resulted in the company holding stocks in excess of £200,000. Significant additional purchases may be required to satisfy the January–March 1987 production schedule.
(d) The lead time for certain components is, we understand, up to eleven weeks after placing the order. The company has not yet reviewed its material requirements to ensure that the material will arrive in time to meet its production schedule.
(e) No adequate review has been undertaken to establish the amount of provision required against slow-moving stocks.

2.5 The significance of the matters referred to in the paragraph above renders all financial projections a broad estimate, at best. Due regard must be taken of these matters when drawing any conclusions from this report.

2.6 Should the company have a receiver appointed or enter insolvent liquidation it is likely that a significant deficit would exist. The estimated statement of affairs shows a deficit of £573,000 on a break-up basis and £450,000 if the assets were sold to achieve a going concern sale. These amounts are, however, inclusive of £379,000 of finance provided by the shareholders.

2.7 The directors are confident that the projected output of 500 units per week from 1 January 1987 can be achieved.

Conclusion

2.8 The company is likely to experience severe financial pressure during the period January–March 1987.
2.9 We recommend that we monitor the performance of the company upon a weekly basis, and are kept informed of significant developments daily if necessary.
2.10 If the company cannot solve the problems facing it within a very short period of time then we fear that the only option available to it would be to request the bank to appoint a receiver or, alternatively, to call meetings of members and creditors with a view to placing the company into liquidation.
2.11 The directors should be mindful of the personal risk associated with taking additional credit and must form a view as to the prospects of the company being able to pay for the goods and services acquired.

Estimated cash flow

3.1 Trade creditors in the past have been paid two months after invoicing. Consequently, goods and services received in September 1986 would normally have been paid for on 30 November 1986. To remain within the agreed overdraft facilities, cheques to suppliers have been held back, thus extending creditor payment periods.
3.2 If we assume the maintenance of the current overdraft facilities, payment of suppliers' invoices will not be made, thus extending payment periods by approximately three to four weeks. Consequently, the company will be taking some three months' credit from suppliers. This extension of payment period is also at a time when the company is significantly increasing its production schedule and thus requiring significantly more raw materials. The combination of these factors is likely to encounter some resistance from suppliers.
3.3 Debtors must be pressed for payment more quickly and those who are withholding payment due to unresolved queries *must* have their problems resolved immediately so as to encourage payment. At 18 December 1986 some £50,000 of debtors were withholding payment due to snagging problems, late delivery or unresolved queries. The collection of these amounts must be a priority.
3.4 Stocks have increased significantly to over £200,000. This level of stockholding is unacceptable. Significant quantities of goods were purchased in October and November 1986 which are not immediately usable for production. As a result some £282,000 of credit (October £132,000 and November £150,000) was incurred, a significant proportion of which could have been avoided. The reduction of stock levels must be given priority. If excessive stocks of profiles or components are being held which are not immediately usable for production, these goods should be exchanged – if possible for stocks that are currently required.

[*The estimated cash flow is shown in Table 8.1.*]

Table 8.1 Any Windows Limited: Estimated cash flow to 31 March 1987

	January 1987 £	February 1987 £	March 1987 £	Total £
Receipts				
Debtors	175,473	172,469	—	347,942
Sales (incl. VAT)	—	32,760	221,778	254,538
	175,473	205,229	221,778	602,480
Payments				
Creditors	169,000	119,500	65,000	353,500
Material purchases (incl. VAT)	18,360	24,280	38,671	81,311
Overheads (incl. VAT)	56,351	55,216	62,147	173,714
VAT Creditor	—	20,000	—	20,000
	243,711	218,996	165,818	628,525
Cash movement	(68,238)	(13,767)	55,960	(26,045)
Opening balance	(130,000)	(198,238)	(212,005)	(130,000)
Closing balance	(198,238)	(212,005)	(156,045)	(156,045)

Profit forecast

4.1 The essential feature of the profit forecast [*see Table 8.2*] is the forecast of units produced. In the past 500 units have rarely been achieved, but management are confident that with increasing experience and improved efficiency an average of 500 units will be consistently achieved from January 1987 onwards.

4.2 Based on the projected production, each contract has been evaluated to determine the sales value and the cost of sales (excluding direct labour and overhead recovery).

4.3 The gross margin shows a substantial increase of 5 per cent, from 25 to 29 per cent of total sales. This is mainly due to the assumption that production will be more efficient. The increase in contract work means that there are fewer 'one-off' windows, set-up times are reduced and stocks can be standardized.

4.4 The major alteration to administration expenses is the recruitment of the new general manager. At present Mr X is not an employee of the company, but is remunerated as a consultant. It is estimated that his cost to the company is approximately £2,500 per month.

4.5 The company is undergoing a period of change. To improve efficiency, certain improvements can be made at no cost to the company. Other

Table 8.2 Any Windows Limited: Budgeted profit forecast to 31 March 1987

	Budget January	Budget February	Budget March	Budget Total	Actual 3 months to 3.9.86
Sales (units)	2,000	2,107	2,500	6,607	3,393
	£	£	£	£	£
Sales (value)	175,207	199,943	220,884	596,034	317,453
Materials (+ direct fixing)	99,825	115,566	112,823	328,214	163,592
Labour	24,200	24,200	30,250	78,650	43,231
Direct selling	2,487	2,487	2,641	7,615	14,735
Direct installation	2,170	2,170	2,170	6,510	17,163
	128,682	144,423	147,884	420,989	238,721
Gross margin	46,525	55,520	73,000	175,045 (29%)	78,732 (25%)
Works costs	11,595	11,645	11,645	34,885	31,315
Indirect selling	3,355	3,355	3,355	10,065	12,786
Indirect installation	4,895	4,895	4,895	14,685	14,792
Admin & general	17,870	17,870	17,870	53,610	45,757
Special projects	5,000	2,500	2,500	10,000	—
	42,715	40,265	40,265	123,245	104,650
Trading profit/ (loss)	3,810	15,255	32,735	51,800	(25,918)

improvements will require a cash input or a temporary halt to production to effect a reorganization. As a result we have provided £10,000 for 'special projects'.

Production and costing systems

5.1 The company uses standard units as a basis of its production system. A 'unit' is basically a single frame plus an outward-opening window. The company manufactures many types of windows with many types of opening systems; accordingly, there are numerous combinations of one production unit.

5.2 The costing system is designed to cost the material content and labour content of each product. However, it suffers from the following drawbacks.

(a) The material content of production is based upon the actual material required together with 10 per cent allowance for wastage. The company has not verified the accuracy of this waste content.
(b) Estimated labour hours are costed into product costing. The actual labour hours of producing each unit have not been verified by the company. Overall production targets are, however, in force.

5.3 The company's costing systems are designed to generate a 30–40 per cent gross profit from each order. However, the estimates incorporated in the costing system in respect of materials and labour place a significant question mark over the reliability of the costing systems.

5.4 The company's budgets are not integrated with the costing systems; consequently, the budgeted profit and loss and the budgeted balance sheet must be suspect.

5.5 There has been little or no control over the materials ordered from suppliers. Consequently, stocks have risen from £145,000 at 30 September 1986 to £224,000 at 30 November 1986.

5.6 The company does not yet operate adequate control over material requirements. Consequently, although the company is holding stock in excess of £200,000 it estimates that a further £80,000 of materials will be acquired in January 1987.

5.7 The company has traditionally manufactured to supply three markets, namely the contract, trade and retail markets. Recently, however, the company has switched to almost total reliance upon the contract market. The budgeted production for January–March 1987 shows an 85 per cent supply to the contract market.

5.8 To produce units for the contract market requires the supply of profiles and components which may not be readily available from stocks. Consequently, significant amounts of material are required to meet the January–March 1987 production schedule.

5.9 The company is attempting to increase weekly production to 500 units per week. However, the company has been unable to sustain this level of production over the seven weeks prior to our investigation.

Although we have no specific information upon which to assess the break-even position of the company, from our review of the financial information and budgets it would be reasonable to assess the break-even position at 400 units per week. Any regular sustained production above this would contribute to profit.

5.10 The poor organization within the factory has resulted in a poor flow of work around the factory and a lack of co-ordination between the different processes. This has resulted in the following problems:

(a) extra and unnecessary labour time is incurred in sanding and polishing frames which are damaged due to excessive handling;
(b) labour-saving machines have broken down and have been out of use for several months, resulting in certain work requiring to be done by hand;

(c) there has been a lack of co-ordination between the factory and warehouse and also within the factory, resulting in delays and holding up production.

5.11 We appreciate that the directors and the general manager are aware of all these problems, and in some cases they have started to correct them, but we must emphasize that these changes must be made in the very short term in order to achieve the required levels of production.

Any Windows Limited: Estimated statement of affairs as at 18 December 1986

	NBV	Break-up value	Going concern value
	£	£	£
Assets subject to fixed charge			
Leasehold property		Nil	Nil
Debtors		144,200	250,000
Less amount due to Goodbank plc		(129,390)	(129,390)
		14,810	120,610
Assets subject to hire purchase			
Motor cars		22,700	29,500
Commercial vehicles		3,900	5,000
Less amount due to HP company		(30,200)	(30,200)
		(3,600)	4,300
Assets subject to floating charge			
Fixtures and fittings	23,065	1,000	1,300
Plant and machinery and tools	45,774	30,000	39,000
Office equipment	1,012	1,400	1,800
Motor cars	10,139	3,500	4,500
Commercial vehicles	8,823	500	600
Stock	260,000	120,000	120,000
		156,400	167,200
		171,210	292,110
Preferential creditors			
PAYE and NIC		23,000	23,000
VAT		6,000	6,000
Rates		—	—
Wages and holiday pay		10,000	10,000
		39,000	39,000
		132,210	253,110

	Break-up value	Going concern value
	£	£
Unsecured creditors		
Trade creditors	323,300	323,300
Loans	204,000	204,000
Hire-purchase balance	3,600	
	530,900	527,300
Deficiency as regards creditors	(398,690)	(274,190)
Share capital	175,000	175,000
Deficiency as regards members	(573,690)	(449,190)

Document 2: Deed of appointment of administrative receiver

WHEREAS by a Debenture dated   19   made between Any Windows Limited (hereinafter called 'the Company') of the one part and the Goodbank plc (hereinafter called 'the Bank') of the other part

WHEREAS the Company has charged to the Bank the premises therein more precisely defined with payment to the bank on demand of monies and other liabilities described in the Debenture, together with interest thereon

AND WHEREAS despite the demand of the Bank for repayment of the monies so described default has been made by the Company in the payment to the Bank of such monies and liabilities

NOW THEREFORE in exercise of the powers conferred on it by the said Debenture and pursuant to the Law of Property Act 1925 the Bank hereby appoints [*name of receiver*] of [*address*] to be the Administrative Receiver of the premises charged in the Debenture with power to exercise in the name of the Company (notwithstanding the liquidation of the Company) or at his option (but only with the specific written approval of the Bank) in the name of the Bank or at his option in his own name all the powers conferred on a receiver specifically by the Debenture or by virtue of the Insolvency Act 1986 or the Law of Property Act 1925 or otherwise by the law. The Administrative Receiver so appointed shall without prejudice to the extent of his said powers be deemed to be the agent of the Company which alone shall be responsible for the Administrative Receiver's acts or defaults.

DATED this   day of   19

[*Executed by Goodbank plc*]

Document 3: Estimated statement of affairs as at 21 July 1987

[*Note:* After the appointment of an administrative receiver, Any Windows Ltd traded for a short time, but the projections, as listed in the viability report were optimistic.

The administrative receiver decided to try to sell the business on a going concern basis so that the purchaser could inject the much-needed working capital. A business profile was produced and the business advertised in various trade magazines. Twelve interested parties visited the company's premises, resulting in four offers. There were retention of title claims over some items of property, and the eventual buyer agreed to settle these for approximately £30,000.

The administrative receiver continued to trade and realized approximately £40,000 from the sale of stock. He expended some £20,000–30,000 in completing work in progress. This resulted in a trading surplus of £10,000.

A small reduction of staff was made, to thirty employees.

The administrative receiver requested claims from the preferential creditors. These amounted to some £19,000, but had not yet been confirmed at the time of the completion of the estimated statement of affairs.

The majority of the bank's debt had been repaid.

A meeting of members and creditors was called for a date in August 1987, at which a resolution was to be passed to place the company into liquidation.]

Any Windows Limited – in administrative receivership: Estimated statement of affairs as at 21 July 1987

	Book value	Going concern realizable value
	£	£
Fixed charge		
Book debts	350,000	150,000
Goodbank plc (inclusive of guarantee)	—	(83,000)
		67,000
Floating charge		
Plant and machinery		90,000
Stock and work in progress		49,000
Motor vehicles		5,000
Trading surplus		10,000
		154,000
Preferential creditors		(25,000)
		129,000
Estimated surplus to Goodbank plc (before receiver's fees, costs and interest)		196,000

REFERENCES AND FURTHER READING

Crabb, L. (1988) Receivers, administrators, agency and capacity, *Company Lawyer*, Vol. 9, pp. 124–9.
Goode, R. M. (1988) *Legal Problems of Credit and Security*, 2nd edn, Sweet and Maxwell, London.
Gough, W. J. (1978) *Company Charges*, Butterworth, London.
Grier, I. S. and Floyd, R. E. (1987) *Voluntary Liquidation, Receivership and Administration*, 2nd edn, Longman, Harlow.
Kerr, W. W. (1989) *The Law and Practice of Receivers and Administrators*, 17th edn, Sweet and Maxwell, London.
Lange, and Hartwig, (1989) *The Law and Practice of Administrative Receivers*, Sweet and Maxwell, London.
Lightman, G. and Moss, G. (1986) *The Law of Receivers of Companies*, Sweet and Maxwell, London.
Milman, D. and Rushworth, J. (1987) *Receivers and Receivership*, Jordans, Bristol.
Moss, G. (1989) Receivers of companies and bankers under the Insolvency Act 1986, *Insolvency Law & Practice*, Vol. 6, pp. 35–7.
Samwell, S. (1987) *Corporate Receiverships*, 2nd edn, Institute of Chartered Accountants.
Stewart, G. (1987) *Administrative Receivers and Administrators*, CCH Editions, Bicester.
Tolley, (1988) *Receivership Manual*,
Totty, P. and Jordan, M. (1987) *Insolvency Law*, Longman, Harlow.

NOTES

1 See Kerr (1989), pp. 49–59.
2 *Burt, Boulton and Hayward* v. *Bull* [1895] 1 QB 276; *Re Botibol* [1947] 1 All ER 26.
3 *Edwards* v. *Standard Rolling Stock Syndicate* [1893] 1 Ch 574; *Re Victoria Steamboats* [1897] 1 Ch 158. See Kerr, op. cit., pp. 195–207 and Chap. 9.
4 S. 42(1) and Sched. 1 (this latter is reproduced in the case study in Chap. 9).
5 Gough (1978).
6 [1979] 2 Lloyd's Rep 142; see also *Re Keenan Bros* [1986] BCLC 242 (a case in the Irish courts decided on similar principles).
7 He has no power to carry on the business of the company. The court can order a sale of the property comprised in the security, LPA, ss. 90 and 91.
8 IA, s. 40.
9 For a full list of statutorily preferred creditors, see Sched. 6, which is reproduced in the case study in Chap. 10.
10 *Wheatley* v. *Silkstone & Haigh Moor Coal Co.* (1885) 29 Ch D 715.
11 See pp. 108–9.
12 See Chap. 10, p. 166–8.
13 Defined in s. 249 to include a director or a shadow director or an 'associate' of such a person, or an 'associate' of the company. The term 'associate' is defined in wide terms in CA 1985, s. 435.
14 S. 239(5).
15 S. 245(3); the time before the onset of insolvency during which a floating charge may be declared invalid is extended to two years in the case of a charge created in favour of a 'connected person'.
16 As to an interesting case in which a managing director was appointed as a receiver of assets covered in a charge granted to himself, see *Mace (Builders) Glasgow Ltd*

Administrative Receivers: Purposes and Procedures 129

v. *Lunn* [1987] BCLC 55. Such an appointment could not now be made, because the charge was a floating charge and an administrative receiver must be a licensed insolvency practitioner. But it would still be the case as regards receivership under the terms of a fixed charge.

17 [1904] AC 355, 358.
18 *Re Yorkshire Woolcombers Association Ltd* [1903] 2 Ch 284.
19 CA 1985, s. 395.
20 For a discussion of the problems relating to notice in this area see Farrar (1976) The crystallisation of a floating charge, *The Conveyancer*, Vol. 40, p. 397, and for a contrary view Goode (1988). When implemented, the CA 1989 will abolish the doctrine of constructive notice so far as it relates to documents registered with the Registrar of Companies.
21 *Re Crompton & Co. Ltd* [1914] 1 Ch 954.
22 *Wallace v. Automatic Machines Co.* [1894] 2 Ch 547.
23 *Re Woodroffes (Musical Instruments) Ltd* [1985] 2 All ER 908.
24 *Re Brightlife Ltd* [1986] 3 All ER 673.
25 *Re Woodroffes (Musical Instruments) Ltd* [1985] 2 All ER 908.
26 For example, other charges may be caused to crystallize and leases may be forfeited.
27 [1986] 3 All ER 673.
28 Under s. 40(3) the receiver can recoup any payments made to preferential creditors out of the assets of the company that are available for payment to the general creditors. Contrast the position of a floating charge administrative receiver with that of a receiver appointed under a fixed charge, who may pay his secured creditor without making payments to statutorily preferred creditors, see *Re G. L. Saunders Ltd* [1986] 1 WLR 215.
29 See Chap. 9, p. 135.
30 See Chap. 9, p. 134.
31 See Chap. 10, p. 170.
32 Care must be taken in expressing the compass of such a charge to ensure that it effectively covers the property required, see *Re Hi-Fi Equipment (Cabinets) Ltd* [1988] BCLC 65.
33 S. 245(3).
34 S. 245(2).
35 S. 245(4).
36 [1987] BCLC 55.
37 See Chap. 10, p. 167.
38 *Mercantile Bank of India Ltd v. Chartered Bank of India, Australia and China* [1937] 1 All ER 231.
39 *Bank of Baroda v. Panessar* [1987] Ch 338.
40 Lightman and Moss, *The Law of Receivers of Companies*, p. 57.
41 *Bank of Baroda v. Panessar* [1987] Ch 338.
42 *NRG Vision Ltd v. Churchfield Leasing Ltd* [1988] BCLC 624.
43 *Byblos Bank SaL v. Al-Khudairy* (1986) 2 BCC 99.
44 *Cyrne v. Barclays Bank plc* [1987] BCLC 548.
45 *Edwards v. Standard Rolling Stock Syndicate* [1893] 1 Ch 574; *Re London Pressed Hinge Co.* [1905] 1 Ch 576.
46 *Re Woodroffes (Musical Instruments) Ltd* [1985] 2 All ER 908.
47 S. 9(3).
48 *Byblos Bank SaL v. Al-Khudhairy* (1986) 2 BBC 99.
49 This section will validate the acts of a receiver notwithstanding a defect in his appointment, nomination or qualifications, but it will not validate acts done by a receiver appointed under an invalid security or where the receiver has acted without being appointed at all; see *Morris v. Kanssen* [1946] AC 459 (on a comparable provision relating to directors).

50 (1986) 2 BCC 98, 910.
51 An example of a deed of appointment is given in the case study in this chapter.
52 S. 33.
53 S. 230(2).
54 CA 1985, S. 405.
55 IA 1986, S. 46(1).
56 *Rother Iron Works* v. *Canterbury Precision Engineers Ltd* [1974] QB 1; as to leases, see *Re Offshore Ventilations Ltd* [1989] BCLC 318; as to liability for rates (now the uniform business rate) see *Ratford* v. *Northavon District Council* [1987] QB 357.
57 [1986] 3 All ER 94.
58 [1970] Ch 193.
59 *Lathia* v. *Dronsfield Bros* [1987] BCLC 321.
60 *Airlines Airspares Ltd* v. *Handley Page Ltd* [1970] Ch 193; *Telemetrix plc* v. *Modern Engineers of Bristol (Holdings) plc* [1985] BCLC 213.
61 S. 48.
62 S. 44(1).
63 S. 9(1).
64 S. 11(1)(b).
65 *Westminister Corporation* v. *Haste* [1950] Ch 442; *IRC* v. *Goldblatt* [1972] 1 Ch 498; *Woods* v. *Windskill* [1913] 2 Ch 303.
66 IA 1986, Sched. 1, para. 21.
67 IR, r. 3.33.
68 S. 45(4).

9
Trading and Sale by Administrators and Administrative Receivers

INTRODUCTION

In this chapter we shall examine the powers and duties of administrators and administrative receivers in relation to both trading and sale of the corporate assets over which they have control. Both insolvency procedures have much in common: they must both be operated by licensed insolvency practitioners; the powers of such practitioners concerning trading and sale of the company's assets are specified in the same Schedule 1 to the Insolvency Act, which is reproduced in the case study in this chapter; both have adequate powers to achieve a rescue of the business or to sell it as a going concern and achieve a better realization than would be available on a winding up; and both are office-holders within the meaning of section 233 of the Insolvency Act and will have the same powers and duties which flow from that position.[1] In many ways the position of the administrator mirrors that of the administrative receiver, and this is not surprising as the concept of administration was conceived as a procedure for achieving a rescue or sale of the business where the assets were not covered by a floating charge which would have enabled a secured creditor to appoint an administrative receiver.[2]

However, having stated that there are similarities in the powers of administrators and receivers, there are significant differences between their positions both in the range of assets under their respective control and in the nature and extent of the duties which they owe in relation to trading and sale. Rather than dealing with their position separately, we deal with them in the same chapter in order to highlight these similarities and differences and so enable an assessment to be made of the most appropriate insolvency procedure to deal with the circumstances of a particular case.

PRELIMINARY STAGES

When an administrator or administrative receiver has been appointed, the powers of the directors in relation to the management of the corporate assets are suspended.[3] Nevertheless, the insolvency practitioner will usually need the directors' assistance with the initial assessment of the causes of insolvency; to help in any remedial action necessary to stem losses; to evaluate the company's financial position and to identify the viable core of the business.[4] The insolvency practitioner will be particularly concerned during this initial period to assess the ability of management – indeed, the administrator (but not the administrative receiver) has the unusual power of being able to remove any director of the company and appoint any person to be a director should this assist in achieving the objective of the administration order.[5] The incoming practitioner will also consider the position of employees, to determine whether any organizational change is required in the workforce for any economic or technical reasons.[6] These changes might require redundancies. Finally, he will evaluate the company's cash-flow needs if there is to be continued trading, and make arrangements for additional financing through further capital input by the management and/or shareholders, through loans or continued support from secured creditors or cash receipts from trading.

To assess the company's current financial position and formulate a rescue plan, both the administrator and the administrative receiver will require the directors to prepare a detailed statement of affairs.[7] The insolvency practitioner can require the following persons to contribute to the statement of affairs: those who are or who have been directors or officers of the company; those who have taken part in the company's formation at any time within one year before the date of the appointment of the insolvency practitioner; those who are employed by the company or who have been in its employment within that year and who are, in the practitioner's opinion, capable of giving the required information.[8] Employment under this provision is to be construed as including employment under a contract for services and thus will include accountants who have prepared a management plan for the company within the past year.

The statement of affairs, an example of which is given in the case study in this chapter, is required to set out particulars of the company's assets, debts and liabilities; the names and addresses of its creditors and the securities held by them together with the dates on which the securities were given; and any further information prescribed in the Insolvency Rules or felt to be of use by the insolvency practitioner.[9] The statement of affairs, which must be verified by affidavit, must be prepared within twenty-one days after it has been requested by the insolvency practitioner.[10] The courts have power to impose fines for non-performance of the duty to provide the information requested.[11]

Both insolvency practitioners may face practical and legal problems in relation to their plans for trading and/or sale. Although the Insolvency Act gives an administrator extensive trading powers and the moratorium provides a breathing space against creditors' claims, he may experience practical problems relating to the financing of trading because there is no positive duty on outsiders to co-operate with an administrator and his rescue proposals may quite easily founder if banks or financial institutions cut off funds, perhaps by terminating overdraft facilities. Also, the suppliers of goods and services may cut off vital supplies. Probably the most important immediate action to be taken on (or preferably before) his appointment is for the administrator to assess the company's financial requirements for continued trading and to secure the availability of funds. He may do this by agreeing continued or extended overdraft facilities; trading through the receipts from sales or commissions – as, for example, the administrator in the case study in Chapter 7 was able to do – or trading on the proceeds of collection of book debts, provided that these are not subject to a fixed charge.[12] All these methods of financing involve sensitive negotiations in the light of the company's insolvency and the complex and uncertain state of the law.

Particular legal problems may be faced by an administrator who hopes to trade either on current receipts or on the proceeds of collection of book debts where a bank or other institution holds a floating charge over all the company's assets (and has yet consented to the appointment of the administrator) or there exists a fixed charge over book debts. If the administrator trades on the receipts from current trading which would otherwise be 'caught' by the bank's floating charge (which he can use as if the receipts were not caught by the charge by virtue of section 15(1)),[13] the bank has the same priority in respect of any property (which includes debts and money) which directly or indirectly represents the property disposed of as it would have had in respect of the property subject to the charge, and the administrator must account to the chargee for this. This may be a satisfactory option if the administrator is confident that his trading will be profitable, but is much more problematic if he makes a loss. Similarly, the administrator might not be able to utilize the proceeds of collection of book debts which are subject to a fixed charge, without a court order under section 15(2).[14] However, such an order could be fruitless due to the working of section 15(5), which requires the proceeds of collection to be applied in discharging the sums secured by the security.

However, a bank with a fixed charge over book debts is itself in a complicated position upon the presentation of an administration petition, in that any attempt to collect the debts may be caught by the pre- and post-hearing moratorium.[15] A solution to this stalemate may well be for the bank to agree to permit the administrator to collect and use the proceeds of debts generated after the administration order, while the bank retains the right to collect the debts up to that date.[16]

An administrative receiver, too, has problems in relation to the decision to trade. First, he is under a duty to pay the statutorily preferred creditors before repaying the debt owed to the secured creditor,[17] and if he trades he will be under a duty not to diminish the assets available for those preferred creditors – if he does trade at a loss he may incur personal liability for payment of their accrued entitlement.[18]

The second mixed practical and legal problem facing an incoming administrative receiver is to determine the extent of the corporate assets caught within the ambit of the floating charge and thus available for use in any trading or included in the negotiations for a sale of the business. An administrative receiver must take care to deal only with assets over which he has authority, otherwise he may find himself liable to third parties in an action for trespass to goods.[19] Property held on trust for those outside the company and property held under retention of title clauses are excluded from the corporate assets over which a floating charge would crystallize.

In the case of a trust, the person lending money to a company, who claims that it is held by the company on trust for a particular purpose, will have to show that the money which has been lent was not intended to become part of the assets of the company available for it to use as and when it wished. Rather, the lender must show that the money was paid over for a special purpose, was to be applied only for that purpose and was not to be mixed with the company's general assets. The case of *Carreras Rothmans Ltd* v. *Freeman Mathews Treasure Ltd*[20] will illustrate how the concept of the trust can operate to isolate money from the corporate assets and insulate it from being used by an administrative receiver (or administrator or liquidator). In that case FMT, in providing advertising services for Carreras Rothmans, purchased advertising space in the media. It booked the advertising space in its own name and paid for this from its own funds. When FMT experienced financial difficulties, Carreras Rothmans was unwilling to jeopardize its advertising campaign and business reputation in the event that FMT should default on payments to media clients. Carreras Rothmans thus agreed that it should pay a sum to FMT to cover the expenses FMT had incurred towards media clients. This sum was to be paid into a separate, special bank account which was to be used only for the payment of media creditors, and Carreras Rothmans stipulated that it should receive written confirmation from the bank that the latter was aware of the purpose for which the account was established.

When FMT went into creditors' voluntary liquidation and all its bank accounts were frozen, the question arose (which would have been pertinent in the case of an administrative receivership) as to the status of the special bank account.

The court held, following earlier decisions on the creation of trusts,[21] that the way in which the payments had been made was sufficient to constitute a trust of the money in the special account. It was clear that there was an intention to create a trust for the benefit of media creditors; there was certainty as to the property comprised in the trust and as to the ultimate recipients. The money in the trust account never became part of the assets of FMT and thus would not have fallen within the terms of a floating charge.

If the lender fails to establish the creation of a trust, money lent to the company will become part of the company's assets over which a floating charge will crystallize and which the administrative receiver can utilize in trading or include in the negotiations for sale of the business.[22]

Also excluded from the assets over which the administrative receiver has authority are goods supplied to the company subject to retention of title clauses.[23] These clauses, which are often incorporated into contracts of supply, enable the supplier of goods and materials to be used by the company in its manufacturing or processing operations, to determine the time when ownership of the goods supplied is to pass to the company. Until such time as ownership passes, the supplier retains the legal ownership of the goods and is entitled to recover them from the company. The supplier's title to the goods is superior to that of any administrative receiver (or liquidator). Because the supplier will have retained legal ownership of the goods, he can retake possession of his goods which are on the company's premises and which are in an identifiable form[24] and can also take possession of his goods which have been the subject of some manufacturing process – provided that they retain their essence, remain in identifiable form and can be severed from other property.[25] Once the supplier's goods have become incorporated into other goods, the supplier ceases to be able to assert ownership over them:[26] they become the company's assets and as such will be caught by any general floating charge. The administrative receiver will be able to use and sell the manufactured products as part of the company's assets.

Retention of title clauses may also be sufficiently well drafted to cover the proceeds of sale of the supplier's goods, provided that they have been sold in their original state and provided that the company sold them as agent for the supplier and in some 'fiduciary capacity'.[27] This is, however, unusual as the company will normally sell the goods on its own account or as a buyer in possession of them, and this will defeat the supplier's claim to the proceeds of sale.[28]

Once goods have been manufactured or incorporated into other items, the supplier loses legal ownership and cannot claim to be entitled to the proceeds of sale of these manufactured items.[29]

The position of an administrative receiver in relation to goods subject to a retention of title clause should be contrasted with the powers of an administrator in relation to such property. As soon as a petition for an administration order has been presented, no steps may be taken to retake possession of goods subject to a retention of title clause unless the court consents to this action.[30] After the making of an administration order, the administrator has power to apply to the court for an order enabling him to sell property under a retention of title clause or on hire purchase or subject to some other security interest.[31] The powers of the administrator to deal with property subject to security interests are dealt with later in this chapter.[32]

Under section 234 both the administrator and administrative receiver are relieved from liability to any person for loss or damage resulting from the wrongful seizure or disposal of goods except in so far as the loss or damage was caused by the insolvency practitioner's own negligence.

POWERS IN RELATION TO TRADING

The powers of the administrator so far as the management of the company's assets are concerned are contained in section 14, which states in general terms that he 'may do all such things as may be necessary for the management of the affairs, business and property' of the company. This general power is amplified by Schedule 1 to the Act.

By section 42 an administrative receiver is deemed to have all the powers of management and sale conferred by Schedule 1 to the Act, and these powers may be enhanced by additional powers in the receiver's instrument of appointment.

Among the most significant trading powers are the ability to carry on the business of the company; the power to raise or borrow money and grant security therefor over the company's property; the power to appoint an agent to do any business which the insolvency practitioner is unable to do himself; the power to establish subsidiaries; and the power to present a petition for the winding up of the company.

Administrators

In exercising his powers, the administrator is deemed to act as the company's agent[33] and those dealing with him in good faith and for value are not concerned to inquire whether he is acting within his powers.[34] Although he acts as an agent, his position is somewhat unusual in that he is not subject to the control of his principal – the company – but must, in the first place, act subject to any directions given by the court,[35] and after the approval of his proposals by the creditors' meeting, in accordance with those agreed proposals.[36]

So far as existing contracts are concerned, the appointment of an administrator is neutral, that is, existing contracts continue unaffected by the appointment.[37]

There are two matters which the administrator should consider carefully in relation to the company's existing contracts with suppliers and customers. The first is the extent of 'set-off' rights which the other contracting parties may have against the company. A set-off right means that those outside contractors who are in debt to the company may seek to set off debts owed to them by the company against their own liability to pay. In relation to administrators, such a set-off claim, not being a 'step to enforce a security' or a 'proceeding' against the company, may not be caught within the moratorium provisions[38] and, consequently, an administrator should try to exclude any right of set-off in contracts of supply. If such a set-off is successfully claimed it may considerably reduce the proceeds of collection of book debts which the administrator could use for trading.

The second concern with regard to existing contracts and commitments which the incoming administrator inherits is to assess whether it is profitable for the company to continue to perform those existing contracts which may be burdensome or loss-making. In relation to his trading and sale plans, the administrator must decide whether it is profitable to continue such contracts to preserve goodwill and continuing trading relations or whether it would be better to repudiate the contracts, leaving the other contracting party to claim damages for breach of contract against the insolvent company.[39]

The administrator will not be personally liable on new contracts he makes during the course of the administration unless he specifically undertakes such liability or is asked to guarantee the company's contracts, and in this respect his position should be contrasted with that of an administrative receiver.

Administrative receivers

So far as the company has existing and continuing contracts, the appointment of a receiver as agent for the company is a neutral event, and such contracts remain binding on the company and enforceable by and against the company in the normal way. This is because the administrative receiver is deemed to be the agent of the company and his appointment does not disturb existing contractual relations.[40]

In relation to new contracts, the receiver should be wary of incurring personal liability. This automatically attaches to new contracts by virtue of the wording of section 44(1)(b) unless the receiver expressly stipulates that he undertakes no personal liability on the contract. In such a case the company alone will be liable. Should the receiver not be able to negotiate to contract out of personal liability, he may claim an indemnity from the company's assets to cover any claim which may subsequently be made against him.[41]

Employment contracts

The contractual position of an administrative receiver in relation to employment contracts is complex.[42] When the receiver takes office, he is simply continuing such contracts as agent for the company.[43] However, there may be circumstances where the appointment of a receiver operates to terminate the employment of people, such as a managing director, whose position is rendered untenable in the light of the receiver's control over the company's assets.[44]

However, in relation to contracts of employment, the receiver must carefully consider the impact of section 44(1)(b) of the Insolvency Act, which states that he is personally liable 'on any contract entered into by him in carrying out his functions (except insofar as the contract otherwise provides) and on any contract of employment adopted by him in the carrying out of those functions'.

Section 44(2) provides that a receiver is not to be taken to have adopted a contract of employment by reason of anything done or omitted to be done within fourteen days after his appointment.

Thus, the receiver has a breathing space during which he should consider whether to dismiss the employees or some of them, whether to continue their employment on exactly the same terms as before, making it clear that he is not 'adopting' their contracts or whether to adopt their contracts directly (which will probably never be an option) or indirectly by negotiating a change in the terms of their employment.

Should he choose to dismiss the employees (or some of them), they would be entitled both to preferential payments to which they would have been entitled had the company been in liquidation[45] and to payments from the Redundancy Fund under the provisions of the Employment Protection (Consolidation) Act 1978. The latter covers arrears of pay in excess of the statutorily preferred amounts payable under the former, payment in lieu of notice and redundancy payments. The payments of such lump sums as are due to the employees are made by the administrative receiver acting as agent for the Department of Employment.

The receiver may well be in some difficulty if he wishes to continue the employment of some of the employees prior to the sale of the business as a going concern. He would ideally wish to avoid 'adopting' their contracts of employment and thus becoming personally liable for such contracts. There is some doubt among lawyers as to the meaning of the term 'adoption' in section 44(1)(b). Kerr[46] (1989) suggests that 'mere inaction' in relation to current employees cannot be sufficient to adopt their contracts. Some positive act of adoption, it is suggested, is required, such as negotiating new terms or modifying existing employment conditions. It is suggested that this interpretation is necessary otherwise receivers will be in the unenviable position of being saddled with all the employment liabilities simply by failing to dismiss the employees at the end of the fourteen-day breathing space.

It would appear that there are two ways of avoiding the difficulties associated with personal liability for contracts of employment. First, the receiver may dismiss employees within the fourteen-day period (in so doing he will act as agent of the company, and the company will be liable for any consequent unfair dismissal claims); then, he would re-engage those employees required by the business on the same terms but expressly excluding his personal liability. However, such dismissals may be counter-productive when it comes to putting into effect a rescue, as key employees might be unwilling to agree to the re-engagement terms where their employment rights have been undermined. Alternatively, the receiver may simply continue the employment of existing workers but make it plain by notice or letter to such employees that he does not intend to adopt their contracts. Stewart[47] (1987) notes the case of *Re Specialised Mouldings Ltd* (unreported), in which the meaning of the term 'adoption' in relation to contracts of employment was examined. The joint administrative receivers in that case sought the directions of the court[48] as to the effect of a letter they proposed to send to employees in which they would make it clear that the employees would continue in the company's employment on the same terms as before the administrative receivers' appointment and that there was no intention to adopt the employees' contracts of employment.

The court held that it was possible for an administrative receiver to exclude liability for adoption of employees' contracts and personal liability that would otherwise attach by virtue of section 44(1)(b). The letter the receiver proposed to send was approved as conveying a sufficient intention not to adopt the employees' contracts.

As is the case in relation to trading by the administrator, so also an administrative receiver might face problems in relation to set-off rights which other contracting parties have against the company. The most significant point with regard to set-off rights is whether they have accrued when the floating charge under which the receiver was appointed crystallized. If the set-off right had accrued by that date, it can be set up against the receiver.[49] But set-off will not be permitted in respect of contract rights accruing after the crystallization of the charge.[50]

Loss-making contracts

The administrative receiver, like the administrator, should consider whether, in order to preserve the goodwill of the company and to promote an effective turnaround or sale, he will continue to honour existing loss-making contracts or whether he should repudiate them. From the case law on this point, it seems that the receiver has a free hand to decide whether to continue or whether to repudiate such contracts. For example, in *Airlines Airspares Ltd v. Handley Page Ltd*,[51] prior to the appointment of a receiver the company had entered into a contract to pay a commission to an individual. The benefit of this commission payment was later assigned to Airline Airspares. When the receiver took control of the assets of Handley Page, he decided to hive-down[52] the profitable parts of the business and sell these to an American purchaser. He did not include in the sale the burdensome agreement between Handley Page and Airline Airspares. The latter company tried to sue for an injunction to prevent the receiver from carrying out the hive-down, but failed. The receiver, it was held, was in a stronger position than the company in that he could cause the company to repudiate existing burdensome contracts and no action could be taken against him to prevent him from so doing. Furthermore, the courts have confirmed that there can be no claim against the administrative receiver personally for inducing breach of contract should he decide that the company repudiate a contract.[53] Where, however, prior to the commencement of the receivership the company has entered into a contract for the sale of land or where a third party has acquired some proprietary interest in the company's property, the receiver will be prevented by injunction or by an order for specific performance from overriding those acquired proprietary rights.[54]

DUTIES IN RELATION TO TRADING

Administrators

In the period immediately after his appointment and before acceptance of his proposals by the creditors' meeting, the administrator is under an obligation to manage the affairs of the company in accordance with any orders given by the court.[55] If he is in doubt about any of his powers or wishes to take some immediate action before he can call a creditors' meeting, he can apply to court for directions.[56]

Once the proposals have been agreed by the creditors' meeting,[57] the administrator is then under a duty to put into effect those proposals subject to any modifications agreed to be the creditors.

Administrative receivers

In Chapter 8 it was emphasized that the status of an administrative receiver is complex; he is deemed to be an agent for the company and, as such, owes a duty of care in trading and managing the company's business, but he also has a responsibility and duty of care towards the secured creditor who appointed him. This divided loyalty must be taken into account by a receiver in deciding whether he should continue to trade or whether the interests of the secured creditor demand that he tries to sell the business as quickly as is reasonably possible or simply closes it down and realizes the assets on a break-up basis.

The courts, faced with the problems caused by this divided loyalty, have indicated that the administrative receiver owes no duty to the company or the unsecured creditors to continue to trade.[58] However, if the company is not hopelessly insolvent, and there is a chance that it may continue in business at the conclusion of the receivership, there may be a duty to preserve the goodwill.[59]

The administrative receiver as well as the administrator must exercise due care in their trading activities because any subsequent liquidator may examine their dealings and, if they have misapplied or retained or become accountable for any money or property of the company or are guilty of any misfeasance or breach of fiduciary or other duty, they may be called upon to make such contribution to the company's assets as the court thinks fit.[60]

In carrying on any business, both an administrator and an administrative receiver must be aware of the technical difficulties that may arise from the nature of the company's operations. There may be particular problems with regard to product liability and obligations to employees under the Health and Safety at Work etc. Act. In deciding whether to continue trading in such an environment, the insolvency practitioner must ensure that the company is adequately insured and that there is satisfactory expertise and supervision within the business.

POWERS IN RELATION TO SALE

Both administrators and receivers will be conscious that the decision to continue trading is a short-term one, being in the nature of a preparation either to hand the business back to the existing (perhaps augmented) management or to sell it as a going concern. There are a number of matters that both insolvency practitioners will have to consider in negotiating the sale of the business. The insolvency practitioner may either sell the business directly to a transferee company, in which case all the assets, undertaking and liabilities (including the employees' accrued employment rights) will be transferred, or the sale may be achieved through a hive-down company. In the latter case, the valuable assets of the company and its profitable contracts, together with key employees, are transferred to a newly formed or purchased subsidiary company[61] while burdensome contracts and business losses are excluded from the transfer. The transferee of either the shares or the assets and undertaking of the subsidiary then acquires a profitable and 'clean' company and the purchase price is held by the administrator or receiver to be passed on to the directors, if the company is still solvent after the sale, or more likely to the liquidator of the insolvent transferor company for distribution to that company's creditors.

The use of the hive-down technique enables the administrator or receiver to establish the profitability of the subsidiary's trading, which can continue to operate even if a petition to wind up the parent company is presented. Similarly, trading through the medium of a subsidiary will enable the insolvency practitioner to obtain new trading supplies without danger of being hampered by set-off rights (because the contracts will be with the newly formed company), to obtain supplies of utilities without the necessity of a personal guarantee, and to attract purchasers to a viable business.

In relation to hive-down sales, particular care needs to be exercised in negotiating with the transferee company about the rights of the transferor company's employees.

Both administrators and administrative receivers need to be aware of the impact of the Transfer of Undertakings (Protection of Employment) Regulations 1981.[62] The problem encountered by many insolvency practitioners in the past has been that potential purchasers of a hive-down subsidiary would be unwilling to pay the costs entailed in taking over the accumulated employment rights of the employees of the insolvent transferor company. Similarly, a potential purchaser may not be willing to take over liabilities with regard to redundancy payments or possible claims in relation to unfair dismissal. Yet many potential purchasers may wish to take over a trimmed-down workforce or integrate new employees into their corporate organization after the purchase. Regulation 5 of the Transfer of Undertakings Regulations deals with the rights of employees on the transfer of a business, and specifies that as regards employees 'employed in the undertaking immediately before the transfer', the transfer shall not operate to terminate the employment of any person employed by the transferor in the undertaking transferred, but any such contract will be automatically transferred to the purchaser company. It was thought that the 'automatic transfer' provisions applied only to employees employed by the transferor company immediately before transfer and so if there was any break in employment before the purchaser acquired the company, the automatic transfer provisions would not apply. Administrative receivers sometimes exploited this provision by dismissing employees very shortly before the transfer of the business to a purchasing company.[63] However, in *Litster* v. *Forth Dry Docks & Engineering Co. Ltd*[64] the House of Lords held that if the dismissals prior to the sale of the business are rendered automatically unfair by virtue of regulation 8 of the Transfer of Undertakings Regulations, that is, because the dismissal was connected with the transfer of a business but was *not* made for an economic, technical or organizational reason entailing changes in the workforce, then the automatic transfer provisions of regulation 5 will operate to transfer the contracts of employment from the transferor company to the purchaser.

The result of the *Litster* case is that if dismissal of the employees of the insolvent transferor company was not for an economic, technical or organizational reason entailing changes in the workforce, it will be unfair and the employees' contractual rights will automatically be transferred to the purchasing company. Where such transfer takes place, all rights, duties, powers and liabilities connected with the employees' contracts are transferred.[65]

If the dismissal of employees by an administrator or administrative receiver prior to the sale of the business is related to economic, technical or organizational reasons, the dismissed employees would not be automatically transferred to the purchasing company. The words 'economic, technical and organisational reasons' give the purchasing company considerable leeway to negotiate with the administrator/receiver on the redundancy of staff for economic reasons and to ensure that if genuine redundancies are necessary and agreed, due notice can be given to terminate contracts of employment. The responsibility for redundancy payments, unfair dismissal claims or protective awards then falls on the insolvent transferor company. The employees have a direct claim against the Secretary of State for payment out of the Redundancy Fund, and the payments are administered on the Department of Employment's behalf by the administrator/receiver. To guard against possible future liability in respect of redundancy or unfair dismissal claims, the transferee company purchasing a business from an administrator or administrative receiver will usually seek to protect its position by requiring the transferor company to give an indemnity, possibly guaranteed by the insolvency practitioner, in respect of any dismissals made in advance of the business transfer.

Also, in negotiating a successful sale of the business, the insolvency practitioner would wish to be able to sell the whole or substantially the whole of the company's undertaking shorn of any prior security interests and incumbrances. The Insolvency Act gives administrators very extensive powers in relation to prior security interests, and receivers somewhat less authority.

As regards administrators, a power to deal with charged property is conferred by section 15, permitting them to dispose of or otherwise deal with property subject to a floating charge as if the property were not subject to that security. The administrator does not require the consent of the court for such a disposition.

The security holder's position is preserved by the provision in section 15(4) giving him the same priority in respect of any property of the company directly or indirectly representing the property disposed of as he would have had in respect of the property subject to the security. Thus, the secured creditor who had a floating charge has his interest transferred to the proceeds of sale.

The administrator can also dispose of property which is subject to a fixed charge or any goods in possession of the company which are subject to a hire-purchase, chattel-leasing or conditional sale agreement or held subject to a retention of title clause.[66] However, in this case, unless the interest holder consents, the administrator must apply to the court for an order for sale and the court must be satisfied that the disposal, taken alone or with other assets, would be likely to promote one or more of the purposes specified in the administration order. Where the court orders a sale, it is a condition of sale that the proceeds of sale shall be applied in discharging the sums secured by the security or payable under the hire-purchase agreement, etc. To protect the security holder from the effects of a sale at below market value, as, for example, where the administrator sells the going concern business for a price which is at a discount on account of the global sale of assets, whereas the items included in the fixed charge could have been sold individually without an element of discount, the court may order 'such sums as may be required to make good the deficiency' to be paid to the security holder.[67] This power to sell assets which are incumbered by hire-purchase and retention of title agreements is a very useful one, enabling the administrator to negotiate a global sale quickly and without undue legal complications. The interests of the claimants to the proceeds of sale can be sorted out after the sale has been completed.

As regards administrative receivers, section 43 gives the court jurisdiction, on application by the receiver, to authorize him to dispose of property subject to a prior or equal-ranking charge if this is likely to promote a more advantageous realization of the assets. It will be a condition of the sale that the net proceeds of sale together with any such other sum as the court shall determine to be necessary to make up any deficiency between the sale price and open market price, shall be applied towards discharging the prior security. This provision does not apply to property subject to a later-ranking charge, because a sale of property by the administrative receiver will automatically overcome later security interests.

Although the power to apply to court to sell property subject to a charge is valuable to an administrative receiver, the comparable powers of administrators are much wider because the administrator does not require the leave of the court to overreach floating charges and, additionally, he can sell property subject to hire-purchase and chattel-leasing agreements and subject to retention of title clauses.

DUTIES IN RELATION TO SALE

The administrator's duty in relation to sale is to follow the proposals agreed to by creditors together with any modifications to those proposals.

The administrative receiver is in a more complex situation in relation to the sale of the business. This complexity results from a potential conflict between, on the one hand, the interest of the secured creditor in having a sale concluded with all due speed in order that the loan be repaid as quickly as possible and, on the other, the interest of the company and any guarantor of the company's debts, in achieving the highest possible sale price – which might mean delaying sale for a time. If the realization value is maximized, any surplus over and above repayments to the secured creditor is available for distribution to the unsecured creditors and the potential liability of guarantors for any deficit on the sale is kept to a minimum.

There has been considerable case law on administrative receivers' duties in relation to sale, the tenor of which is that the receiver owes a duty of care, first, to guarantors of the company's debts and also to the company itself to conduct any sale in such a way as to achieve the best possible market price as the circumstances of the case permit.[68] Thus, if the administrative receiver acts negligently in relation to the sale, for example by choosing an adverse time[68] or by failing to advertise effectively,[69] he may be personally liable in an action for negligence brought by the company for any loss caused by the negligent sale.[70] Similarly, a guarantor of the loan may set up the negligent sale as a defence to a claim for any deficit under the terms of the guarantee.[71] There may be circumstances – as, for example, where subsequent liquidation has brought an end to the receiver's agency for the company or where the secured creditor has interfered with the administrative receiver's decision as to when to sell – where the secured creditor himself, as the receiver's appointor and instructor, may also be liable to the company for loss occasioned by a negligent sale of the business.[72]

The recent cases, extending the potential liability of receivers for negligent sales, emphasize the need for such insolvency practitioners to concentrate on obtaining the best possible price, thus providing a further impetus towards rescuing the viable parts of a business.

Finally, when trading and realization are complete, administrative receivers are under an obligation to pay the proceeds in accordance with legal entitlement. First, payment should be made to any security holder whose interest ranked in priority to the charge under which the receiver was appointed;[73] thereafter, there will be payment of the trading expenses incurred in the receivership and the expenses of realization of the assets together with the receiver's own remuneration; then, if the receiver is appointed under the terms of a debenture containing both fixed and floating charges, realizations to the amount of the fixed charge are paid to the secured creditor; thereafter, the receiver must pay the statutorily preferred creditors; finally, payment to cover the floating charge element of the security will be made to the secured creditor who appointed the receiver. If there is any surplus, this must be paid to any subsequent secured creditor (or his receiver) and, if there is no such creditor, to the directors or, if the company is in liquidation, to the liquidator.

The administrator is in a more complex position with regard to payment of receipts from trading or sale of the business. If one of the purposes of the administration was a voluntary arrangement with creditors,[74] payments may be made to such creditors as have consented to the arrangement in accordance with its terms. However, it must be remembered that voluntary arrangements bind only consenting creditors – those outside the scheme are entitled to petition for a winding-up order.[75] Alternatively, at the conclusion of the administration, the administrator, acting under his statutory powers,[76] may cause the company to petition for winding up or may propose a voluntary winding-up resolution. Thereafter, payments are made to creditors within the liquidation proceedings.[77]

ENFORCEMENT OF DUTIES IN RELATION TO TRADING AND SALE

The administrator has very wide and to some extent unfettered powers with regard to decisions about the future of the company. In his rescue plans he can deal with and dispose of property which is subject to the rights of secured creditors; he need not consult shareholders and he can dismiss directors. In the light of this all-embracing power, it is not surprising that the Insolvency Act provides some protection for creditors and shareholders who feel that their interests have been unfairly prejudiced by decisions proposed or taken by the administrator.

Section 27(1) provides a means of redress for any creditors or group of creditors or any member who complains that, during the course of the administration:

(a) ... that the company's affairs, business or property are being or have been managed by the administrator in a manner which is unfairly prejudicial to the interests of its creditors or members generally, or some part of its creditors or members (including at least himself), or
(b) that any actual or proposed act or omission of the administrator is or would be so prejudicial.

Once the petitioner has made out a case of unfair treatment, the court has almost unlimited powers to take remedial action. There is an unlimited discretion under section 27(2) to 'make such order as it thinks fit' for giving relief in respect of the matter complained of, and section 27(4) lists the types of action which may be appropriate:

Subject as above, an order under this section may in particular—
(a) regulate the future management by the administrator of the company's affairs, business and property;
(b) require the administrator to refrain from doing or continuing an act complained of by the petitioner, or to do an act which the petitioner has complained he has omitted to do;
(c) require the summoning of a meeting of creditors or members for the purpose of considering such matters as the court may direct;

(d) discharge the administration order and make such consequential provision as the court thinks fit.

Thus, secured creditors, whose rights have been overridden by powers in section 15 may apply under section 27 if they feel that the administrator's decision with regard to their security was unfairly prejudicial.

There is, however, a limitation on actions under the section, in that an order made under section 27 shall not prejudice or prevent the implementation of a voluntary arrangement approved under section 4, or any compromise or arrangement sanctioned under section 425 of the Companies Act. This limitation is sensible given that creditors who complain that their interests have been prejudiced by such proceedings have separate rights of redress under the relevant provisions. Furthermore, no application may be made under section 27 more than twenty-eight days after the approval of the administrator's proposals under section 24 or 25.

There is no guidance yet as to how the court will exercise its jurisdiction under section 27. If comparisons can be drawn with the analogous jurisdiction under section 459 of the Companies Act 1985, it would seem that the petitioner must show that he has suffered, objectively speaking, some prejudice whereby his position is worsened as a result of the administrator's actions or omissions. Mere disagreement on a policy to be pursued will not suffice. However, the petitioner will not bear the burden of showing that the administrator acted fraudulently or in bad faith, rather, the case will turn on the effect of the administrator's decisions on the applicant's interests.

As regards the enforcement of an administrative receiver's duty, we have seen that his duty to the company is subordinate to that owed to the secured creditor who appointed him. In the absence of a negligent sale, the directors cannot sue the administrative receiver in connection with any of his trading or sale decisions. Similarly, unsecured creditors have no cause of action against the administrative receiver, though it is always open to them to petition for a winding-up order, which will have the effect of terminating the receiver's agency and enable the liquidator to examine the administrative receiver's conduct.

Even though the administrative receiver has been appointed by the secured creditor, he is insulated from interference from his appointor. If the secured creditor meddles with the receiver's decisions, the creditor himself may find that he incurs liability towards third parties whose interests have been affected.[78] Also, in order to protect his independence, the administrative receiver can be removed only by court order.[79]

POWERS AND DUTIES AS OFFICE-HOLDERS

In addition to their trading and sale powers, administrators and administrative receivers are 'office-holders' and as such have certain rights and duties as defined within Part VI of the Insolvency Act.

Both types of insolvency practitioner have the right to require persons connected with a company to submit a detailed statement of affairs in the prescribed form.[80]

To ensure compliance with the office-holder's request, section 235 imposes on those requested an obligation to give the officer the information required and, if necessary, to attend and answer questions. Failure to comply with such a request, without reasonable excuse, renders a person liable to a fine and, for continued breach, to a daily default fine.

In their capacity as office-holders, both administrators and receivers enjoy certain advantages in their dealings with public utility suppliers. Prior to the Insolvency Act, receivers and liquidators wishing to continue trading for a period prior to the sale of the business were in a weak position in relation to public utility suppliers, who, although they were not preferential creditors, could effectively paralyse the company by cutting off supplies unless arrears were paid. Now, by section 233, if a request is made by an administrator or administrative receiver for the supply of gas, electricity, water or telecommunication services, the supplier may make it a condition of continued supply that the insolvency practitioner personally guarantees the payment of charges for services supplied after the effective date,[81] but cannot make it a condition, or do anything that has the effect of making it a condition, that outstanding charges are paid before new supplies will be made.

Both administrators and receivers have limited investigatory powers,[82] though both these insolvency practitioners, unlike the Official Receiver or a liquidator, will be primarily concerned with future trading plans or negotiating a profitable sale, and to this end will usually require, if not value, the assistance of the existing management to achieve their objectives, and as a consequence will not be unduly concerned to investigate previous management decisions. Unlike liquidators, administrators and receivers have no powers to bring proceedings under sections 212–214 for misfeasance or fraudulent or wrongful trading.

Under powers conferred by section 234, the office-holders may apply to the court for an order that any person having in his possession or control any property, books, papers or records to which the company appears to be entitled, shall deliver them to the office-holder. This power is underpinned by section 236, which enables the court to summon before it any person who is known or suspected to have in his possession property of the company or is indebted to the company or is capable of giving information concerning the company's affairs.

Finally, there is a duty imposed on both administrators and receivers to report on the conduct of directors of insolvent companies. Both types of insolvency practitioner are required to report on the conduct of directors, former directors and shadow directors with regard to their conduct in the period leading up to and after the onset of insolvency.[83]

Detailed rules contained in the Insolvent Companies (Reports on the Conduct of Directors) No. 2 Rules 1986[84] set out the matters to be taken into account by insolvency practitioners in preparing their reports and the time scale for the reports' presentation.

CONCLUSION

The extensive trading and sale powers given by the Insolvency Act represent a formidable challenge to the skill of insolvency practitioners in achieving a rescue beneficial to creditors, employees, customers, suppliers, shareholders and ultimately the community at large. Operated effectively, that is where management co-operates by bringing potential insolvency situations to the attention of an insolvency practitioner at the earliest possible date, and where the insolvency practitioner himself operates with speed and care in diagnosing problems and negotiating solutions, the Insolvency Act may provide the mechanisms whereby genuine commercial advantages can be achieved.

Case Study
[Any Yarn Ltd.]

This case study contains an example of an administration whose purpose was to continue trading for a while during which time the administrator negotiated for the sale of the business as a going concern.

Since the business was partly a mail order business selling knitting yarns and partly a retail business selling yarns and associated products, it was important for the administrator to continue trading so that the customer base and goodwill could be preserved. This would lead to a much better realization value than would have been achieved on the sale of the assets on a break-up basis.

The administrator utilized his powers under Schedule 1 to the Insolvency Act and continued trading for some two months, during which time he advertised the business and obtained offers for the mail order business and an offer for the retail shop.

The documents included are:

(1) statement of administrator's proposals pursuant to section 23 of the Insolvency Act 1986;
(2) estimated statement of affairs as at the date of the administration order 23 September 1988;
(3) administrator's receipts and payments to 25 November 1988;
(4) estimated balance sheet as at 31 August 1988;
(5) Schedule 1 to the Insolvency Act 1986 – Powers of Administrator or Administrative Receiver.

Document 1: Statement of administrator's proposals pursuant to section 23 of the Insolvency Act 1986 – Any Yarn Limited

Introduction

1 The following proposals have been prepared for the purpose of a creditors' meeting to be held at [*place*] on [*date and time*].

2 The meeting has been called pursuant to section 23 of the Insolvency Act 1986. The purpose of the meeting is as follows:

(1) to consider whether to approve the administrator's proposals;
(2) to consider such modifications as the creditors may deem necessary;
(3) to elect a creditors' committee (in accordance with section 26 of the Insolvency Act 1986).

Statutory information

1 Company number: 0000000
2 Date of incorporation: 19
3 Directors: [*names*]
4 Share capital:
   Authorized: 10,000 ordinary shares of £1 each
   Issued and fully paid: 7,600 ordinary shares of £1 each
5 Registered office: 15 West Street, Anytown.

Business profile

1 Any Yarn Limited was established in 1947 to trade as wool merchants and importers.
2 Its business was as a mail order knitting machine and machine yarn seller; in 1986 it acquired a retail shop and in May 1987 it acquired the Anytown Sewing and Knitting Centre.
3 In July 1986 it was appreciated that in order to establish itself in the retail trading business it would require vigorous promotion, which would be costly. To finance this a further £170,000 was introduced to the business by one of the directors.
4 Business in the first year, to August 1987, failed to come up to expectations and the predicted loss was greater than expected. The staffing level was reduced and a more cost-effective programme was planned for the next year. Budgeted sales were anticipated at the level experienced in the previous year and cost savings should have resulted in a profit of £50,000.
5 By February 1988 it was clear that sales were significantly below budget and again steps were taken to reduce costs further. In addition, a further £90,000 was introduced into the company by Mr X. It was hoped that the trading losses could be accommodated until the autumn catalogue was mailed at the end of August 1988, but sales were immediately hit by the postal strike.
6 On 22 August 1988, when financial information was presented to the company, it became clear that Any Yarn was likely to be insolvent and arrangements were made to place the company into administration.

Recent financial history

1 For the year ended 31 August 1986 the company had turnover of £139,866 and incurred an operating loss of £25,570, which after interest of £3,069 resulted in a loss for the year of £28,639.

2 In the year to 31 August 1987 the company significantly increased turnover, to £956,003, and incurred an operating loss of £137,375, which with the addition of interest payable of £26,255 resulted in a loss for the period of £163,630. The accounts to 31 August 1987 are in a draft unaudited state.

3 The estimated unaudited balance sheet at 31 August 1988 indicates that the trading loss for the period was in the region of £127,879.

4 In retrospect, a significant reduction in overheads was necessary during 1986/7. This was not done until after August 1987, and that reduction and the further reduction in February 1988 did not have the anticipated effect of bringing the company back into profit.

Reasons for seeking an administration order

1 An administration will produce a more advantageous realization of the company's assets than would be effected on a winding up for the following reasons.

(1) The mail order business has been profitable. It was of considerable interest to companies presently involved with mail order business which are able to stand the high overheads which, in this company, have turned a high gross profit into a net loss. At the beginning of the busy season for the yarn retail trade the autumn catalogue was circulated to customers. Orders were being received and it was essential to continue to service these if a sale of this part of the business as a going concern was to be achieved.

(2) The company had a high stock level of yarns which have been acquired for the beginning of the autumn season when trade traditionally increases. If the stock is sold through the shops, even at a discount on the retail price, this is likely to exceed the proceeds of an auction sale, at which even wholesale prices would probably not be achieved.

(3) While the shops continue to trade the administrator has marketed them for sale as a going concern and has commenced negotiations with the parties who had expressed interest.

(4) Although his agents advised that it is unlikely any premium could be achieved for the leasehold premises, the administration prevented the landlords forfeiting the leases, which they could have done upon liquidation of the company. If the leases are preserved, the administrator will be able to assign certain leases as part of a sale as a going concern, thus reducing potential further claims against the company.

2 As the company continues to trade it is anticipated that the difference in realizations would be substantial, as shown in the statement of affairs [*Document 2*]. If the company had gone into liquidation a liquidator would not have been prepared to continue trading the business as it would involve personal liability for any contracts which the company entered into.

3 Accordingly, if the company was to achieve the enhanced realization

predicted as a result of continuing to trade, this would have to be under an administrator.

Administrator's actions to date

1 Immediately upon my appointment I commenced negotiations with the various parties who had expressed an interest in parts of the business.
2 Because of the nature of the types of business it was important that they be disposed of as soon as possible in order to maintain them as a 'going concern' and retain the customer base.
3 Details of the mail order business were given to eleven potentially interested purchasers, of whom five showed an initial interest and visited the company's premises. The mail order stock and business were finally sold to X Limited for a total of £69,500, including £14,000 for goodwill, on 17 October 1988.
4 There was very little interest in the shop business, mainly due to the nature of the lease and the fact that this shop had only recently been established and there was therefore no trading record. Following advice from my agents the stock and business at [. . .] was sold to the former manageress for £20,000, on 8 November 1988.
5 Four interested parties considered purchasing the Knitting and Sewing Centre but then withdrew. Having obtained my agent's advice, the remaining stock at these shops was sold to Mr Y on 28 November 1988, for £30,000.
6 Administrator's trading receipts (net of stock purchased) amount to £43,056.
7 Total stock realization therefore amounts to £148,556 (net of stock purchases).
8 My agents have in the meantime disposed of the company vehicles for £22,000, out of which approximately £8,000 will be available for the creditors after repayment of the hire-purchase liability.
9 Employees were made redundant as the various parts of the business were sold. Currently one employee remains to clear outstanding paperwork in the very short term.

Conclusion and further proposals

1 Following the ceasing of trading I shall instruct my agents to dispose of the computer and other remaining office equipment and surrender the office lease, which I am advised has no premium value.
2 Debtors, which relate mainly to short-term credit sale agreements, will take another four to six months to collect.
3 Following the sale of the remaining equipment the company can then proceed into liquidation in order that creditors can obtain VAT bad debt relief and the surplus funds can be distributed. I expect these proceedings to commence in early 1989.

152 Corporate Insolvency in Practice

4 I am pleased to report that the administrator of the company has achieved the purposes set out in section 8(3)(d) of the Insolvency Act, namely a more advantageous realization of the company's assets than would have been effected on a winding up.

Document 2: Any Yarn Limited – Estimated statement of affairs as at 23 September 1988

	WDV	Admin 'going concern'	Liquidation 'break-up'
	£	£	£
Assets specifically pledged			
Motor vehicles	20,269	21,000	21,000
Due to HP creditor	(14,226)	14,000	14,000
	6,043	7,000	7,000
Assets not specifically pledged			
Cash in hands of accountant	3,000	3,000	3,000
Fixtures and fittings	1,215	2,000	—
Stocks	215,000	130,000	75,000
Debtors	52,700	30,000	25,000
Other trade debtors	19,300	14,000	10,000
Goodwill	—	10,000	—
Total assets available		196,000	120,000
Preferential creditors			
PAYE/NIC		4,600	4,600
VAT		5,500	5,500
Wages and holiday pay		3,000	3,000
Bank's claim for wages		—	—
		13,100	13,100
Surplus as regards preferential creditors		182,900	106,900
Unsecured creditors			
X Limited		293,911	293,911
Director's loan account		10,622	10,622
Bank overdraft		175,000	175,000
Redundancy/pay in lieu		10,000	10,000
		489,533	489,533
Deficiency as regards unsecured creditors		(306,633)	(382,633)
Share capital		7,600	7,600
Total deficiency		314,233	390,233

Document 3: Any Yarn Limited – in administration: Administrator's receipts and payment to 25 November 1988

Receipts (£)		
Sale proceeds – Mail order business		
Goodwill		14,000
Stock		55,500
– Shop business		20,000
– Knitting and Sewing Centre		30,000
Administrator's trading		62,637
Debtors		13,658
HP debtors		9,697
Interest received		565
VAT		9,395
		215,452
Payments (£)		
Trading expenses – Wages	8,565	
– Purchases	19,581	
– Expenses	1,271	29,417
Reservation of title/lien claims		3,542
Administrator's fees on account		5,000
Legal fees		2,937
Statement of affairs fee		2,000
VAT		4,704
		47,600
Funds in hand		£167,852

Document 4: Any Yarn Limited – Estimated balance sheet as at 31 August 1988

	1988		*1987*	
	£	£	£	£
Fixed assets				
Motor vehicles		20,269		24,995
Fixtures and fittings		1,215		1,641
		21,484		26,636
Current assets				
Stocks	225,000		220,987	
HP debtors	50,386		106,224	
Trade debtors	18,043		2,420	
Prepayments	—		39,098	
Cash at bank	560		—	
Cash in hand	—		1,882	
	293,989		370,611	

Continued

	1988		1987	
	£	£	£	£
Current liabilities				
Bank overdrafts				
– Giro	423			
– Any Bank	1,035		230,743	
– Current a/c	198,759			
PAYE and NI	3,404		2,842	
VAT	82,632		119,204	
HP creditors	10,850		19,976	
Director's loan a/c	10,621		10,621	
Accruals	—		15,143	
Inter-co. guarantee	293,911		157,001	
	601,635		555,530	
		(307,646)		(184,919)
		(286,162)		(158,283)
Share capital		7,600		7,600
Profit and loss account				
Balance	(165,883)			
Estimated profit/(loss)	(127,879)	(293,762)		(165,883)
		(286,162)		(158,283)

Document 5: Schedule 1 to the Insolvency Act 1986 – Powers of Administrator or Administrative Receiver

1. Power to take possession of, collect and get in the property of the company and for that purpose, to take such proceedings as may seem to him expedient.
2. Power to sell or otherwise dispose of the property of the company by public auction or private auction or private contract or, in Scotland, to sell, feu, hire out or otherwise dispose of the property of the company by public roup or private bargain.
3. Power to raise or borrow money and grant security therefor over the property of the company.
4. Power to appoint a solicitor or accountant or other professionally qualified person to assist him in the performance of his functions.
5. Power to bring or defend any action or other legal proceedings in the name and on behalf of the company.
6. Power to refer to arbitration any question affecting the company.
7. Power to effect and maintain insurances in respect of the business and property of the company.

8. Power to use the company's seal.
9. Power to do all acts and to execute in the name and on behalf of the company any deed, receipt or other document.
10. Power to draw, accept, make and endorse any bill of exchange or promissory note in the name and on behalf of the company.
11. Power to appoint any agent to do any business which he is unable to do himself or which can more conveniently be done by an agent and power to employ and dismiss employees.
12. Power to do all such things (including the carrying out of works) as may be necessary for the realization of the property of the company.
13. Power to make any payment which is necessary or incidental to the performance of his functions.
14. Power to carry on the business of the company.
15. Power to establish subsidiaries of the company.
16. Power to transfer to subsidiaries of the company the whole or any part of the business and property of the company.
17. Power to grant or accept a surrender of a lease or tenancy of any of the property of the company, and to take a lease or tenancy of any property required or convenient for the business of the company.
18. Power to make any arrangement or compromise on behalf of the company.
19. Power to call up any uncalled capital of the company.
20. Power to rank and claim in the bankruptcy, insolvency, sequestration or liquidation of any person indebted to the company and to receive dividends, and to accede to trust deeds for the creditors of any such person.
21. Power to present or defend a petition for the winding up of the company.
22. Power to change the situation of the company's registered office.
23. Power to do all other things incidental to the exercise of the foregoing powers.

REFERENCES AND FURTHER READING

Anderson, H. (1987) *Administrators: Part II of the Insolvency Act 1986*, Sweet and Maxwell, London.
Goode, R. M. (1988) *Legal Problems of Credit and Security*, 2nd edn, Sweet and Maxwell, London.
Grier, I.S. and Floyd, R. E. (1987) *Voluntary Liquidation, Receivership and Administration*, 2nd edn, Longman, Harlow.
Kerr, W. W. (1989) *The Law and Practice of Receivers and Administrators*, 17th edn, Sweet and Maxwell, London.
Lightman, G. and Moss, G. (1986) *The Law of Receivers of Companies*, Sweet and Maxwell, London.
Lingard, J. R. (1989) *Corporate Rescues and Insolvencies*, 2nd edn, Butterworth, London.
McMullen, J. (1987) *Business Transfers and Employee Rights*, Butterworth, London.
Milman, D. and Durrant, C. (1987) *Corporate Insolvency: Law and Practice*, Sweet and Maxwell, London.
Stewart, G. (1987) *Administrative Receivers and Administrators*, CCH Editions, Bicester.

NOTES

1 Ss. 230–237.
2 Insolvency Law Review Committee, *Insolvency Law and Practice*, Cmnd. 8558, paras. 495–7.
3 As to administrators, see s. 14(1) and (4); as to administrative receivers, see *Re Emmadart Ltd* [1979] Ch 450.
4 See Chap. 5, pp. 62–5.
5 S. 14(2)(a).
6 This would enable the dismissal of employees to be treated as 'fair' under the exception provided by reg. 8(2) of the Transfer of Undertakings (Protection of Employment) Regulations 1981 (S.I. 1981 No. 1794); see further p. 137.
7 As to administrators, see s. 22 and IR, r. 2.11; as to administrative receivers, see s. 47 and IR, r. 3.3.
8 Ss. 22(3) and 47(3).
9 Ss. 22(2) and 47(2).
10 Ss. 22(4) and 47(4).
11 Ss. 22(6) and 47(6).
12 See p. 133.
13 See p. 143.
14 Under this provision, the administrator may apply to the court for an order to 'dispose' or otherwise exercise his powers in relation to charged property, and if the court is satisfied that the disposal (or utilization) of the property would be likely to promote the purposes of the administration order, the court may order the sale or utilization of the property.
15 Ss. 10(1)(b) and 11(3)(c). However, as simple collection may constitute a 'self-help' remedy, a bank may be able to make such collections, see Chap. 7, p. 89.
16 See Stewart (1987), para. 1104.
17 S. 40.
18 *IRC* v. *Goldblatt* [1972] Ch 498; *Woods* v. *Winskill* [1913] 2 Ch 303.
19 *Aluminium Industrie Vaassen* v. *Romalpa Aluminium Ltd* [1976] 2 All ER 552.
20 [1985] Ch 207; see also *Re EVTR Ltd* [1987] BCLC 646.
21 *Barclays Bank Ltd* v. *Quistclose Investments Ltd* [1970] AC 567; *Re Kayford Ltd*

(in liquidation) [1975] 1 WLR 279.
22 *Re Multi-Guarantee Co Ltd* [1987] BCLC 257.
23 See generally R. M. Goode (1989) *Proprietary Rights and Insolvency in Sales Transactions*, 2nd edn.
24 *Aluminium Industrie Vaassen* v. *Romalpa Aluminium Ltd* [1976] 2 All ER 552; *Clough Mill Ltd.* v. *Martin* [1984] 3 All ER 982.
25 *Hendy Lennox (Industrial Engines) Ltd* v. *Grahame Puttick Ltd* [1984] 1 WLR 485.
26 *Borden (UK) Ltd* v. *Scottish Timber Products Ltd* [1981] Ch 25; *Re Bond Worth Ltd* [1980] Ch 228; see also a manufacturing process (which did not combine the supplier's products with those of others) *Re Peachdart Ltd* [1984] Ch 131.
27 *Aluminium Industrie Vaassen* v. *Romalpa Aluminium Ltd* [1976] 2 All ER 552.
28 *Re Andrabell Ltd* [1984] 3 All ER 407.
29 *Borden (UK) Ltd* v. *Scottish Timber Products Ltd* [1981] Ch 25; *Re Peachdart Ltd* [1984] Ch 131. Neither can the supplier claim the goods themselves from the purchaser from the company, because the company will be able to pass good title to the purchaser under s. 25(1) of the Sale of Goods Act 1979; see *Four Point Garage Ltd* v. *Carter* [1985] 3 All ER 12.
30 S. 10(1)(b); as to the definition of retention of title agreements, see s. 251.
31 S. 15(2).
32 P. 143.
33 S. 14(5).
34 S. 14(6).
35 S. 17(2)(a).
36 S. 17(2)(b).
37 S. 14(5).
38 See Anderson (1987), pp. 46–8.
39 See p. 139. It would seem that to bring proceedings against the company for breach, the other party would require the leave of the court under s. 11(3)(d).
40 S. 44(1)(a).
41 S. 44(1)(c).
42 See Kerr (1989), Chapter 22.
43 *Re Mack Trucks (Britain) Ltd* [1967] 1 WLR 780; *Nicoll* v. *Cutts* [1985] BCLC 322.
44 *Griffiths* v. *Social Services Secretary* [1974] QB 468.
45 As to the extent of their preference, see IA, Sched. 6 (reproduced in the case study in Chap. 10).
46 Kerr (1989), pp. 378–9.
47 Stewart (1987), para. 512.
48 Under S. 35.
49 *Rother Iron Works Ltd* v. *Canterbury Precision Engineers Ltd* [1974] QB 1.
50 *N. W. Robbie & Co. Ltd* v. *Witney Warehouse Co Ltd* [1963] 1 WLR 1324; *Business Computers Ltd* v. *Anglo-African Leasing Ltd* [1977] 1 WLR 578.
51 [1970] 1 Ch 193.
52 p. 141.
53 *Lathia* v. *Dronsfield Bros Ltd* [1987] BCLC 321; see also *Edwin Hill & Partners* v. *First National Finance Corp. plc* [1989] BCLC 89.
54 *Freevale Ltd* v. *Metrostore Holdings Ltd* [1984] Ch 199; *Telemetrix plc* v. *Modern Engineers of Bristol (Holdings) plc* [1985] BCLC 213.
55 S. 17(2).
56 S. 14(3).
57 S. 24(1).
58 *Lathia* v. *Dronsfield Bros Ltd* [1987] BCLC 321.
59 *Re Newdigate Colliery Co.* [1912] 1 Ch 468.
60 S. 212.
61 The techniques of 'hive downs' are well documented in Lange and Hartwig, *The*

Law and Practice of Administrative Receivership, pp. 92–104.
62 S.I. 1981 No. 1794.
63 *Secretary of State for Employment* v. *Spence* [1986] 3 WLR 380.
64 [1989] 2 WLR 634. See Collins, H. (1989) Transfer of undertakings and insolvency, *Industrial Law Journal*, Vol. 18, p. 144; Drake, R. S. (1989) Transfer of Undertakings (Protection of Employment) Regulations after *Litster* – effect on insolvency practitioners, *Insolvency Intelligence*, Vol. 2, p. 59.
65 Transfer Regs, reg. 5(2)(a). Excluded from transfer are rights under or in connection with an occupational pension scheme (reg. 7) and criminal liability (reg. 5(4)).
66 S. 15(2).
67 S. 15(5).
68 *Standard Chartered Bank Ltd* v. *Walker* [1982] 3 All ER 938.
69 *American Express International Banking Corp.* v. *Hurley* [1985] 3 All ER 564.
70 *Cuckmere Brick Co. Ltd* v. *Mutual Finance Ltd* [1971] Ch 949.
71 *Standard Chartered Bank Ltd* v. *Walker* [1982] 3 All ER 938.
72 *American Express International Banking Corp.* v. *Hurley* [1985] 3 All ER 564.
73 Provided that this was a fixed charge (if there is a prior floating charge, the administrative receiver will be obliged to pay the statutorily preferred creditors first (s. 40)).
74 See Chap. 6, pp. 76–7.
75 S. 5(2).
76 IA, Sched. 1, para. 21.
77 See Chap. 10, p. 163–5.
78 *American Express International Banking Corp* v. *Hurley* [1985] 3 All ER 564.
79 S. 45(1).
80 See p. 132.
81 In the case of an administrator, the effective date is the date of the administration order; in the case of receivership, the effective date is the date of the receiver's appointment.
82 Ss. 234 and 235.
83 CDDA 1986, s. 7(3).
84 S.I. 1986 No. 2134.

10
Liquidations

INTRODUCTION

There are two types of liquidation procedure for insolvent companies. First, by far the most usual form is the creditors' voluntary liquidation. This is commenced by a resolution of the shareholders in general meeting that the company be wound up.[1] Thus, the procedure is dependent on the willingness of the directors and shareholders to pass the necessary resolutions, acknowledging that the company is insolvent and unable to continue trading. Since, in an insolvency, the directors will not be in a position to make a declaration of solvency[2] the liquidation will be a creditors' voluntary winding up.[3] A meeting of creditors is then held to appoint the liquidator, to examine the statement of affairs and the report on the causes of the insolvency and, if it is felt necessary, to elect a liquidation committee to assist the liquidator in his task of investigating the affairs of the company and the conduct of directors and to advise as to the realization of the assets.

Alternatively, if the members are not willing to pass the resolution necessary for a voluntary winding up, a creditor (or creditors) who fulfils the criteria set out in sections 122 and 123 of the Insolvency Act[4] may petition the court to grant a compulsory winding-up order. In this event, once the winding-up order has been granted, the Official Receiver, an officer of the Insolvency Service of the DTI, will be appointed as a provisional liquidator of the company. His role will be to examine the affairs of the company, and, if he thinks it necessary, to call a meeting of creditors:[5] the Official Receiver may be required to call a meeting of creditors if he is at any time requested to do so by a quarter or more in value of the company's creditors,[6] thereafter either continuing the process of the liquidation himself or standing down after the creditors' meeting has appointed their own liquidator.[7] The main ground for applying for a compulsory winding-up order, so far as the creditors are concerned, is that the company is unable to pay its debts. The statutory definition of this inability is given in section 123.[8] A debt owed by the company in excess of £750 for which a statutory demand has been served on the company and which remains unpaid for a three-week period will suffice.[9] Alternatively, in the absence of a statutory demand, the creditor may bring forward other proof that the company is unable to pay its debts.[10]

The relative advantages and disadvantages of the two procedures have been examined in Chapter 6.[11]

PROCEDURES

Preliminary considerations

As with all forms of insolvency procedures, the directors must carefully consider all the options open to them. Liquidation is most clearly indicated where a company is constantly operating at a loss, creditors have been pressing for payment and their demands are unmet or cannot be met, or where rescue plans under the auspices of an administration or receivership have failed through lack of adequate finance or for any other reason.

Once the decision to liquidate has been taken, the directors, acting on the advice of an insolvency practitioner, should move quickly so as to avoid trading further into debt, thus incurring criticism from creditors and facing a possible claim for wrongful trading.[12] The company should cease trading; to continue trading is justified only where this would lead to a significant increase in the realization value of the company. Indeed, if this is a serious consideration, the trading might best be pursued under the protection of an administration order.[13] If there is any viable part of the business, the insolvency practitioner might well advise the directors to hive down the profitable or saleable parts to a subsidiary prior to the commencement of the liquidation. This is because after the commencement of winding up, the company ceases to be the beneficial owner of its assets: they are held on trust to be distributed according to the statutory order of distribution.[14] The shares in the subsidiary could then be sold, prior to liquidation, to a purchaser and the proceeds of sale held for distribution to creditors by a subsequently appointed liquidator.

Summoning meetings

The board meeting, after recording its recommendation to liquidate, will call shareholders' meetings to pass the necessary resolutions. Time may be of the essence here. If the resolution is to be passed as a special resolution, twenty-one days' notice must be given to the shareholders,[15] but if, as is more usual, an extraordinary resolution is to be passed the period of notice required will be fourteen days.[16] However, it is common in a company where the agreement of all the shareholders can be obtained quickly – as, for example, where the shares are held by two or three shareholders – for the winding-up resolution to be passed on short notice[17] and the liquidator to be appointed by the shareholders almost as soon as there has been a decision to wind up the company. Prior to the Insolvency Act, the ability to put a company into liquidation by this expedited procedure was abused by some unscrupulous directors and liquidators so as to carry out a sale of the assets before the creditors could be called to a meeting where a liquidator could be appointed to protect their interests. Now, under section 166 of the Insolvency Act, a liquidator, appointed by the members, is limited in the powers that he can exercise in the period prior to the holding of creditors' meeting. He may only:[18]

3 (a) take into his custody or under his control all the property to which the company appears to be entitled;
   (b) dispose of perishable goods and any other goods the value of which is likely to diminish if they are not immediately disposed of; and
   (c) do all such things as are necessary for the protection of the company's assets.

Any other exercise of power by the liquidator during the period prior to the creditors' meeting requires the sanction of the court.[19]

The creditors' meeting must be held not more than fourteen days after the date when the company resolved to go into voluntary liquidation.[20] Notice of the meeting must be sent to the creditors not less than seven days before the date on which the meeting is to be held;[21] the notice should contain details of the name and address of the insolvency practitioner handling the proceedings to whom interested creditors can refer, or a place where creditors can inspect a list of the names and addresses of creditors prior to the meeting.[22] In practice, creditors' meetings are often scheduled to take place immediately after the shareholders' meetings called to pass the winding-up resolution.

The main purposes of the creditors' meeting are to receive the statement of affairs prepared by the insolvency practitioner, to consider the report into the insolvency and to appoint the liquidator. This outline does not convey the nature of such meetings, which may be acrimonious affairs in which creditors seek explanations for the losses that they have sustained. Blame will be apportioned. The liquidator will be called on to act with skill and diplomacy so as not to impeach the conduct of the directors or suggest that an adverse report to the Department of Trade and Industry will be made, if such is not the case.

Ultimately, although the insolvency practitioner may have done much work in investigating the company's affairs, arranging for valuations of its property and preparing the statement of affairs, he is not the liquidator until his appointment is confirmed by the meeting. Thus, the practitioner preparing this material must be satisfied that he has enough in the way of funds to cover his fees in case he is not appointed by the meeting.

The directors must prepare and lay before the meeting the statement of affairs,[23] for which they, and not the insolvency practitioner are responsible. The meeting will then vote on the appointment of the liquidator.[24] The creditors, who have lodged proof of their debts[25] within the requisite time, may vote at the meeting and any resolution must be passed by a majority in value of those present and voting in person or by proxy.[26] The Insolvency Rules deal in detail with such questions as the admission of proofs of debts for voting purposes, and whether unquantified claims may be admitted.[27]

In addition, a liquidation committee may be elected consisting of not less than three or more than five members.[28] The role of such committee is advisory only; its establishment is most appropriate in a situation where the liquidator may have to undertake a detailed examination of the directors' conduct prior to the liquidation, where there might be a suspicion of fraud or misapplication of company assets. Also, such a committee may be apt in a complex insolvency where the liquidator may need to consult the creditors. If he does not have a liquidation committee, he may have to convene meetings of creditors to give the necessary consents to his actions.

There are a number of administrative matters to be dealt with at the conclusion of the meeting. A notice of the liquidator's appointment must be sent to the Registrar of Companies[29] together with copies of the winding-up resolution.[30] A notice of his appointment must also be published in the *London Gazette*[31] and the liquidator must prepare a report on the meeting for presentation to members and creditors within twenty-eight days.[32]

STATUS, POWERS AND DUTIES OF THE LIQUIDATOR

Upon his appointment, the liquidator becomes an officer of the company and the powers of the directors cease.[33] He deals as an agent of the company in his transactions with third parties.

The results of winding up are drastic. Section 87 of the Insolvency Act provides:

> (1) In the case of a voluntary winding up, the company shall from the commencement of the winding up cease to carry on its business, except so far as may be required for its beneficial winding up.
> (2) However, the corporate state and corporate powers of the company notwithstanding anything to the contrary in its articles, continue until the company is dissolved.

Usually, depending on their terms, the company's contracts with customers and suppliers will be automatically terminated by the winding-up resolution and employees' contracts will also normally be discharged.

Thus, although the liquidator may carry on the business if he reasonably believes that this is necessary for the beneficial winding up of the company, it would appear that he would have to re-engage the workforce and trade on precarious contracts with suppliers and customers.

Generally, a liquidator's powers are geared towards achieving the best realization of assets in the shortest time so that they can be distributed to creditors in accordance with the priorities set out by law. Under powers granted in Schedule 4 to the Insolvency Act (which is appended in the case study), the liquidator may sell any of the company's property by public auction or private sale. The liquidator has a free hand to decide when and how to sell and, in the absence of fraud, the court will not grant an injunction to stop a sale.[34]

In disposing of assets, he must be careful that he does not interfere with the rights of others who have ownership or possessory interests in the property. For example, those with effective retention of title clauses[35] in their contracts of supply of raw materials or other goods will need to be informed that their unused materials/goods are available for collection. Likewise, those with a lien, that is, a right to retain possession of goods which are owned by the company, may need to have their claims settled before the company can retake possession of the goods prior to sale. The liquidator may pay off such creditors immediately but, in so doing, he requires the sanction of the court or the liquidation committee.[36] As regards liens over the company's books, papers and records, section 246 of the Insolvency Act has considerably strengthened the liquidator's hand, in that it provides that such liens are unenforceable against him.[37]

The liquidator is empowered to enter into all kinds of ancillary deals, such as arranging for banking facilities for the purposes of financing the costs of sales (the company's bank account will have been frozen by the winding-up resolution), making the plant and stock secure against theft and arranging insurance cover, countermanding new deliveries of stock and refusing to make any deliveries on current orders.

A voluntary winding up does not automatically stay litigation which is pending or proceeding against the company. However, the liquidator has power to refer any question arising in the liquidation (including the continuing of legal proceedings) to the court for decision, and the court may stay proceedings or restrain execution against the company's assets.[38]

The liquidator also has wide powers to disclaim onerous property notwithstanding that he has taken possession of such property and exercised ownership rights, for example tried to sell the property. Section 178 defines onerous property to include unprofitable contracts, property which is not readily saleable (such as land held on a short lease) or assets which will cost money to continue to operate. Upon disclaimer, the company's rights and liabilities in respect of the property cease and the other party with an interest in the disclaimed property may claim simply as a creditor in the liquidation for the value of the rights disclaimed.[39] Since this is an extensive power, section 178(3) permits a person interested in the property (for example the landlord of premises the company leases) to serve a notice on the liquidator requiring him to decide whether to disclaim the interest. The liquidator then has twenty-eight days in which to exercise his power of disclaimer.[40]

The liquidator's primary duty is to settle the list of creditors and, after realization of the assets, to distribute such final dividend as is available to them in accordance with their statutory entitlement. To prove their entitlement, creditors must submit a claim either in the form provided for in the insolvency forms[41] or in any other form.[42] If the claim is unquantified – as, for example, a claim for faulty workmanship in relation to goods supplied by the company – the liquidator may estimate the value of the debt. This estimate may be challenged by the creditor in court proceedings.[43]

Having received the proofs of claims against the assets, the liquidator's first task is to ascertain the total entitlement of the preferential creditors, because he is obliged to pay such claims in priority to all others save the expenses incurred in liquidation and his own fees.[44] The list of preferential creditors is contained in Schedule 6 to the Insolvency Act (which is reproduced in the case study in this chapter), and contains the following categories of persons whose entitlement is assessed as at the date of the resolution for winding up (known as the 'relevant date').[45]

Category 1: Debts due to the Inland Revenue
Sums due at the relevant date on account of deductions of income tax from pay (PAYE) for the twelve-month period immediately preceding the winding-up resolution are preferred debts. The Inland Revenue's claim is also extended to cover deductions required on the part of subcontractors in the construction industry.

Category 2: Debts due to the Customs & Excise
Any VAT amount which is referable to the period of six months before the relevant date is also preferred; as is any car tax or betting levy due at the relevant date from the debtor company and which became due within a twelve-month period prior to winding up.

Category 3: Social security contributions
All contributions due under the Social Security Act 1975 (national insurance contributions) which became due in the twelve-month period prior to the winding-up resolution are preferential debts.

(Category 4 relates to contributions to occupational pension schemes.)

Category 5: Employee's remuneration
Any amount that is owed by the company to any person who is or has been an employee of the company and is payable by way of remuneration in respect of the whole or part of the four-month period prior to the relevant date is a preferential debt.

This is subject to a limit of £800 per employee.[46] Also in the category of preferential payments are any amounts owed by the company by way of accrued holiday pay.

Normally, so far as employees' preferential claims are concerned, the liquidator will contact the Department of Employment, which deals with employees' claims under the insolvency provisions of the Employment Protection (Consolidation) Act 1978, as amended. The liquidator, acting as agent for the Department of Employment, will pay the employees the amounts owing to them within the statutory limits imposed by the 1978 Act. The Department of Employment is entitled to claim to be in the same preferential position in the liquidation as the employees to whom payment has been made. If there is a shortfall owing to the employees, this may be claimed directly from the liquidator as a preferential payment, but will rank after the Department of Employment's claim.

The position of any person who has lent the company money specifically to pay a preferred creditor (most likely a bank which has loaned the company money to pay the employees' wages) is protected, in that that person will be treated as a preferential creditor for so much as has been advanced for the purpose of paying the preferential creditor.[47] Any bank which lends for this purpose will usually ensure that such payments from 'wages accounts' are strictly applied for preferential payments only and are not used to pay other creditors, and in any case do not exceed the statutory limit on preferential claims, otherwise the bank will not be eligible to be treated as a preferential creditor.

A number of useful booklets have been prepared by the Department of Employment to guide both liquidators and employees as to their rights and duties. The most relevant ones are: No. 3, *Employees' Rights on the Insolvency of an Employer*, and No. 13, *Redundancy Payments*.

All the preferential creditors rank equally among themselves after the payment of the expenses of the winding up, and if there are insufficient funds to pay them in full, they abate in equal proportions.[48]

The liquidator must ascertain the full extent of liability to preferential creditors because he will be justified in paying *any* dividend to ordinary creditors only if the preferential creditors have been paid in full. It may happen that the Inland Revenue and Department of Employment take some time in investigating their preferential claims. This can cause frustration because the liquidator is obliged to wait until the position of the preferential creditors is clear before he can deal with the non-preferential claims.

Something which a liquidator can do to relieve any immediate hardship for unsecured creditors is to issue a certificate to them indicating that the company is insolvent. This will enable them to claim relief from VAT payments in respect of the bad debts.[49]

Once the expenses of liquidation and the preferential creditors have been paid, the ordinary trade creditors will be entitled to payment.[50] They rank equally among themselves and will abate equally if the realizations are insufficient to meet their debts in full.

It is in the creditors' and liquidator's interests that the winding up be completed as quickly as the circumstances will permit. If the winding up continues for more than a year, the liquidator is under an obligation to call meetings of the shareholders and creditors in order to lay accounts before them and to give an explanation of his dealings during the year.[51] When the liquidator is ready to make his final distribution, he is under a duty to call meetings to lay his final accounts before the members and creditors and to summarize his conduct of the liquidation.[52]

In addition to these duties the liquidator in a creditors' voluntary winding up has a wide range of investigatory powers and duties both in relation to the company's assets and antecedent transactions and in connection with the stewardship of the directors. We will examine these investigating and reporting obligations in the next section.

COMPULSORY LIQUIDATIONS

Much of what has been said concerning voluntary liquidations applies also to compulsory liquidations. However, the whole tenor of the Insolvency Act is towards the avoidance of compulsory liquidation proceedings except where some detailed investigation is required. If there is a chance of a turnaround, administration or receivership should be utilized, and if the company has clearly and irreversibly failed, the creditors' voluntary winding up is the preferred procedure. Compulsory liquidation is geared towards a more investigative approach to business failure and the conduct of directors.

This is highlighted by section 132 of the Insolvency Act, which provides:

(1) Where a winding up order is made by the court in England and Wales, it is the duty of the Official Receiver to investigate –
 (a) if the company has failed, the causes of the failure; and
 (b) generally, the promotion, formation, business, dealings and affairs of the company,
 and to make such report (if any) to the court as he thinks fit.
(2) The report is, in any proceedings, prima facie evidence of the facts stated in it.

Three main lines of inquiry may be pursued during the course of these investigations:

(1) investigation of antecedent transactions with a view to setting these aside and recovering benefits for the creditors at large;
(2) investigation into the causes of the failure and the conduct of directors: this may result in misfeasance proceedings or actions for fraudulent or wrongful trading;
(3) investigations prior to a report on directors required under the Company Directors Disqualification Act 1986 or inquiries leading to civil or criminal proceedings against the officers of the company, administrators or receivers or the company's auditors.

In carrying out these duties, the Official Receiver, and any liquidator who is appointed by the creditors' meeting in a creditors' voluntary winding up, has extensive powers to require the co-operation of the company's officers.

Investigation into antecedent transactions

The Official Receiver, as well as any liquidator or administrator appointed to the company, has power to investigate preferences given before winding up (section 239); transactions entered into at an undervalue (section 238); extortionate credit transactions (section 244); and to set aside a floating charge created within a certain time before winding up (section 245). The aim of these investigations and subsequent actions is to ensure that all creditors are treated equally and fairly.

Preferences

The aim of the law relating to the recovery of preferences is to enable the liquidator or administrator to apply to the court to set aside a transaction which has been entered into in the period leading up to the insolvency proceedings, as a result of which the creditor who has been preferred has been put in a better position in the liquidation than he would otherwise have been. In entering into the transaction, the company must have been influenced by the desire to better the creditor's position,[53] but such a desire is presumed in the case of a person connected with the company.

Before an order can be made under section 239, the liquidator must show that the following conditions are satisfied.

(1) The company gave a preference, as defined in section 239(4); that is:

> For the purposes of this section and section 241, a company gives a preference to a person if –
> (a) that person is one of the company's creditors or a surety or guarantor for any of the company's debts or other liabilities, and
> (b) the company does anything or suffers anything to be done which (in either case) has the effect of putting that person into a position which, in the event of the company going into insolvent liquidation, will be better than the position he would have been in if that thing had not been done.

(2) The company was influenced in entering into the transaction by a desire to bring about the preference. This expression has been examined recently in the case of *Re M. C. Bacon Ltd*.[54] The company involved, which was experiencing severe financial difficulties and which had exceeded the limit on its unsecured overdraft, negotiated a continuance of its bank's support on condition that the bank was granted a fixed and floating charge over the company's property. The necessary documents were executed on 20 May 1987. The company continued trading at a loss and went into creditors' voluntary liquidation in August 1987.

The liquidator sought to set aside the bank's charges on the grounds that they were preferences, in that the directors were influenced in granting the charges by a desire to put the bank in a better position than it would otherwise have been in. This claim did not succeed. The court held that the liquidator had failed to show that the directors were motivated, in giving the preference, by a desire to prefer the bank. Furthermore, the mere presence of a desire to prefer was not sufficient in itself – the liquidator must show that the desire to prefer must have influenced the decision to enter into the transaction.

Applying this interpretation of section 239 to the facts of the case, the court concluded that the directors were influenced by a desire to continue trading and to further the prospects of a turnaround, and since they thought that this was entirely dependent on continued support from the bank, they granted the charges to ensure this continued support rather than to better the bank's position in any subsequent insolvency.

Where a company has given a preference to a person connected with the company[55] it is presumed to have been influenced by the desire to prefer that creditor.[56]

(3) The company gave the preference at a 'relevant time'. In the case of a person connected with the company (otherwise than by reason only of being its employee) this is within two years ending with the onset of

insolvency,[57] and in the case of a preference given to any other person, within a period of six months ending with the onset of insolvency.
(4) The liquidator or administrator must show, finally, either that the company was unable to pay its debts within the meaning of section 123 at the time it entered into the transaction, or that it became unable to do so as a result of entering into it.[58]

The typical type of situation which would amount to a preference is where the directors have given personal guarantees in respect of the company's overdraft, and, at a time when liquidation is imminent, payments are made into the company's bank account to lessen or pay off the overdraft and thus wipe out the liability on the directors' guarantees.

The main difficulty facing a liquidator investigating possible preferences, as the case of *Re M. C. Bacon Ltd* highlights, lies in the interpretation of section 239(5), which requires that in order to prove the existence of a preference, it is necessary to establish that the company was influenced by a desire to put the creditor in a better position.[59]

Transactions at an undervalue

A company which is in financial straits may transfer property to third parties prior to the liquidation so that those persons receive a benefit but give the company little or nothing in return. Similarly, the company may pay for services where the price it pays is significantly more than the value of the services rendered. In these and other circumstances, section 238 permits the liquidator or administrator to examine prior contracts, purchases, guarantees and commitments and, if they amount to transactions at an undervalue, to apply to the court for an order restoring the position to what it would have been if the company had not entered into the transaction.

The liquidator must establish the following points in his application to set a transaction aside.

(1) The transaction is at an undervalue within the definition contained in section 238(4):

a company enters into a transaction at an undervalue if –
(a) the company makes a gift to that person or otherwise enters into a transaction with that person on terms that provide for the company to receive no consideration, or
(b) the company enters into a transaction with that person for a consideration the value of which, in money or money's worth, is significantly less than the value in money or money's worth, of the consideration provided by the company.

(2) The company entered into the transaction either within two years ending with the onset of insolvency[60] or between the presentation of a petition for the making of an administration order and the making of such an order.[61]

(3) The company was unable to pay its debts as defined by section 123 at the time that it entered into the transaction, or became unable so to do as a result of the transaction.

However, the court may not make an order reversing the effect of such a transaction, if it is satisfied that the company entered the transaction in good faith and for the purpose of carrying on its business and, at the time it did so, there were reasonable grounds for believing that the transaction would benefit the company.[62]

The chief problem for the liquidator in setting aside such transactions is to demonstrate that the value received by the company was 'significantly less' than the value of the property transferred. If there would have been no 'willing buyers' for the property or it was sold on a 'forced sale' it would be difficult to establish that what was paid to the company was significantly less than the worth of the asset.

If the liquidator makes out a satisfactory case against the transaction, the court is given very extensive powers to restore the position to what it would have been had the transaction not been entered into. This will enable all the creditors to share in the assets which would otherwise have been dissipated. By section 238(3) the court has a virtually unlimited discretion to reverse the effects of the transaction. This is amplified by section 241, which gives examples of the types of court order that can be made. For example, if property has been transferred as part of a transaction at an undervalue, the court may order that it is transferred back to the company. Similarly, if the property has been sold by the transferee, the proceeds of sale may be vested in the company.

However, there are limits on the liquidator's power of recovery under this court order. Any such order must not prejudice any interest in property which was acquired from a person, other than the company, and was acquired in good faith, for value and without notice of the relevant circumstances.[63] Furthermore, a court order may not require a person who received a benefit from the transaction in good faith, for value and without notice of the relevant circumstances to pay a sum to the office-holder except where that person was a party to the transaction.[64] There is some overlap between the provisions relating to preferences and those concerned with transactions at an undervalue, because the latter type of transaction may be entered into with a desire to prefer the creditor involved.

The liquidator will have to consider under which provision to attack the transaction. Section 238 on transactions at an undervalue is wider than section 239, in that transactions at an undervalue entered into within two years of the onset of insolvency can be investigated and their effects reversed. Furthermore, the aim of setting aside transactions at an undervalue is to redress the imbalance in the bargain made between the company and a creditor – there is no need for the liquidator to show that the company was influenced by a desire to create that imbalance or prefer the creditor.

Only preferences during the six months prior to the onset of insolvency may be examined (unless they are in favour of a connected person, in which case the period is two years). However, the provisions relating to setting aside preferences are not concerned with the value that has been given by the creditor, but with the improvement of the creditor's position in the insolvency proceedings.

Floating charges

Those who take a floating charge on the company's assets at a time when the company is close to the onset of insolvency and do not inject any new funds into the company in return for the charge, may find that the liquidator (or administrator) challenges their security and treats them as unsecured creditors.

This is because their security may be caught within the terms of section 245(2), which states:

> Subject as follows, a floating charge on the company's undertaking or property created at a relevant time is invalid except to the extent of the aggregate of –
> (a) the value of so much consideration for the creation of the charge as consists of money paid or goods or services supplied, to the company at the same time as, or after, the creation of the charge.
> (b) the value of so much of that consideration as consists of the discharge or reduction, at the same time as, or after, the creation of the charge, of any debt of the company.
> (c) the amount of such interest (if any) as is payable on the amount falling within paragraph (a) or (b) . . .

Thus, the floating charge will be valid notwithstanding that it is given close to the onset of insolvency, to the extent that new cash is lent to the company and also to the extent of goods or services supplied in return for the charge. The money must be paid or goods or services supplied at the same time as or subsequently to the creation of the charge and the payments must be genuine and not merely 'book entries' made for the purposes of validating otherwise unsecured amounts. The courts have given considerable protection to banks which pay cheques to third parties and the company's existing unsecured overdraft is then secured by floating charge. The continued payment of cheques is regarded as being made 'in consideration for the charge' and is 'cash paid to the company'. Thus, the security will be validated by the continued operation of the account.[65]

Furthermore, section 245 provides that, except in the case of a connected person, the charge will not be invalidated unless the company was unable to pay its debts or became unable to do so as a result of the transaction. So far as 'connected persons' are concerned, there is a presumption that the company was insolvent at the time when the security was given and it is up to the connected person to prove the company's solvency at the time. The relevant period during which floating charges can be invalidated is twelve months prior to the onset of insolvency or, in the case of a charge granted to a person connected with the company, two years.

It is important to remember that it is only after the liquidator or administrator has been appointed that a floating charge can be invalidated under section 245. So, if an administrative receiver has realized the assets covered by the charge and paid the secured creditors and later the company goes into liquidation, the liquidator cannot retrospectively invalidate the charge and claim back the payments made to the erstwhile secured creditors.[66]

Extortionate credit transactions

The liquidator can also apply to the court for an order setting aside certain credit transactions or varying the terms on which credit has been given to the company or security has been provided in respect of such credit deals.[67] The period during which the transaction can be examined is three years prior to the day on which an administration order was made or the company went into liquidation.

The term 'extortionate' is defined in section 244(3):

> For the purposes of this section a transaction is extortionate if, having regard to the risk accepted by the person providing the credit –
> (a) the terms of it are or were such as to require grossly exorbitant payments to be made (whether unconditionally or in certain contingencies) in respect of the provision of the credit, or
> (b) it otherwise grossly contravened ordinary principles of fair dealing:
> and it shall be presumed, unless the contrary is proved, that a transaction with respect to which an application is made under this section is or, as the case may be, was extortionate.

Once the court is satisfied that the terms on which credit was given were extortionate, it has a wide discretion in the type of order it may make remedying the effects of the credit terms.[68]

The powers conferred under section 244 are exercisable concurrently with the power to apply to court to set aside a transaction at an undervalue.[69]

Transactions defrauding creditors

Under section 423 the liquidator, Official Receiver or administrator may apply to court for an order setting aside a transaction at an undervalue which was entered into with the intention of defrauding creditors. The types of transaction envisaged include gifts of corporate property and transactions in which the company receives significantly less than the value of the property transferred.

To fall within this section, the court must be satisfied that the transaction was entered into for the purpose of putting the assets beyond the reach of a person who is making, or may at some time make, a claim against the company or otherwise prejudicing the interests of such person in relation to the claim which he is making or may make.

Under this section there is no time limit on the transactions which may be examined and in this sense, the section is wider than section 238. Once the nature of a transaction has been proved, the court may make a wide range of orders reversing the transaction or otherwise making arrangements for compensating the company's creditors whose interests have been harmed.[70]

Investigations into the conduct of management

The liquidator may question the past and present directors, officers and shadow directors of the company whose conduct is relevant to the insolvency. The purpose of such investigation is to establish the cause of the insolvency and the extent of the directors' culpability.

Examination of the conduct of directors may lead the liquidator to consider whether any of the following civil actions should be taken against the director(s) or shadow directors(s).

Fraudulent trading

If it appears to the liquidator that the business of the company has been carried on with the intention of defrauding creditors of the company or of any other person or for any fraudulent purpose, then the directors may be liable for fraudulent trading.[71]

The earlier case law, which is still of relevance in the interpretation of section 213, indicated that some positive action on the part of the directors was required,[72] mere inaction not sufficing to demonstrate a fraudulent intent. The types of conduct that are likely to fall within the ambit of the section include, for example, ordering supplies knowing that the company could not pay for them[73] or obtaining credit knowing that there is no reason to believe that the company would ever have funds to repay such credit.[74]

The main difficulty facing a liquidator in mounting such a case is to establish the requisite state of mind of the director concerned. Fraud is a difficult allegation to maintain as the onus is on the liquidator to show that the director was subjectively dishonest, not merely negligent or reckless. If the allegation of fraud is satisfactorily made out, the court may declare that anyone who was knowingly a party to carrying out fraudulent trading is liable to make such contributions to the company's assets as the court thinks proper.[75]

Wrongful trading

This civil action has already been examined in some detail in Chapter 1.[76] Suffice it to say that the liquidator will bear the less onerous burden of showing that at some time before the commencement of winding up, a director or shadow director knew or ought to have concluded that there was no reasonable prospect that the company would avoid going into insolvent liquidation.

In assessing the person's[77] responsibility the liquidator will apply an objective standard in that he will assess the person by taking into account the general knowledge, skill and experience which may reasonably be expected from a person carrying out the same functions as are carried out by the director in relation to the company. If the director has any special skill, for example as an accountant or lawyer, this will be taken into account to increase the overall standard of skill expected from him.

The court will not make a declaration of wrongful trading if it is satisfied that the director or shadow director has taken every step to minimize the potential loss to the company's creditors. This would seem to place a considerable burden of proof on the director seeking to escape liability under section 214.

It remains to be seen whether the section 214 remedy will be used against careless or reckless directors who should have foreseen that the company was insolvent and who failed to take steps to minimize the eventual loss to creditors. The *Produce Marketing* case[78] will no doubt send warning ripples to the insolvency profession and those advising directors as to their responsibilities.

Misfeasance

It may be that at a time prior to the insolvency the directors have acted in a way which is in breach of their duties to the company, for example by misapplying company property, and yet the shareholders have been powerless to take action against the directors.

Section 212 provides a summary way in which the Official Receiver or liquidator (or indeed any creditor or contributory) may apply to the court to examine the conduct of the directors. If, following the examination, it appears that the director (or any officer of the company or liquidator, administrator or administrative receiver) has misapplied or retained or become accountable for any of the company's money or property or has been guilty of any misfeasance or breach of duty in relation to the company, the court may make any of the orders specified in section 212(3).

These include orders requiring repayment of money and contribution to the assets of the company by way of compensation for the loss caused by the misfeasance or breach of duty.

Though the main duty of the liquidator will be to achieve the best realization of assets for the creditors, and the investigation of both antecedent transactions relating to assets and the civil liability of directors is focused towards this end, it may be that in the course of his investigations the liquidator uncovers facts which indicate that the past or present officers of the company may be guilty of a criminal offence in relation to the company. The liquidator, in the case of a voluntary liquidation, should report such matters to the Director of Public Prosecutions,[79] and in the case of a compulsory liquidation he should report the matter to the Official Receiver.

Report on the conduct of directors

The liquidator, in common with other office-holders, is under an obligation to examine the conduct of directors and if it appears that conduct on the part of the director or past director, either taken alone or in conjunction with conduct in relation to any other company, renders him unfit to be concerned in the management of a company, a report to this effect should be made to the DTI.[80] The detailed provisions of the Company Directors Disqualification Act have been examined in Chapter 1.

The manner in which such report should be made is specified by the Insolvent Companies (Reports on Conduct of Directors) No. 2 Rules 1986. The insolvency practitioner should complete his investigation into the director's conduct within six months of the relevant date.[81] In the case of a company in voluntary liquidation this is the date of the winding-up resolution; in the case of a compulsory liquidation it is the date when the winding-up order is made. Penalties may be imposed on insolvency practitioners who fail to fulfil their reporting obligations.

Clearly, the details of the director's conduct and matters to be brought to the attention of the Disqualification Unit of the DTI will vary from case to case, but the practitioner will derive some guidance as to the types of conduct considered important in determining the question of fitness from the case law in process of development.[82] The ultimate decision whether to apply for a disqualification order rests with the DTI. Directors of insolvent companies are placed under considerable pressure knowing that their conduct is being investigated, but section 7(2) of the Company Directors Disqualification Act provides that the threat of possible disqualification should not hang over them indefinitely. That section provides that the application for a disqualification order must be brought within two years of the company becoming insolvent,[83] unless the court gives leave for the application to be brought outside the time limit.

Once an application for a disqualification order has been made, section 6 of the Company Directors Disqualification Act provides that the court *shall* make an order if it is satisfied:

(a) that he is or has been a director of a company which has at any time become insolvent (whether while he was a director or subsequently), and
(b) that his conduct as a director of that company (either taken alone or taken together with his conduct as a director of any other company or companies) makes him unfit to be concerned in the management of a company.

The court has no discretion in the matter. By section 6(4) the *minimum* period of disqualification is two years and there is a maximum period of fifteen years.

TERMINATION OF LIQUIDATION

Although the main aim of liquidation is to maximize realizations so as to achieve the best dividend possible for creditors, and a secondary purpose is to examine the causes of insolvency and responsibility of the directors for the company's failure, the liquidator must bear in mind that he must close the liquidation as rapidly as possible while trying to achieve these objectives. In practice, it is very much a question of balance where the liquidator must appraise the costs of continuing the liquidation against the benefits of closing it and declaring a final dividend.

The liquidator, having paid his fees and the costs of the liquidation, will distribute the remaining funds to the creditors and call a final meeting of creditors.[84] Thereafter, the liquidator must send his final accounts to the Registrar of Companies.

The dissolution of the company and removal of its name from the register occurs automatically three months after the Registrar has received the final accounts and return of the final meeting.[85] The liquidator or any other interested party may apply to the court for an order deferring dissolution for such time as the court thinks fit.[86]

In the case of a compulsory liquidation, it is possible for the Official Receiver or liquidator to apply to the Registrar for an early dissolution of the company where it appears that the realizable assets of the company are insufficient to cover the costs of winding up and the affairs of the company do not require any further investigation.[87] The company is then dissolved three months after the Official Receiver's application. It is open to any creditor or contributory to apply to the Secretary of State to review the situation if there is any reason to consider that early dissolution is not appropriate.

Case Study
[Any Name Ltd.]

The following documents constitute some of the records of a creditors' voluntary liquidation. They are extracted to indicate the procedures which led to the winding up and the narrative account of the circumstances, prepared by the liquidator.

They also include statutory material relating to the powers of liquidators and the categories of preferential debts.

The documents are:

(1) statutory demand under section 123(1)(a) or section 222(1)(a) of the Insolvency Act 1986 (Form 4.1 of the insolvency forms);
(2) notice to shareholders of an EGM to resolve on winding up;
(3) notice to creditors of a meeting called under section 98 of the Insolvency Act 1986;
(4) documents presented to the creditors' meeting:
    (a) statutory information;
    (b) company history;
    (c) trading information;
    (d) statement of affairs;
    (e) deficiency account.
(5) Schedule 4 to the Insolvency Act – Powers of a Liquidator in a Winding Up;
(6) Schedule 6 to the Insolvency Act – The Categories of Preferential Debts.

Document 1: Statutory demand under section 123(1)(a) or 222(1)(a)

Form 4.1

Rule 4.5 Statutory Demand under section 123(1)(a) or 221(1)(a) of the Insolvency Act 1986

> **Warning**
> - This is an **important** document. This demand must be dealt with **within 21 days** after its service upon the company or a winding-up order could be made in respect of the company.
> - Please read the demand and notes carefully.

Notes for Creditor
- If the creditor is entitled to the debt by way of assignment, details of the original creditor and any intermediary assignees should be given in part B on page 3.
- If the amount of debt includes interest not previously notified to the company as included in its liability, details should be given, including the grounds upon which interest is charged. The amount of interest must be shown separately.
- Any other charge accruing due from time to time may be claimed. The amount or rate of the charge must be identified and the grounds on which it is claimed must be stated.
- In either case the amount claimed must be limited to that which has accrued due at the date of the demand.
- If signatory of the demand is a solicitor or other agent of the creditor the name of his/her firm should be given.

Demand

To _____

Address _____

_____

This demand is served on you by the creditor:

Name _____

Address _____

_____

The creditor claims that the company owes the sum of £_____ , full particulars of which are set out on page 2.

The creditor demands that the company do pay the above debt or secure or compound for it to the creditor's satisfaction.

Signature of individual _____

Name _____
(BLOCK LETTERS)

Date _____

*Position with or relationship to creditor _____

_____

*Delete if signed by the creditor himself

*I am authorised to make this demand on the creditor's behalf.

Address _____

_____

Tel. No. _____ Ref. _____

N.B. The person making this demand must complete the whole of this page, page 2 and parts A and B (as applicable) on page 3.

JWU1
1.88

Jordans Jordan & Sons Limited
LAW STATIONERS 21 St. Thomas Street, Bristol BS1 6JS Telephone 0272 230600 Telex 449119

Liquidations 177

Form 4.1 contd.

PART A

The individual or individuals to whom any communication regarding this demand may be addressed is/are:—

Name
(BLOCK LETTERS)
Address

Telephone Number
Reference

PART B

For completion if the creditor is entitled to the debt by way of assignment

	Name	Date(s) of Assignment
Original creditor		
Assignees		

How to comply with a statutory demand

If the company wishes to avoid a winding-up petition being presented it must pay the debt shown on page 1, particulars of which are set out on page 2 of this notice, within the period of **21 days after** its service upon the company. Alternatively, the company can attempt to come to a settlement with the creditor. To do this the company should:

- inform the individual (or one of the individuals) named in part A above immediately that it is willing and able to offer security for the debt to the creditor's satisfaction; or
- inform the individual (or one of the individuals) named in part A immediately that it is willing and able to compound for the debt to the creditor's satisfaction.

If the company disputes the demand in whole or in part it should:

- contact the individual (or one of the individuals) named in part A immediately.

REMEMBER! The company has only 21 days after the date of service on it of this document before the creditor may present a winding-up petition.

Form 4.1 contd.

Particulars of Debt.
(These particulars must include (a) when the debt was incurred, (b) the consideration for the debt (or if there is no consideration the way in which it arose) and (c) the amount due as at the date of this demand.)

Notes for Creditor
Please make sure that you have read the notes on page 1 before completing this page.

Note:
If space is insufficient continue on reverse of page 3 and clearly indicate on this page that you are doing so.

Document 2: Notice of shareholders' meeting to resolve on winding up

IN THE MATTER of the INSOLVENCY ACT 1986

and

IN THE MATTER of Anyname Ltd
Registered Office: 14 East Street, Anytown

NOTICE IS HEREBY GIVEN that an Extraordinary General Meeting of the shareholders of the above-named company will be held at the office of [name for organization and address] at [date and time of meeting] for the purpose of considering and, if thought fit, passing the following resolutions as Extraordinary Resolutions:

> THAT it has been proved to the satisfaction of this meeting that this company cannot by reason of its liabilities continue in business, and that it is advisable that the same should be wound up; and that the company be wound up accordingly.

> THAT [name of liquidator] of [address of liquidator] be and is hereby appointed as the liquidator of the company for the purpose of such winding up.

DATED this   day of   19

BY ORDER OF THE BOARD

....
Director

Document 3: Notice to creditors of a meeting called under section 98 of the Insolvency Act

IN THE MATTER of the INSOLVENCY ACT 1986

and

IN THE MATTER of Anyname Ltd
Registered Office: 14 East Street, Anytown

NOTICE IS HEREBY GIVEN pursuant to section 98 of the Insolvency Act 1986, that a meeting of the creditors of the above-named company will be held at the offices of [name of organization and address] on [date of meeting] at [time of meeting] for the purpose mentioned in section 99 et seq. of the said Act.

A form of proxy is enclosed which, if intended to be used, must be duly completed and lodged at the registered office of the company as above, not later than 4.00 p.m. on [date].

A list of the names and addresses of the company's creditors will be available for inspection at [*address*] on [*date(s)*] between the hours of 10.00 a.m. and 4.00 p.m.

DATED this   day of   19

BY ORDER OF THE BOARD

....
Director

Document 4: Meeting of creditors held on 4 January 1990 at 11.30 a.m. – Anyname Ltd (trading as 'Big Eat')

Statutory information

Name of company: Anyname Limited
Trading as: Big Eat
Date of incorporation: 4 July 1983
Company number: 00000000
Registered office: 14 East Street, Anytown
Trading address: 45 Juniper Lane, Stockstown
                 56 Stores Road, Lightvale
Share capital:
  Authorized: 12,000 ordinary shares of £1 each
  Issues and fully paid: 12,000 ordinary shares of £1 each
Directors and shareholders:
  A. Brown   6,000
  B. Green   6,000 (company secretary)
              _____
              12,000

Company history

After test-marketing Mexican food at outside catering venues throughout Britain, the company was formed in 1983 to operate Mexican-style restaurants. A forty-seater restaurant was opened in October 1983. The venture proved extremely popular, but the site was too small to cater for the demand and consequently the company made only a marginal profit at the location.

An eighty-seater restaurant was found in Stockstown in November 1985. The move was immediately successful: in the first year profits before tax were of the order of £20,000-plus, and the company has continued to trade profitably from the Stockstown location since that time.

In March 1987 the company opened a further Mexican restaurant in Lightvale. Escalation of building costs during conversion, coupled with a much slower build-up of trade than had been previously experienced, forced the directors to apply for overdraft facilities to be increased from £10,000 to

£26,000 in late 1987. The application was supported by joint and several personal guarantees from the directors totalling £30,000.

During 1988 trade continued steadily from both premises, but the Lightvale location was subject to a substantial rent review. Subsequently the site became less viable as a potential profit-making entity.

The company experienced a comparatively small loss in the year ending August 1988 and the cash-flow projection indicated that a short-term increase in the overdraft facility to £40,000 would be required for the first three months of 1989. In October 1989 the facility was again increased to £45,000, and the directors' personal guarantees were likewise increased.

While trade in Lightvale increased in 1989, the Stockstown site has experienced a reduction in trade as the credit squeeze and high interest rates continue. This, coupled with increasing costs linked to general inflation and lack of credit control, has caused the company to suffer a loss of over £28,000 in the year to August 1989. The Lightvale restaurant was placed on the market throughout 1989 and a buyer was found at £85,000. However, in October 1989 the sale fell through.

Other potential buyers were actively pursued during November 1989. At the end of December 1989, in view of the company's financial situation, the directors resolved to place the company in voluntary liquidation.

Trading information

Audited accounts for 1985–88 and draft accounts for 1989 (£)

	1985	1986	1987	1988	1989
Turnover	95,999	197,472	302,179	355,226	363,085
Gross profit	24,832	42,010	26,188	50,206	30,216
Net profit (loss) before tax	13,985	21,526	(20,913)	(7,027)	(28,221)
Profit (loss) after tax	9,093	13,988	(19,237)	(4,329)	(28,221)
Cumulative profit (loss)	10,423	24,411	(19,226)	(23,553)	(51,774)
Directors' emoluments	12,241	17,208	25,612	35,171	40,042

Statement of affairs

IN THE MATTER of Anyname Ltd (trading as 'Big Eat')

and

IN THE MATTER of the INSOLVENCY ACT 1986

Statement of affairs of Anyname Ltd on 4 January 1990, the date of the resolution for winding up.

AFFIDAVIT

[*This affidavit must be sworn or affirmed before a solicitor or commissioner for oaths when you have completed the rest of this form.*]

I, A. Brown of 14 Main Street, Anytown MAKE OATH and say that the pages exhibited hereto are to the best of my knowledge and belief a full, true and complete statement as to the affairs of the above-named company as at 4 January 1990, the date of the resolution for winding up, and that the said company carried on business as a Mexican-style restaurant.

Sworn at

Date [*Signature of deponent*]
Before me,
[*signature*]
(Solicitor/Commissioner for Oaths)

A – Summary of assets

Assets	Book value	Estimated to realize
	£	£
Assets specifically pledged		
Motor vehicle	3,145	2,750
Hire-purchase creditor		(2,750)
Leasehold properties	35,081	35,000
Anybank		(56,724)
		(21,724)
Assets not specifically pledged		
Stocks	7,386	—
Equipment, fixtures and fittings	61,161	1,500
Cash at bank	—	4,521
Cash in hands of accountants	—	9,423
Debtors	—	6,777
Estimated total assets available for preferential creditors		22,221

A1 – Summary of liabilities

		Estimated to realize
		£
Estimated total assets available for preferential creditors (carried from page A)		22,221
Liabilities	£	
Preferential creditors:		
PAYE/NIC	5,145	
VAT	11,266	
Arrears of wages/holidays pay	1,545	
Anybank plc	1,316	
		19,272
Estimated surplus as regards preferential creditors		2,949
Debts secured by a floating charge:		
Estimated deficiency/surplus of assets available for non-preferential creditors		
Non-preferential claims:		
Anybank plc	20,408	
Redundancy/pay in lieu	12,479	
Trade creditors	34,224	
Directors' loan account	38,190	
		105,301
Estimated deficiency as regards creditors		(102,352)
Issued and called-up capital		
12,000 ordinary shares of £1 each	12,000	12,000
Estimated total deficiency as regards members		£114,352

Deficiency account

	£	£
Excess of capital and liabilities over assets at 31.8.89		14,774
Amounts written off in preparation of statement of affairs:		
Goodwill	6,771	
Motor vehicle	395	
Equipment, fixtures and fittings	59,661	
Stocks	7,386	74,213
Other items:		
Redundancy/pay in lieu		12,479
Trading losses 1.9.89–28.12.89 (balance)		12,886
Estimated deficiency as per Statement of Affairs		114,352

Document 5: Schedule 4 – powers of liquidator in a winding up

Part I – Powers exercisable with sanction

1. Power to pay any class of creditors in full.
2. Power to make any compromise or arrangement with creditors or persons claiming to be creditors, or having or alleging themselves to have any claim (present or future, certain or contingent, ascertained or sounding only in damages) against the company, or whereby the company may be rendered liable.
3. Power to comprise, on such terms as may be agreed:
   (a) all calls and liabilities to calls, all debts and liabilities capable of resulting in debts, and all claims (present or future, certain or contingent, ascertained or sounding only in damages) subsisting or supposed to subsist between the company and a contributory or alleged contributory or other debtor or person apprehending liability to the company, and
   (b) all questions in any way relating to or affecting the assets or the winding up of the company,
   and take any security for the discharge of any such call, debt liability or claim and give a complete discharge in respect of it.

Part II – Powers exercisable without sanction in voluntary winding up, with sanction in winding up by the court

4. Power to bring or defend any action or other legal proceeding in the name and on behalf of the company.

5. Power to carry on the business of the company so far as may be necessary for its beneficial winding up.

Part III – Powers exercisable without sanction in any winding up

6. Power to sell any of the company's property by public auction or private contract, with power to transfer the whole of it to any person or to sell the same in parcels.
7. Power to do all acts and execute, in the name and on behalf of the company, all deeds, receipts and other documents and for that purpose to use, when necessary, the company's seal.
8. Power to prove, rank and claim in the bankruptcy, insolvency or sequestration of any contributory for any balance against his estate, and to receive dividends in the bankruptcy, insolvency or sequestration in respect of that balance, as a separate debt due from the bankrupt or insolvent, and rateably with the other separate creditors.
9. Power to draw, accept, make and indorse any bill of exchange or promissory note in the name and on behalf of the company, with the same effect with respect to the company's liability as if the bill or note had been drawn, accepted, made or indorsed by or on behalf of the company in the course of its business.
10. Power to raise on the security of the assets of the company any money requisite.
11. Power to take out in his official name letters of administration to any deceased contributory, and to do in his official name any other act necessary for obtaining payment of any money due from a contributory or his estate which cannot conveniently be done in the name of the company.

    In all such cases the money due is deemed, for the purpose of enabling the liquidator to take out the letters of administration or recover the money, to be due to the liquidator himself.
12. Power to appoint an agent to do any business which the liquidator is unable to do himself.
13. Power to do all such other things as may be necessary for winding up the company's affairs and distributing its assets.

Document 6: Schedule 6 – the categories of preferential debts

Category 1 : Debts due to Inland Revenue

1. Sums due at the relevant date from the debtor on account of deductions of income tax from emoluments paid during the period of 12 months next before that date.

    The deductions here referred to are those which the debtor was liable to make under section 203 of the Income and Corporation Taxes Act 1988 (pay as you earn), less the amount of the repayments of income tax which the debtor was liable to make during that period.

2. Sums due at the relevant date from the debtor in respect of such deductions as are required to be made by the debtor for that period under section 559 of the Income and Corporation Taxes Act 1988 (subcontractors in the construction industry).

Category 2: Debts due to Customs and Excise

3. Any value added tax which is referable to the period of 6 months next before the relevant date (which period is referred to below as 'the 6-month period').
   For the purposes of this paragraph –
   (a) where the whole of the prescribed period to which any value added tax is attributable falls within the 6-month period, the whole amount of that tax is referable to that period; and
   (b) in any other case the amount of any value added tax which is referable to the 6-month period is the proportion of the tax which is equal to such proportion (if any) of the accounting reference period in question as falls within the 6-month period;
   and in sub-paragraph (a) 'prescribed' means prescribed by regulations under the Value Added Tax Act 1983.
4. The amount of any car tax which is due at the relevant date from the debtor and which became due within a period of 12 months next before that date.
5. Any amount which is due –
   (a) by way of general betting duty or bingo duty, or
   (b) under section 12(1) of the Betting and Gaming Duties Act 1981 (general betting duty and pool betting duty recoverable from agent collecting stakes), or
   (c) under section 14 of, or Schedule 2 to, that Act (gaming licence duty), from the debtor at the relevant date and which became due within the period of 12 months next before that date.

Category 3: Social security contributions

6. All sums which on the relevant date are due from the debtor on account of Class 1 or Class 2 contributions under the Social Security Act 1975 or the Social Security (Northern Ireland) Act 1975 and which became due from the debtor in the 12 months next before the relevant date.
7. All sums which on the relevant date have been assessed on and are due from the debtor on account of Class 4 contributions under either of those Acts of 1975 being sums which –
   (a) are due to the Commissioners of Inland Revenue (rather than to the Secretary of State or a Northern Ireland department), and
   (b) are assessed on the debtor up to 5th April next before the relevant date,
   but not exceeding, in the whole, any one year's assessment.

Category 4: Contributions to occupational pension schemes, etc.

8. Any sum which is owed by the debtor and is a sum to which Schedule 3 to the Social Security Pensions Act 1975 applies (contributions to occupational pension schemes and state scheme premiums).

Category 5: Remuneration, etc. of employees

9. So much of any amount which –
   (a) is owed by the debtor to a person who is or has been an employee of the debtor, and
   (b) is payable by way of remuneration in respect of the whole or any part of the period of 4 months next before the relevant date,
   as does not exceed so much as may be prescribed by order made by the Secretary of State.
10. An amount owed by way of accrued holiday remuneration, in respect of any period of employment before the relevant date, to a person whose employment by the debtor has been terminated, whether before, on or after that date.
11. So much of any sum owed in respect of money advanced for the purpose as has been applied for the payment of a debt which, if it had not been paid, would have been a debt falling within paragraph 9 or 10.
12. So much of any amount which –
    (a) is ordered (whether before or after the relevant date) to be paid by the debtor under the Reserve Forces (Safeguard of Employment) Act 1985, and
    (b) is so ordered in respect of a default made by the debtor before that date in the discharge of his obligations under that Act,
    as does not exceed such amounts as may be prescribed by order made by the Secretary of State.

Interpretation for category 5

13(1). For the purposes of paragraphs 8 to 12 a sum is payable by the debtor to a person by way of remuneration in respect of any period if –
   (a) it is paid as wages or salary (whether payable for time or for piece work or earned wholly or partly by way of commission) in respect of services rendered to the debtor in that period, or
   (b) it is an amount falling within the following sub-paragraph and is payable by the debtor in respect of that period.

13(2). An amount falls within this sub-paragraph if it is –
   (a) a guarantee payment under section 12(1) of the Employment Protection (Consolidation) Act 1978 (employee without work to do for a day or part of a day);
   (b) remuneration on suspension on medical grounds under section 19 of that Act;

(c) any payment for time off under section 27(3) (trade union duties), 31(3) (looking for work, etc.) or 31A(4) (ante-natal care) of that Act; or
(d) remuneration under a protective award made by an industrial tribunal under section 101 of the Employment Protection Act 1975 (redundancy dismissal with compensation).

14(1). This paragraph relates to a case in which a person's employment has been terminated by or in consequence of his employer going into liquidation or being adjudged bankrupt or (his employer being a company not in liquidation) by or in consequence of –
(a) a receiver being appointed as mentioned in section 40 of this Act (debenture-holders secured by floating charge), or
(b) the appointment of a receiver under section 53(6) or 54(5) of this Act (Scottish company with property subject to floating charge), or
(c) the taking of possession by debenture-holders (so secured), as mentioned in section 196 of the Companies Act.

14(2). For the purposes of paragraphs 9 to 12, holiday remuneration is deemed to have accrued to that person in respect of any period of employment if, by virtue of his contract of employment or of any enactment, that remuneration would have accrued in respect of that period if his employment had continued until he became entitled to be allowed the holiday.

14(3). The reference in sub-paragraph (2) to any enactment includes an order or direction made under an enactment.

15. Without prejudice to paragraphs 13 and 14 –
(a) any remuneration payable by the debtor to a person in respect of a period of holiday or of absence from work through sickness or other good cause is deemed to be wages or (as the case may be) salary in respect of services rendered to the debtor in that period, and
(b) references here and in those paragraphs to remuneration in respect of a period of holiday include any sums which, if they had been paid, would have been treated for the purposes of the enactments relating to social security as earnings in respect of that period.

Category 6: Levies on coal and steel production

15A. Any sums due at the relevant date from the debtor in respect of –
(a) the levies on the production of coal and steel referred to in Article 49 and 50 of the ECSC Treaty, or
(b) any surcharge for delay provided for in Article 50(3) of that Treaty and Article 6 of Decision 3/52 of the High Authority of the Coal and Steel Community.

Orders

16. An order made under paragraph 9 or 12 –
    (a) may contain such transitional provisions as may appear to the Secretary of State necessary or expedient;
    (b) shall be made by statutory instrument subject to annulment in pursuance of a resolution of either House of Parliament.

REFERENCES AND FURTHER READING

Frieze, S. A. (1987) *Compulsory Winding-Up Procedure*, 2nd edn, Longman, Harlow.
Loose, P. and Griffiths, M. (1989) *Loose on Liquidators*, 3rd edn, Jordans, Bristol.
Milman, D. and Durrant, C. (1987) *Corporate Insolvency: Law and Practice*, Sweet and Maxwell, London.
Pennington, R. R. (1987a) *Company Liquidations: The Substantive Law*, Jordans, Poristol.
Pennington, R. R. (1987b) *Company Liquidations: The Procedure*, Jordans, Bristol.

NOTES

1. Either a special resolution under s. 84(1)(b) or an extraordinary resolution under s. 84(1)(c).
2. S. 89.
3. S. 90.
4. See Chap. 1, p. 11.
5. S. 136.
6. S. 136(5)(c).
7. S. 139.
8. See Chap. 1, p. 11.
9. As to the form of the statutory demand, see IR, Form 4.5.
10. S. 122(1)(f); *Re Taylor's Industrial Flooring Ltd* (1990) 6 BCC 44.
11. Chap. 6, p. 80.
12. Chap. 1, p. 4 et seq.
13. Chap. 7, p. 88.
14. *Ayerst (Inspector of Taxes)* v. *C & K (Construction) Ltd* [1987] AC 167.
15. CA 1985, s. 378(2).
16. CA 1985, s. 369(1)(b).
17. CA 1985, s. 378(3) – this applies where 95 per cent of the shareholders will consent to the short notice.
18. IA, s. 166(3).
19. S. 166(2).
20. S. 98(1)(a).
21. S. 98(1)(b) – for details of the contents of the notice, see IR (as amended), r. 4.51.
22. S. 98(2).
23. S. 99.
24. S. 100(2).
25. IR, r. 4.67.
26. IR, r. 4.63.
27. IR, r. 4.73–4.94. As for the form of 'proof of debts', see Form 4.1 (in the case study in this chapter); as to claims which are not quantified, see r. 4.86; as to mutual set-off rights, see r. 4.90.

28 S. 101.
29 S. 109.
30 CA 1985, s. 380.
31 S. 109.
32 IR, r. 4.49. Note that if the liquidator was formerly the company's administrator, in addition to the material required to be sent under r. 4.49, he must also send copies of the report and proposals that he prepared as administrator; r. 4.49A.
33 S. 103.
34 *Harold M. Pitman & Co.* v. *Top Business Systems (Nottingham) Ltd* [1984] BCLC 593.
35 See Chap. 9, p. 135.
36 For powers which the liquidator can exercise with the sanction of the court or liquidation committee, see IA, Sched. 4, Part I.
37 Also they are unenforceable against the administrator, but they are enforceable against the administrative receiver.
38 S. 112.
39 S. 178(6).
40 S. 178(5).
41 See note 27, above.
42 IR, r. 4.73(6).
43 S. 168(5).
44 S. 175(2).
45 S. 387; this is unless an administrative receiver has already been appointed, in which case the relevant date for determining the amounts owed to preferential creditors is the date of his appointment: s. 40.
46 Insolvency Proceedings (Monetary Limits) Order 1986 (S.I. 1986 No. 1996).
47 IA, Sched. 6, para. 11.
48 S. 175(2).
49 VAT Bad Debt Regulations 1986 (S.I. 1986 No. 335).
50 S. 107.
51 S. 105.
52 S. 106.
53 S. 239(5).
54 (1990) 6 BCC 78.
55 S. 249 (this is defined to include a director or shadow director or an associate of the company; for the definition of the latter term, see s. 435.)
56 S. 239(6).
57 S. 240(3).
58 S. 240(2).
59 See discussion on this point in Goode (1990) *Principles of Corporate Insolvency Law*, pp. 172–3.
60 S. 240(3).
61 S. 240(1)(c).
62 S. 238(5).
63 S. 241(2).
64 S. 241(2)(b).
65 *Re Yeovil Glove Co. Ltd* [1965] Ch 148.
66 *Mace Builders (Glasgow) Ltd* v. *Lunn* [1985] 3 WLR 465, affirmed [1987] Ch 191.
67 S. 244.
68 S. 244(4).
69 S. 244(5).
70 S. 425.
71 S. 213.
72 *Re Patrick & Lyon Ltd* [1933] Ch 786.
73 *Re Gerald Cooper (Chemicals) Ltd* [1978] 1 Ch 262.

74 *R* v. *Grantham* [1984] QB 675.
75 Ss. 213(2) and 215.
76 See pp. 4–6.
77 It must be remembered that an allegation of wrongful trading may be made against a director or shadow director: ss. 214(7), 251 and CA 1985, s. 741(2).
78 *Re Produce Marketing Consortium Ltd* [1989] BCLC 520.
79 S. 218.
80 CDDA 1986, ss. 6 and 7(3).
81 Insolvent Companies (Reports on Conduct of Directors) No. 2 Rules 1986 (S.I. 1986 No. 2134)
82 Chap. 1, p. 7.
83 CDDA 1986, s. 22 (referring to IA 1986, s. 247, i.e. approval of a voluntary arrangement; the making of an administration order or the appointment of an administrative receiver as well as the passing of a resolution for a voluntary winding up or the presentation of a compulsory winding-up petition).
84 S. 106 and IR, r. 4.126.
85 S. 201(2).
86 S. 201(3).
87 S. 202.

Table of Cases

(*Note:* The page numbers in ordinary type refer to the reference in the Notes sections at the end of chapters; the page numbers in brackets (in **bold**) refer to the page of the text where the case is discussed or referred to.)

Abbreviations

AC	Appeal Cases
All ER	All England Law Reports
BCC	British Company Cases
BCLC	Butterworths Company Law Cases
Ch	Chancery Division (1891–)
Ch D	Chancery Division (1875–90)
Co Law	The Company Lawyer
Lloyd's Rep	Lloyd's Law Reports
QB	Queen's Bench
WLR	Weekly Law Reports

Air Écosse *v.* Civil Aviation Authority (1987) 3 BCC 492 103
Airlines Airspares Ltd *v.* Handley Page Ltd [1970] Ch 193 .... 130 (**116, 117**), 157 (**139**)
Aluminium Industrie Vaassen BV *v.* Romalpa Aluminium Ltd [1976]
2 All ER 552; [1976] 1 WLR 676 .... 156 (**134, 135**)
American Express Banking Corp. *v.* Hurley [1985] 3 All ER 564 .... 103 (**87**), 158 (**144, 146**)
Andrabell Ltd, *Re* [1984] 3 All ER 407 .... 157 (**135**)
Anglo-Continental Supply Co. Ltd, *Re* [1922] 2 Ch 723 .... 82 (**75**)
Arctic Engineering Ltd, *Re* [1986] 1 WLR 686 .... 15 (**10**)
Ayerst (Inspector of Taxes) *v.* C & K (Construction) Ltd [1987] AC 167... 188 (**160**)

Bacon (M. C.) Ltd, *Re* (1990) 6 BCC 78......................... 189 (**167, 168**)
Bank of Baroda *v.* Panessar [1987] Ch 338; [1987] 2 WLR 208;
[1986] 3 All ER 751 .... 129 (**114**)
Barclays Bank Ltd *v.* Quistclose Investments Ltd [1970] AC 567; [1968]
3 WLR 1097; [1968] 3 All ER 651 .... 156 (**134**)
Bond Worth Ltd, *Re* [1980] Ch 228; [1979] 3 WLR 629; [1979]
3 All ER 919 .... 156 (**135**)

Table of Cases

Borden (UK) Ltd v. Scottish Timber Products Ltd [1981] Ch 25; [1979]
3 WLR 672; [1979] 3 All ER 961 .... 157 **(135)**
Botibol Ltd, *Re* [1947] 1 All ER 26 .... 128 **(105)**
Brightlife Ltd, *Re* [1987] Ch 200; [1986] 3 All ER 673; [1987] 2 WLR 197 .. 82 **(79)**, 129 **(109)**
Brooke Marine Ltd, *Re* [1988] BCLC 546 .... 104 **(92)**
Burt, Boulton and Hayward v. Bull [1895] 1 QB 276 .... 128 **(105)**
Business Computers Ltd v. Anglo-African Leasing Ltd [1977]
1 WLR 578 .... 157 **(139)**
Business Properties Ltd, *Re* (1988) 4 BCC 684 .... 103 **(88)**
Byblos Bank v. Al-Khudhairy (1986) 2 BCC 99 .... 15 **(11)**, 129 **(114, 115)**

Carreras Rothmans Ltd v. Freeman Mathews Treasure Ltd [1985] Ch 207;
[1984] 3 WLR 1016; [1985] 1 All ER 155 .... 156 **(134)**
Charnley Davies Business Services Ltd, *Re* (1987) 3 BCC 408 .... 102 **(84)**, 103 **(90, 91)**
Churchill Hotel (Plymouth) Ltd, *Re* [1988] BCLC 341 .... 15 **(8)**
Cladrose Ltd, *Re* (1990) 6 BCC 11 .... 15 **(8)**
Clough Mill Ltd v. Martin [1984] 1 WLR 111; [1984] 3 All ER 982 .... 157 **(135)**
Company A, *Re* (No. 00175 of 1987) (1987) 3 BCC 124 .... 103 **(88, 89)**
Company A, *Re* (No. 005009 of 1987) [1989] BCLC 13 .... 15 **(9)**
Company A, *Re* (No. 001992 of 1988) [1989] BCLC 9 .... 103 **(89)**
Consumer and Industrial Press Ltd, *Re* (1988) 4 BCC 72 .... 82 **(77)**, 102 **(85)**, 103 **(91)**
Cuckmere Brick Co. Ltd v. Mutual Finance Ltd [1971] Ch 949;
[1971] 2 WLR 1207; [1971] 2 All ER 633 .... 158 **(144)**
Cyrne v. Barclays Bank plc [1987] BCLC 548 .... 129 **(114)**

Dawson Print Group Ltd, *Re* [1987] BCLC 601 .... 15 **(8)**

Edwards v. Standard Rolling Stock Syndicate [1893] 1 Ch 574 .... 128 **(105)**, 129 **(114)**
Edwin Hill & Partners v. First National Finance Corp. plc [1989]
BCLC 89 .... 157 **(139)**
Emmadart Ltd, *Re* [1979] Ch 540; [1979] 2 WLR 868; [1979] 1 All ER 599
156 **(132)**
Equiticorp International plc, *Re* [1989] 1 WLR 1010; (1989)
5 BCC 599 .... 102 **(83)**
EVTR Ltd, *Re* [1987] BCLC 646 .... 156 **(134)**

Four Point Garage Ltd v. Carter [1985] 3 All ER 12 .... 157 **(135)**
Freevale Ltd v. Metrostore Holdings Ltd [1984] Ch 199; [1984]
2 WLR 496; [1984] 1 All ER 495 .... 157 **(139)**

Gerald Cooper (Chemicals) Ltd, *Re* [1978] Ch 262; [1978]
2 WLR 866; [1978] 2 All ER 49 .... 189 **(172)**
Gomba Holdings UK Ltd v. Homan [1986] 1 WLR 1301; [1986]
3 All ER 94 .... 130 **(116)**
Great Eastern Electric Co. Ltd, *Re* [1941] Ch 241 .... 82 **(80)**
Griffiths v. Secretary of State for Social Services [1974] QB 468; [1973]
3 WLR 831; [1973] 3 All ER 1184 .... 157 **(137)**

Harold M. Pitman & Co. v. Top Business Systems (Nottingham) Ltd
[1984] BCLC 593 .... 189 **(162)**
Harris Simons Construction Ltd, *Re* [1989] 1 WLR 368; [1989]
BCLC 202 .... 82 **(77)**, 102 **(85)**, 103 **(87)**

Table of Cases

Hendy Lennox (Industrial Engines) Ltd v. Grahame Puttick Ltd [1984]
1 WLR 485; [1984] 2 All ER 152 .... 156 **(135)**
Hi-Fi Equipment (Cabinets) Ltd, Re [1988] BCLC 55 .... 129 **(111)**

Illingworth v. Houldsworth [1904] AC 355.......................... 129 **(108)**
Imperial Motors (UK) Ltd, Re (1989) 5 BCC 214 .... 102 **(86)**
IRC v. Goldblatt [1972] Ch 498; [1972] 2 WLR 953 .... 130 **(118)**, 156 **(133)**

Kayford Ltd (In Liquidation), Re [1975] 1 WLR 279; [1975]
1 All ER 604 .... 156 **(134)**
Keenan Bros Ltd, Re [1986] BCLC 242 .... 128 **(106)**

Lathia v. Dronsfield Bros Ltd [1987] BCLC 321 .... 130 **(117)**, 157 **(139, 140)**
Litster v. Forth Dry Dock & Engineering Co. Ltd [1989] 2 WLR 634
104 **(97)**, 158 **(141)**
Lo-Line Electric Motors Ltd, Re [1988] BCLC 698...................... 15 **(8)**
London Pressed Hinge Co. Ltd, Re [1905] 1 Ch 576 .... 129 **(114)**
Lynch (J. & B.) (Builders) Ltd, Re [1988] BCLC 376 .... 15 **(8)**

Mace Builders (Glasgow) Ltd v. Lunn [1987] Ch 191; [1986]
3 WLR 921; [1987] BCLC 55 .... 129 **(113)**, 189 **(171)**
Mack Trucks (Britain) Ltd, Re [1967] 1 WLR 780; [1967] 1 All ER 977... 157 **(137)**
Majestic Recording Studios Ltd, Re (1988) 4 BCC 519.................... 15 **(8)**
Matthews (D. J.) (Joinery Design) Ltd, Re (1988) 4 BCC 513............... 15 **(8)**
Mercantile Bank of India Ltd v. Chartered Bank of India, Australia and
China [1937] 1 All ER 231 .... 129 **(113)**
Morris v. Kanssen [1946] AC 549; [1946] 1 All ER 586.................... 129
Multi Guarantee Co. Ltd, Re [1987] BCLC 257 .... 157 **(134)**

Newdigate Colliery Co. Ltd, Re [1912] 1 Ch 468 .... 157 **(140)**
Nicoll v. Cutts [1985] BCLC 322 .... 157 **(137)**
NRG Vision Ltd v. Churchfield Leasing Ltd [1988] BCLC 624 .... 129 **(114)**

Offshore Ventilations Ltd, Re [1989] BCLC 318 .... 130 **(116)**

Patrick & Lyon Ltd, Re [1933] Ch 786 .... 189 **(172)**
Peachdart Ltd, Re [1984] Ch 131; [1983] 3 WLR 878; [1983] 3 All ER 204
157 **(135)**
Primlaks (UK) Ltd, Re (1989) 5 BCC 710 102
Produce Marketing Consortium Ltd, Re (1989) 5 BCC 569 .... 15 **(5)**, 190 **(173)**

R v. Georgiu (1988) 4 BCC 322 .... 15 **(7)**
R v. Grantham [1984] QB 675; [1984] 2 WLR 815; [1984] 3 All ER 166.... 190 **(172)**
Ratford v. Northavon District Council [1987] QB 357; [1986] 3 WLR 771;
[1986] 3 All ER 193 .... 130 **(116)**
Robbie (N. W.) & Co. Ltd v. Witney Warehouse Co. Ltd [1963]
1 WLR 1324 .... 157 **(139)**
Rother Iron Works Ltd v. Canterbury Precision Engineers Ltd [1974]
QB 1 .... 130 **(116)**, 157 **(139)**

Saunders (G. L.) Ltd, Re [1986] 1 WLR 215 129
Secretary of State for Employment v. Spence [1986] 3 WLR 380; [1986]
3 All ER 616.. 158 **(141)**
Shamji v. Johnson Matthey Bank Ltd (1986) 2 BCC 98, 910 .... 129 **(115)**
Siebe Gorman & Co. Ltd v. Barclays Bank Ltd [1979] 2 Lloyd's Rep 142.. 128 **(106)**
Smallman Construction Ltd, Re [1989] BCLC 420 .... 103 **(91)**

Table of Cases

Specialised Mouldings Ltd, *Re* (unreported) 138
Standard Chartered Bank Ltd *v*. Walker [1982] 1 WLR 1410; [1982]
   3 All ER 938 .... 103 (**87**), 158 (**144**)
Stanford Services Ltd, *Re* (1987) 3 BCC 326 .... 15 (**8**)

Taylor's Industrial Flooring Ltd, *Re* (1990) 6 BCC 44................. 188 (**159**)
Telemetrix plc *v*. Modern Engineers of Bristol (Holdings) plc [1985]
   BCLC 213 .... 130 (**117**), 157 (**139**)

Victoria Steamboats Ltd, *Re* [1897] 1 Ch 158......................... 128 (**105**)

Wallace *v*. Automatic Machines Co. [1894] 2 Ch 547 .... 129 (**109**)
Westminster Corporation *v*. Haste [1950] Ch 442; [1950] 2 All ER 65 ..... 130 (**118**)
Wheatley *v*. Silkstone & Haigh Moor Coal Co. (1885) 29 Ch D 715 .... 128 (**106**)
Woodroffes (Musical Instruments) Ltd, *Re* [1986] Ch 366; [1985] 3 WLR
   543; [1985] 2 All ER 908 .... 82 (**79**), 129 (**109, 115**)
Woods *v*. Windskill [1913] 2 Ch 303 .... 130 (**118**), 156 (**133**)

Yeovil Glove Co. Ltd, *Re* [1965] Ch 148; [1964] 3 WLR 406; [1964]
   2 All ER 849 .... 189 (**170**)
Yorkshire Woolcombers Association Ltd, *Re* [1903] 2 Ch 284 .... 129 (**108**)

Table of Statutes

(*Note:* The page numbers in ordinary type refer to the reference in the Notes sections at the end of chapters; the page numbers in brackets (in **bold**) refer to the page of the text where the section of the statute is discussed or referred to. In the text all references are to the Insolvency Act 1986 unless otherwise stated.)

Companies Act 1985
  s. 369 .... 188 **(160)**
  s. 378 .... 188 **(160)**
  s. 380 .... 189 **(162)**
  s. 395 .... 129 **(108, 113)**
  s. 405 .... 130 **(115)**
  s. 459 146
  s. 741 .... 190 **(172)**
Companies Act 1989
  s. 93 .... **(113)**
  s. 95 .... **(113)**
  s. 100 .... **(110)**
  s. 103 .... **(110)**
Company Directors Disqualification
  Act 1986
  s. 2 .... 15 **(7)**
  s. 3 .... 15 **(7)**
  s. 6 .... 15 **(7)**, 190 **(174)**
  s. 7 .... 15 **(7)**, 158 **(147)**,
                              190 **(174)**
  s. 9 .... 15 **(7)**
  s. 10 .... 15 **(6)**
  s. 22 .... 190 **(174)**
Employment Protection Consolidation
  Act 1978 .... 102 **(138, 164)**
Financial Services Act 1986
  s. 74 102
Insolvency Act 1986
  s. 1 .... 82 **(76)**
  s. 2 .... 82 **(76)**
  s. 3 .... 104 **(91)**
  s. 4 .... 82 **(76)**, 104 **(91)**, **(146)**

s. 5 .... 82 **(76)**, 158 **(145)**
s. 6 .... 82 **(76)**
s. 8 .... 16 **(13)**, 82 **(75, 83)**,
                    102 **(85)**, 103 **(92)**
s. 9 .... 82 **(77, 80)**, 102 **(83)**,
     103 **(87, 89)**, 129 **(115)**, 130 **(117)**
s. 10 ..... 16 **(13)**, 82 **(77)**, 103 **(87,
          88, 89)**, 156 **(133)**, 157 **(135)**
s. 11 .... 16 **(13)**, 82 **(77, 78)**,
       103 **(89)**, 130 **(117)**, 156 **(133)**
s. 14 .... 82 **(77)**, 102 **(85)**,
       103 **(91)**, **(135–6)**, 156 **(132)**
                              157 **(140)**
s. 15 .... 82 **(77)**, 157 **(133)**,
         158 **(135)**, **(142–3, 146)**
s. 17 ..... 103 **(90)**, 157 **(136, 139)**
s. 18 .... 104 **(92)**
s. 20 .... 104 **(92)**
s. 22 .... 156 **(132)**
s. 23 .... 103 **(90)**
s. 24 .... 103 **(91)**, 157 **(140)**, **(146)**
s. 25 .... 103 **(91)**, **(146)**
s. 26 .... 103 **(91)**
s. 27 .... 103 **(89)**, **(145, 146)**
s. 29 .... 129 **(112)**
s. 33 .... 130 **(115)**
s. 35 .... 157 **(138)**
ss. 33–38 .... **(107)**
s. 40 ..... 82, 128 **(107)**, 129 **(111)**,
          156 **(133)**, 158 **(144)**
s. 42 .... 128 **(105)**, **(136)**
s. 43 .... **(143)**

Table of Statutes

s. 44 .... 82 (**78, 79**), 103 (**87**), (**116**), 130 (**117**), 157 (**137**)
s. 45 .... 130 (**118**), 158 (**146**)
s. 46 .... 130 (**115**)
s. 47 .... 156 (**132**)
s. 48 .... 130 (**117**)
s. 84 .... 16 (**14**), 188 (**159**)
s. 87 .... (**162**)
s. 89 .... 188 (**159**)
s. 90 .... 188 (**159**)
s. 98 .... 16 (**14**), 188 (**161**)
s. 99 .... 188 (**161**)
s. 100 .... 188 (**161**)
s. 101 .... 189 (**161**)
s. 103 .... 189 (**162**)
s. 105 .... 189 (**165**)
s. 106 .... 189 (**165**), 190 (**175**)
s. 107 .... 189 (**165**)
s. 109 .... 189 (**162**)
s. 112 .... 189 (**163**)
s. 117 .... 102 (**86**)
s. 122 .... (**14**), 82 (**78**), (**159**)
s. 123 .... (**10–11**), (**85**), (**114**), (**159**), (**169**)
s. 132 ...... 16 (**14**), 82 (**81**), (**166**)
s. 133 .... 82 (**81**)
s. 136 .... 188 (**159**)
s. 139 .... 188 (**159**)
s. 166 .... 188 (**161**)
s. 168 .... 189 (**163**)
s. 175 .... 189 (**163, 165**)
s. 178 .... 189 (**163**)
s. 201 .... 190 (**175**)
s. 202 .... 190 (**175**)
s. 212 .... 104 (**93**), 157 (**140**), (**147**), 190 (**173**)
s. 213 .... 189 (**172**)
s. 214 .... 15 (**5, 6**), (**147**), 190 (**172, 173**)

s. 215 .... 15 (**6**)
s. 218 .... 190 (**173**)
s. 230 .... 130 (**115**)
s. 232 .... 129 (**115**)
s. 233 .... 131 (**147**)
s. 234 ..... (**107**), (**135**), 158 (**147**)
s. 235 .... (**147**)
s. 236 .... (**147**)
s. 238 ...... 103 (**87**), (**168–9, 171**)
s. 239 .... 82 (**80**), 103 (**87**), 128 (**107**), 129 (**113**), (**166–8, 169**)
s. 240 .... 189 (**168**)
s. 241 .... 189 (**169**)
s. 244 .... 189 (**171**)
s. 245 .... 82 (**80**), 128 (**111**), (**112–13**), (**170–1**)
s. 246 .... (**163**)
s. 249 .... 128 (**107**), 189 (**167**)
s. 251 .... 81 (**74**), 129 (**109**), 157 (**135**), 190 (**172**)
s. 387 .... 189 (**164**)
s. 388 .... 15 (**12**)
s. 389 .... 15 (**12**)
s. 391 .... 15 (**12**)
s. 423 .... (**171**)
s. 425 .... (**74–5, 77**), (**146**), (**172**)
s. 426 .... 82 (**75**)
s. 435 128

Law of Property Act 1925
s. 90 .... 128 (**106**)
s. 91 .... 128 (**106**)
s. 101 .... (**106**)

Sale of Goods Act 1979
s. 25 .... (**156**)

Table of Statutory Instruments

Insolvency Practitioners (Recognised Professional Bodies) Order 1986
 (S.I. No. 1764) .... **(15)**
Insolvency Practitioners Regulations 1986 (S.I. No. 1995) .... 16 **(12)**
Insolvency Proceedings (Monetary Limits) Order 1986 (S.I. No. 1996) ...... 189 **(164)**
Insolvency Rules 1986 (S.I. No. 1925)
 r. 1 .... 82 **(76)**
 r. 1.19 .... 82 **(76)**
 r. 1.24 .... 104 **(91)**
 r. 2.1 .... 103 **(86)**
 r. 2.2 .... 103 **(84, 86)**
 r. 2.3 .... 103 **(86, 87)**
 r. 2.6 .... 103 **(87, 88)**
 r. 2.6A .... 103 **(91)**
 r. 2.11 .... 156 **(132)**
 r. 2.32 .... 103 **(91)**
 r. 3.3 .... 156 **(132)**
 r. 3.33 .... 130 **(118)**
 r. 4.49 .... 189 **(162)**
 r. 4.49A .... 189 **(162)**
 r. 4.51 .... 188 **(161)**
 r. 4.63 .... 188 **(161, 163)**
 r. 4.67 .... 188 **(161)**
 r. 4.73–94 .... 188 **(161)**
 r. 4.126 .... 190 **(175)**
Insolvent Companies (Reports on the Conduct of Directors) No. 2 Rules
 1986 (S.I. No. 2134) .... **(7)**, **(147)**, **(174)**
Transfer of Undertakings (Protection of Employment) Regulations 1981
 (S.I. No. 1794)
 reg. 5 .... **(141, 142)**
 reg. 7 .... **(157)**
 reg. 8 .... 156 **(132)**, **(142)**
VAT (Bad Debt Relief) Regulations 1986 (S.I. No. 335) .... 189 **(165)**

Index

accountants
  audit qualifications, 9
  detection of insolvency, 9, 47–8
Accounting Standards Committee, 46
acquisitions, 23
administration proceedings
  compared with administrative receivership, 77–8, 87–8
  consequences of a petition, 77, 88–9
  procedure for appointment, 77, 85–8
  purpose of, 12–13, 83–5
  termination of, 92–3
administrative receivership
  compared with administration, 79–80, 111
  cases in which an apointment may be made, 114–15
  definition of, 112
  purpose of, 13
administrative receivers
  duties of, 140–3, 145–6
  liability on employment contracts, 137–8
  powers of, 137–9
  procedure for appointment, 112, 115
  resignation and removal, 117–18
  status of, 116–17
  trading by, 132–5
administrators
  duties of, 90–1, 139–40, 145–6
  powers of, 135–7, 142–3
  release from liability, 92
Aggarwal, A., 53, 60
Altman, E. I., 39–40, 48
Anderson, H., 157
Argenti, J., 17, 21, 23, 32

bankers
  detection of signs of insolvency, 9, 74
Bannock, G., 24, 32
Beaver, W. H., 34, 39, 48

Bibeault, D., 10, 14
bills of exchange, 55
Bolton, S. E., 36, 60
budgetary planning and control
  cash, 51–2
  examples of, 25–31
  importance of, 20

cash budgeting, 51–2
cash flow
  crisis, 1
  forecast, 20
cash management, 51–3
Clutterbuck, D., 62, 72
Cocker, M., 59, 60
composition with creditors, 73–4
compulsory liquidation
  circumstances in which appropriate, 80–1, 166
  termination of, 174–5
concentration banking, 53
Confederation of British Industry, 5, 14
Cork Committee, 4, 12, 21, 32, 83, 156
corporate recovery strategies, 65–8
cost information, 20
cost structure, 22
credit control, 20
creditors' committee
  in administration, 91
creditors' voluntary liquidation
  decision to liquidate, 160
  meetings of creditors, 160–1
  procedure for, 80, 159
  termination of, 174–5
current ratio, 35–7, 39

Dearing Committee, 46, 48
debtors turnover ratio, 35–6
debts – inability to pay, 10–11
disqualification orders

Index

circumstances in which order can be made, 7
meaning and effect, 6
unfitness to manage company, 7, 174

environmental factors affecting company failure, 1–3, 17–19
extortionate credit transactions, 171

factoring debts, 55
financial control, 55
Financial Reporting Council, 20–1
Finkin, E. F., 63, 72
Firth, M., 49, 60
fixed charges, 13, 106–7
floating charges
  advantages and disadvantages, 111
  crystallization, 108–10
  definition of, 78–9, 108
  grounds for invalidity of, 112–13, 170–1
fraudulent trading, 172
Frieze, S., 104
funds flow statement, 43–5

Gaffney, M., 21, 32
Gallinger, G. W., 52, 60
Ganguly, P., 24, 32
gearing
  ratio, 35, 37
  role in company failure, 22
Goldstein, A. S., 25, 32
Goode, R. M., 156, 189
Gough, W. J., 128
Grinyer, P. H., 17, 23, 32

Healey, P. B., 52–60
hive downs, 117, 141, 160
Horngren, C. T., 38, 48

insolvency practitioner
  and company turnaround, 61–2
  definition, 11–12
  reports on the conduct of directors, 7, 174
interest cover, 35
International Accounting Standards Committee, 1, 15
invoice discounting, 55

Johnson, C., 53, 60
Jones, F. L., 41, 48

Kami, M. S., 17, 32
Kerr, W. W., 93, 128, 138, 157

Kharbanda, O. P., 68, 72
Kibel, H. R., 10, 15

Lange, P., 157
Largay, J. A., 42, 48
Lee, T. A., 42–3, 48
liens
  liquidator's powers in connection with, 163
Lightman, G., 114, 129
Lingard, J. R., 82
liquidation committee, role of, 161–2
liquidator
  duties of, 163–5
  powers of, 163
  status of, 162
lock-box services, 53

management
  assessment of ability, 3
  change of, 64
  rescue plan, 6
  role in corporate failure, 18
marketing
  importance of, 21
  improvement of, 67–8
Mayes, D. G., 17, 23, 32
McKinernan, P., 17, 23, 32
Mellman, M., 46, 48
Miles, K., 69, 72
misfeasance proceedings, 173
multiple discriminant analysis, 39–40
Murphy, J., 61, 72

Nelson, R., 62, 72
Norgard, R., 18, 32

office-holder – powers of, 146–7
Official Receiver, 14, 159, 166
Ohlson, J. A., 35, 48
overtrading, 23

Pastera, V., 46, 48
Patton, G. R., 17, 32
Peel, D. A., 47, 48
performance indicators
  examples, 33–48
  role of, 3–9
Peters, T. S., 18, 32
planning, 19–20
Pope, P. F., 47, 48
Porter, M., 66, 72
predictive models, 39–40
preferences – setting aside, 166–8
preferential creditors, 164–5

Index

quick ratio, 35–6

ratio analysis
  gearing, 37
  liquidity, 35–7
  profitability, 37–9
  role of, 34–5
receivers – appointment by the court, 105
reorder point, 59
retention of title clauses, 134–5
Richardson, P., 24, 32
Riggs, J., 17, 32
Robertson, J., 36, 48
Ross, J. E., 17, 32

Sealy, L., 15
schemes of arrangement, 74–5
set-off – rights against administrator, 136, 139
shadow director, 6
Slatter, S., 10, 15, 17, 19, 32, 65, 72
solvency analysis, 33–4
Stallworthy, E. A., 68, 72
statement of affairs
  prepared for administrator/administrative receiver, 132
  prepared for liquidator, 161
Statement of Standard Accounting Practice No. 10, 44
Stencil, J. M., 53, 60
Stewart, G., 138, 156
Stickney, C. P., 42, 48
stock
  control models, 58–9
  importance of, 57
  levels of, 57–8
stock turnover ratio, 35–6

Taffler, R. J., 40, 47, 48
Totty, P., 93

trade debtors
  credit terms, 54–5
  evaluation of, 55–6
  financing, 55
  management of, 53–4
  monitoring, 56–7
trade discounts, 52
transactions at an undervalue, 168–70
transactions defrauding creditors, 171
trust property, 134
Tseung, M., 47, 48
turnaround
  insolvency practitioner's role, 11–12
  scope for, 9–10
  steps leading to, 61–9
Turok, I., 24, 32

unofficial receivership, 74

viable core of business, 62–3
voluntary arrangements
  challenge of decision, 76
  limitations of, 76–7
  payment to creditors in context of, 145
  procedure for, 76
  supervisor of, 75

Waterman, R. H., 18, 32
Whittred, G., 47, 48
winding up – consequences of, 162
working capital management, 49–50
Wright, F. K., 36, 48
wrongful trading
  contribution order, 6
  elements of, 4–5
  standard of knowledge and skill, 6, 74
  steps to avoid liability for, 6

Zimmer, I., 47, 48